CRIME NEWS
AND
THE PUBLIC

CRIME NEWS
AND
THE PUBLIC

DORIS A. GRABER

PRAEGER SPECIAL STUDIES • PRAEGER SCIENTIFIC

Library of Congress Cataloging in Publication Data

Graber, Doris Appel, 1920-
    Crime news and the public.

    Bibliography: p.
    Includes index.
    1. Crime and criminals--United States--Public
opinion. 2. Mass media--Social aspects--United States.
3. Crime and the press--United States. 4. Public
opinion--United States. I. Title.
HV6791.G69   364'.973   80-16032
ISBN 0-03-055756-9

Published in 1980 by Praeger Publishers
CBS Educational and Professional Publishing
A Division of CBS, Inc.
521 Fifth Avenue, New York, New York 10017 U.S.A.

Printed in the United States of America

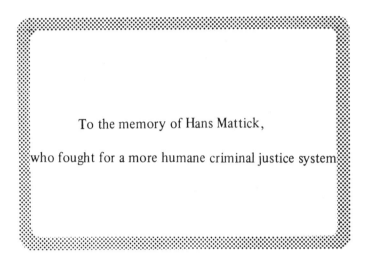

To the memory of Hans Mattick,

who fought for a more humane criminal justice system

PREFACE

To say that this book deals with nonfiction crime news in the United States requires qualification. Nonfiction crime news is fiction, to a certain degree. It does not depict crime in the United States as it really is. The pictures in the minds of media audiences are, in many significant respects, even more remote from reality than the media images. The public lives in a world of unreality when it comes to criminals, victims, and the criminal justice system.

This book reflects this world. It presents media and audience images of crime and the criminal justice system side by side and explains how they are interrelated. Unlike most other studies that deal with the role that the media play in stimulating antisocial behavior, it stresses the media's prosocial role in putting problems on the agenda of concerns, informing citizens, and providing guidance for individuals and for public action. It explores the impact that media images and audience images of the criminal justice process have on life in the United States and the implications for media and public policies. It thus forms part of the major current efforts by government and private organizations to deepen understanding of all facets of the U.S. crime problem. The goal is more enlightened social policy that ameliorates the problem, rather than coping only with its symptoms.

Since this book's purpose is to break new ground, comparatively well-covered subjects have been avoided. This explains the emphasis on nonfiction rather than fictional crime stories, and on images held by adults rather than by children. It also explains the absence of extensive discussion of the question of whether or not crime news stimulates the commission of crime. Cost factors made it imperative to limit the media analysis to selected newspapers and television broadcasts and exclude other print and electronic news sources, such as magazines and radio. The consequences of this omission appear to be minor. Media audiences rely primarily on television and newspapers for crime and justice system news and do not perceive these other sources to be substantially different in substance or approach.

Hans Mattick, director of the Center for Research in Criminal Justice at the University of Illinois at Chicago Circle, played the role of mentor for this book. Along with Broderick Reischl, administrator for the center, he gave encouragement in conducting the project and aided with advice and criticism. The center also arranged for the substantial funding needed for research. Additional material assistance came from the Computer Center at the University of Illinois, Chicago Circle, which made its facilities available.

Among the large number of research assistants who labored diligently on coding and many other tasks involved in this venture, several stand out. Judy Whitaker coded most of the crime stories and helped with interviewing. Jim Marek supervised and assisted with coding and computer operations. Roger Sanders initiated the computer programs and David Mongan viewed and coded television news. Young Yun Kim prepared most of the codebooks for the study and coded all of the interviews. Anne Spray helped in preparing the appendixes and the index and cast a critical editorial eye over the finished manuscript. In its final stages, the book benefited immeasurably from an extensive and highly perceptive critique by Larry Cohen, colleague and friend in the Political Science Department at the University of Illinois, Chicago Circle.

This study would have been impossible without the magnificent cooperation of the panel members, particularly the core panel participants, who gave an average of 20 hours of interview time during the year of the study and many more hours for diary writing. They were refreshingly candid and exceedingly generous in revealing their thoughts. It seemed no exaggeration when one respondent, toward the end of the study, remarked that I now knew more about the pictures in his head than anyone else, including his wife. My pledge to keep the panelists' identities hidden prevents me from naming them. But my thanks to them are public, lasting, and deep.

Portions of Chapter 2 appear in different form in Doris A. Graber, "Is Crime News Coverage Excessive?" in *Journal of Communication* 29 (Summer 1979): 81-92. Reprinted by permission. Portions of chapters 2, 3, and 4 appear in different form in Doris A. Graber, "Evaluating Crime-Fighting Policies: Media Images and Public Perspective," in *Evaluating Alternative Law-Enforcement Policies,* Ralph Baker and Ted A. Meyer, eds. (Lexington, Mass.: Heath, 1979), 179-99.

Doris A. Graber
University of Illinois, Chicago Circle
January 1980

CONTENTS

LIST OF TABLES

LIST OF FIGURES

INTRODUCTION

Most citizens have mental images of crime and the criminal justice system. Relatively little is known about the nature of these images and about the process of image formation. It is known that the information sources from which these images are built come from personal experiences and observations and from vicarious experiences. The vicarious experiences come to the attention of individuals through interpersonal communication, which is largely based on mass media messages, and directly through mass media messages.[1] Although the sources are known, the types of information they supply are not. Nor is it known what parts of the available information are noticed, how they are interpreted, and how they affect attitude formation and overt behavior. This study of the nature of crime news in the mass media and its impact on selected populations sheds some light on these important matters.

The study forms part of the broader effort by social scientists to understand the impact that the mass media have on the opinions, attitudes, and behavior of the general public and its leaders. It sheds light on the manner in which people select and use information and on the reasons for their choices. In this sense, it contributes to the growing body of literature that deals with the uses to which audiences put the media and the gratifications that they derive from them. The book also contributes to another largely unplowed research field: the systematic study of mass media content holistically, in addition to focusing on selected parts. It does this by focusing on crime news in the larger setting of total news provided by the mass media and used by their audiences. This puts crime news into a realistic perspective, rather than distorting it by plucking it from its natural matrix and examining it as if it existed in a vacuum.

Knowledge about the nature of crime news and its impact on the images that people form about crime is needed for several reasons. In the first place, in a democratic society people need to know whether their main information channels provide adequate and accurate news to permit them to be well informed on matters of general concern. Crime is such a matter. It has been a major concern of the U.S. public since the mid-1960s because of its high human and property costs. In Gallup poll reports about the public's choices of the most important issues facing the United States, crime has received from 2 to 29 percent of the votes in the past ten years.[2] In late April 1976, 8 percent of Gallup's sample rated crime as one of the most crucial issues facing the country. This figure excludes the much larger number of people who were highly concerned about crime but did not give it a top rating. Their concern is reflected in polling data that show that the public pays a great deal of attention to news about crime-related matters and has definite ideas about causes of crime and measures that might prevent it.[3]

The respondents in the study reported here typify the opinions recorded by the polls. When questioned further, 64 percent indicated that they were moderately or seriously worried about becoming crime victims, 19 percent were slightly worried, and only 15 percent said that they were not worried at all. Seventy-six percent mentioned specific precautions that they were taking in line with their concerns about victimization. All respondents were familiar with a variety of aspects of crime as a social problem in the United States and with the nature and activities of the police, the courts, and the prison system. All claimed to pay attention to mass media information about crime and the justice system.

Because crime information is so important to people and is so widely used, it is essential to know how adequate and accurate it is at the present time, what systematic biases, if any, distort it, and what corrective measures can and should be taken to correct these biases.

Also, knowledge of crime perception is important for understanding public attitudes about crime and the criminal justice process, particularly those attitudes that are apt to have socially significant consequences. Among likely attitudinal consequences are fear and anxiety about personal safety and the safety of others; general dissatisfaction with the political system because of its perceived inability to protect the individual; distrust at the interpersonal level in social and business relations; and negative attitudes toward specific institutions such as the police, the courts, and the correctional system. Crime and justice news coverage may also engender negative feelings toward the media for allegedly spurring crime through excessive publicity, which glamorizes criminals, and through excessive detail, which provides blueprints for copying crimes.[4] This, in turn, may lead to reduced media credibility and impact and to sympathy for efforts to curb the freedom to publish.

The public's views about crime and crime fighting are taken seriously by politicians because these views measure public satisfaction in a policy area where substantial public cooperation is required to achieve best results.[5] Equally important for many politicians is the fact that public dissatisfaction with the government's capabilities to preserve law and order may lead to electoral sanctions. The 1972 presidential campaign is an example of the prominence that the law and order issue can assume in elections. Concern about these deleterious effects on U.S. society and on public confidence has led to a plethora of government-sponsored investigations into all aspects of the problem.* Many recommendations springing from this research have been widely discussed.

---

*The reports of the Kerner and Eisenhower commissions and voluminous reports by the Surgeon General's office are examples.

xv

Third, the immediate behavioral consequences that may spring from attitudes have a major impact on society. They include such risk-avoidance behavior as limiting one's movements to daytime activities; avoiding certain areas of the community entirely; shunning specific sites, such as high-rise buildings or public parks; avoiding contact with certain types of people, such as juveniles or racial minorities; driving instead of walking; making all outings group affairs; making outings dependent on male escorts; and avoiding public transportation. Special protective devices may be secured, such as dogs, burglar alarms, or private guard services; or people may move to cities that they deem safer or to more secure city locations and buildings.

The economic decay of many residential neighborhoods and business and entertainment sections of cities has been attributed to citizens' perceptions of crime. Likewise, the shut-in lives that many senior citizens and single women live, and the restraints put on interracial social contacts through fear-of-crime engendered housing changes, may well be consequences of the manner in which crime news is conveyed and processed in the United States.

These are just some of the reasons that make it important to take a closer look at the images of crime conveyed by the media and at the impact this information has on individuals and on society in general. Charges by radical criminologists and other critics that mass media images are skewed, unintentionally or deliberately, provide additional impetus for systematic examination of mass media output and its uses by the public. These charges are detailed and analyzed in Chapter 3.

In addition to the broader social purposes of this study, it has served a number of social scientific functions as well. Among these are experimentation with new techniques in the study of small panels of people in natural settings over lengthy periods of time. The data also have lent themselves to the testing of a variety of hypotheses concerning information processing in general and crime information processing in particular. This is particularly important at this juncture because researchers are attempting to go beyond general findings about learning from the mass media to pinpoint the specific conditions under which such learning occurs. Recent mass media studies indicate that there is substantial factual learning from the media and that this knowledge may affect people's attitudes, moods, and behaviors.[6] Furthermore, it has become evident that the breadth and depth of learning and the length of retention for recall vary, depending on subject matter, learning context, and the predisposition of audience members. Numerous field studies involving a variety of news topics will be required to test hypotheses about political learning under specified conditions and to develop models that shed light on the learning process in differential learning situations.

In the course of the project reported here, many hypotheses about learning about politically significant news from the mass media were tested. For example, the hypothesis that the nature of exposure to crime information will vary, depending on demographic characteristics of the audience, was partly confirmed. The same was true for the hypothesis that detailed descriptions of how crimes were executed and what their consequences were make crime news more frightening and produce longer retention. The hypothesis that exceptionally large amounts of crime information numb and desensitize audiences so that the excess amounts of crime information are largely ignored was fully confirmed. The opposite was true for the hypothesis that personal images of crime are more strongly influenced by media images than by official crime data. Whether or not such findings can be generalized to all news, or even to news that matches crime characteristics in terms of appeal and relation to personal experiences, remains to be tested. It does not seem unreasonable, however, to assume that the general learning patterns discerned for crime news are indicative of what researchers are likely to find in other subject areas.

Despite the importance of knowing the bases for the public's images of crime and the criminal justice process, researchers have paid comparatively little attention to this aspect of public attitudes. For the most part, they have failed to investigate what information is made available to the public about the crime and justice process, what the public learns from the data readily available to it, and how it uses this information to form its images and evaluations. The research reported here was undertaken to contribute to the closing of this knowledge gap.

NOTES

1. For data indicating that mass media information is the basis for public reactions to crime problems, see James Garofalo, "Victimization and Fear of Crime in Major American Cities," American Association for Public Opinion Research Paper, 1977. Also see "Public Attitudes Towards Crime and Law Enforcement," in *Task Force Report, Crime and Its Impact: An Assessment,* President's Commission on Law Enforcement and Administration of Justice (Washington, D.C.: U.S. Government Printing Office, 1967), pp. 85-95, especially pp. 86-87; John E. Conklin, *The Impact of Crime* (New York: Macmillan, 1975), pp. 22 ff.; and F. James Davis, "Crime News in Colorado Newspapers," *American Journal of Sociology* 57 (January 1962): 325-30.

2. See *Gallup Opinion Index,* annual volumes, 1967-80. Similar data can be found in the annual volumes of the *Harris Survey Research Yearbook of Public Opinion* and in the National Opinion Research Center's annual *Codebook for the Spring (Year) General Social Survey.*

3. The most complete review of public opinion data on crime is contained in four reports by Hazel Erskine in the spring, summer, fall, and winter issues of *Public Opinion Quarterly* 38 (1974). The reports are entitled "Fear of Violence and Crime," pp. 131-45; "Causes of Crime," pp. 288-98; "Control of Crime and Violence," pp. 490-502; and "Politics and Law and Order," pp. 623-34. Most relevant for this report are pp. 291-94, dealing with causes of crime; p. 493, dealing with social reforms as a way to cope with crime; and pp. 627 and 632-34, dealing with social reforms and attitudes toward the police and the courts. For polling data after 1973 that complement the *Public Opinion Quarterly* data, see *Gallup Opinion Index,* annual volumes, 1967-80. Similar data can be found in the annual volumes of the *Harris Survey Research Yearbook of Public Opinion* and in the National Opinion

Research Center's annual *Codebook for the Spring (Year) General Social Survey*. Also consult U.S. Department of Justice, *Sourcebook of Criminal Justice Statistics, 1978* (Washington, D.C.: Law Enforcement Assistance Administration, 1979), sec. 1, "Public Attitudes Toward Crime and Criminal Justice-Related Topics," pp. 285-359. For suggestions on the limitations of polls, see Terry Baumer and Fred DuBow, "Fear of Crime in the Polls: What They Do and Do Not Tell Us," American Association for Public Opinion Research Paper, 1977. Also see Michael J. Hindelang, "Public Opinion Regarding Crime, Criminal Justice, and Related Topics," *Journal of Research in Crime and Delinquency* 11 (July 1974): 101-16.

4. For data on the contagion effects of crime news, see David and Kay Payne, "Newspapers and Crime in Detroit," *Journalism Quarterly* 47 (1970): 233-35. Lincoln Steffens, in *The Autobiography of Lincoln Steffens* (New York: Harcourt, Brace, 1931), pp. 285-91, notes how media publicity can be used to alert the public to corruption and spark investigations.

5. Douglas Scott, "Measures of Citizen Evaluation of Local Government Services," in *Citizen Preferences and Urban Public Policy*, ed. Terry Nichols Clark (Beverly Hills, Calif.,: Sage, Contemporary Social Science Issues 34, 1976), pp. 111-28. Also see Clark's introduction to the volume, pp. 5-11. Donald J. Black, "The Production of Crime Rates," *American Sociological Review* 35 (1970): 733-48, reports that 76 percent of police responses to crime incidents in Boston, Chicago, and Washington, D.C., resulted from phone calls by citizens.

6. The factors that come into play in learning from the mass media are discussed in chap. 5 of Doris A. Graber, *Mass Media and American Politics* (Washington, D.C.: Congressional Quarterly Press, 1980). Also see Lee B. Becker, Maxwell E. Mc Combs, and Jack M. McLeod, "The Development of Political Cognitions," in *Political Communication: Issues and Strategies for Research*, ed. Steven H. Chaffee (Beverly Hills, Calif.: Sage, 1975), pp. 21-63, and sources cited there.

One

THE STUDY DESIGN

OBJECTIVES

Three major lines of inquiry will be pursued in this study. First of all, an assessment is made of how much and what kind of mass media information is supplied to the public for judging crime and the justice system. Second, we will provide data on the'amount of attention the public pays to this kind of information and on the kind of knowledge it extracts from it. Finally, a comparison is made of the kinds of perceptions and evaluations of crime and crime fighting that different types of people develop with the images and evaluations presented by the media. This will permit us to assess the scope of media impact. After ascertaining the public's perspective on crime and crime-fighting policies and its relationship to crime and justice news, we shall then speculate about the implications and consequences.

DATA SOURCES

The immediate objectives of the study were to analyze the entire content of major print and electronic news sources over the period of one year, on a daily basis, to determine the precise nature of news coverage. The total news supply made available to mass media audiences was analyzed because it provides the context for crime and justice news. Such news competes with other news for placement in the news media and for attention by media audiences. Its impact cannot be fully understood without observing it in a larger setting.

Similarly, the impact of crime and other news is cumulative. Looking at crime news for brief, selected time periods or assessing its impact in one-stage interviews fails to capture reality. It makes it impossible to judge the completeness of news coverage or to gauge the repetition rates of various stories and themes. This is why the present study examined the total news scene on a daily basis over a full year. The need for a full, long-range picture is also the rationale for checking audience perceptions through multiple interviews and through daily reports from respondents.

The media content analysis included an examination of the subject matter discussed by the media, as well as the placement and emphasis given to various types of stories. "Stories" for newspapers were defined as including editorials, letters to the editor, features, and cartoons, as well as ordinary news reports, but excluding advertisements, obituaries, puzzles, radio and television listings, and similar types of announcements. For television, stories encompassed all information conveyed during regularly scheduled newscasts.

The general news analysis undertaken for all the media in the study provides the backdrop for a far more detailed analysis of crime and justice system stories in one of the newspapers of the study: the *Chicago Tribune*. The *Tribune* was selected because it was the paper read by the largest group of panelists interviewed for this study. It also represents a major metropolitan paper that media professionals rate among the top 15 news sources in the United States.[1] Furthermore, it has a sturdy economic base that permits it the luxury to abstain from using sensational crime coverage as bait for boosting circulation. Its crime and justice news coverage is therefore moderate in all respects.

For this detailed analysis, *Tribune* crime and justice stories were coded on such features as the nature of the crimes that were covered, discussion of causes and motivations of crime, details revealed about particular crimes, and apprehension, prosecution, conviction, and penalties. Stories dealing primarily with the police, the courts, and the correctional system were also included in this intensive analysis to provide a comprehensive picture of the images of crime depicted in the *Tribune*. The newspaper codebook and crime story codebook in Appendixes A and C contain detailed information about all of the news features that were captured in the coding.

Table 1.1 outlines the basic research design. It indicates that, besides the *Tribune*, general content analysis was also carried out for the *Indianapolis News*, the *Indianapolis Star*, and the *Lebanon Valley News*. The latter three are papers that served members of two of the panels included in this study, one from a working class neighborhood in Indianapolis and the other from the small town of Lebanon, New Hampshire.* In addition, two constructed weeks of issues of

---

*Three sets of investigators were involved in the analysis. Chicago area print and electronic media were analyzed by a team of research assistants under the author's supervision.

TABLE 1.1
Research Design

Data Sources	Research Tools
Print Media	
Chicago Tribune	General content analysis;* crime content analysis
Indianapolis News	General content analysis
Indianapolis Star	General content analysis
Lebanon Valley News	General content analysis
Television	
Local CBS	Audio and video content analysis
Local NBC	Audio and video content analysis
National ABC	Audio content analysis; partial crime content analysis
National CBS	Audio content analysis
National NBC	Audio content analysis
Audience Panels	
Evanston Core Panel	Taped interviews, diaries, recall stories
Evanston Regular Panel	Telephone interviews
Indianapolis Panel	Telephone interviews
Lebanon Panel	Telephone interviews

Note: Time frame for content analysis: January 15, 1976 to January 14, 1977. Interview dates — January, February, April, May, June, July, August, October, November 1976, and January 1977.

*General content analysis includes semidetailed crime coding. Crime content analysis involves highly detailed crime coding.

Source: Original research.

The Indiana newspapers were analyzed under the supervision of David Weaver of Indiana University. The New Hampshire paper was analyzed under the supervision of Maxwell McCombs of Syracuse University. The first three months of the national television news were analyzed in Syracuse and the remaining nine months in Chicago. Interviews and their analysis were supervised by investigators in each of the panel areas.

The newspaper, television, and interview codebooks in the appendixes to this book are the working documents used in all three locations. The crime news codebook was used in full only for the *Chicago Tribune* and the constructed weeks of the *Sun-Times* and the *Daily News*. Portions were also used to code the *Evanston Review* and ABC national news.

Coding used for the Reactions to Crime project at Northwestern University was partially patterned on this study so that the data are comparable. The Northwestern project involves crime news study for selected periods in San Francisco, Philadelphia, and Chicago. Codebooks are reported in Center for Urban Affairs, Northwestern University, *The Reactions to Crime Papers,* vol. 5, "Crime in the Newspapers and Fear in the Neighborhoods: Some Unintended Consequences" (Evanston, Ill.: Northwestern University, September 1979).

the *Chicago Daily News* and the *Chicago Sun-Times* were coded for comparison with *Chicago Tribune* coverage.* Because two of the panels were located in Evanston, a greater Chicago area town, local crime coverage by the weekly *Evanston Review*, which many of the respondents read, was also recorded. Based on previous studies that indicate the similarity of subject matter of news offerings in major metropolitan centers, there is no reason to believe that the papers selected for this study are atypical, compared to other papers in localities of comparable size.[2]

As Table 1.1 indicates, crime coverage on television was monitored through analysis of news on five separate programs, selected to correspond to viewing habits of the panel of interviewees. The programs were the NBC Chicago local broadcast of television news at 5:00 p.m., the CBS Chicago local broadcast of television news at 10:00 p.m., and the early evening national television news on ABC, CBS, and NBC. Local news was viewed, taped, and coded from the actual telecast. National news was coded from printed abstracts provided by the Vanderbilt Television News Archives. Comparisons between codings from these abstracts and codings done directly from the newscasts showed only very minor differences for the information required for this study. Use of the abstracts simplified coding and reduced costs substantially. At the local level no abstracts were available.

The codebook for television news appended to this study provides details about television news coding. While there was no primary coding of radio broadcasts and of news magazines, information provided during interviews and in the daily news diaries furnished by respondents gives some insights about the crime coverage in these sources. These audience comments suggest that radio newscasts yield information that is quite similar to local television newscasts. Except for sensational crimes, news magazines, on the other hand, provide little crime information. On balance, it appears, the inclusion of radio and news magazine coding would not have altered the substance of findings presented in this book.

The reliability of coding for the content analyses was carefully checked and controlled. Because many different coders were involved in this project, it is difficult to report a single reliability figure. The procedure was to have the same coding supervisor recode a portion of each coder's work following the initial training period and at various times thereafter. Excluding simple identification categories, like paper or station name and date, which could inflate reliability figures, intercoder reliability averaged 85 percent and intracoder reliability averaged 90 percent, using the ratio of coding agreements to the total number of coding decisions. Considering the complexity of coding, these are good results.[3]

The impact of crime news on mass media audiences was ascertained through contact with four separate panels of respondents. As Table 1.1 indicates, these

---

*A constructed week is composed of seven successive weekdays, each drawn from a different week. For the Indiana papers, every fourth day was coded, including Sundays.

panels of 48 respondents each were located in Indianapolis, Indiana, Lebanon, New Hampshire, and Evanston, Illinois. In addition, a "core panel" of 21 respondents in Evanston furnished taped in-depth interviews and provided daily diaries of media usage. The sites were chosen to include residents of a small town, a medium-sized city, and a metropolitan area in locations that were convenient for the investigators. Selection methods for the four panels are discussed below. In addition to the interviews and diaries, the lifestyles and habits of respondents in all panels were observed through regular or periodic personal interviews. Interview data were also supplemented by data on community characteristics.

Repeated interviews of the same people always raise questions about the effects of earlier interviews on later ones. To check on such "sensitization effects," periodic interviews were conducted with nonpanel members, covering selected matters for which data were available from panel members. No significant differences were found between core and regular panel members and the control groups that had been chosen through identical procedures.*

The interview questions used for the core panel and the larger panels overlapped only in part. Core panel questions were more detailed and covered many additional issues, including a far heavier emphasis on the perception of crime and crime stories. However, crime stories were never the dominant interview focus. Substantially more background information was accumulated for members of the core panel, including information about childhood experiences, present lifestyle, personal and political philosophies, attitudes toward the mass media, and use and availability of various media throughout the respondent's life. Information about the respondent's current work and family and friendship circles and about the sources of information used by friends, coworkers, and family members was also included. All of the panels were relatively small in order to investigate knowledge and image formation intensively and over an extended period of time. Also, the high costs involved in this procedure made it mandatory to keep respondent numbers small.[4]

To check the representativeness of the panelists, their responses were compared with results from national surveys that had involved several identical questions. The patterns were sufficiently similar to suggest that this study's findings are fairly typical for demographically matching groups in the general population.†

---

*For instance, a comparison of story recall showed a mean recall of 2.3 points for panel members and 2.4 points for the control group (.05). Recall of stories was scored on a four-point scale, ranging from 1 for "none" to 4 for "a lot." The latter rating was awarded whenever respondents could spontaneously relate three or more aspects of a news story. The stories were randomly selected recent news stories reported by both press and television.

†Comparisons were made by replicating a series of questions asked in the 1976 Election Survey conducted by the Center for Political Studies at the University of Michigan, Ann Arbor, Michigan.

Official police records of crime in the Chicago area and FBI (Federal Bureau of Investigation) crime statistics for 1976 were also collected to provide a basis for comparison with the crime content analyses data, as well as the crime information from individual diaries and interviews. Because the bulk of media stories about crime is sparked by data supplied by the police, the discrepancies between police crime rosters and media stories reflect the gatekeeping process by which the media pick and choose among available stories. Comparisons also disclose the discrepancies that exist between "official" and media reality as it depicts the world of crime in the United States.

RESEARCH PROCEDURES: MEDIA ANALYSIS

Crime story coding had five chief objectives. First of all, we were interested in the types of crime stories reported in the media. Examples might be stories about gang violence, biographies of criminals, court reform stories, or crime prevention stories. Second, we wanted to record what specific crimes were discussed in each story. These crimes were categorized to conform to FBI crime reporting to facilitate comparisons between media and real-world data. We also sought to ascertain the motives, triggering incidents, and causes to which stories linked crimes. Furthermore, we wanted to focus on attributes about the criminals, the crime, and the victims. Factors such as sex, age, race, national background, occupation, previous crime record, location of the crime and details of injuries in crime execution, and subsequent police and court action were important here. Finally, we looked for evaluations provided in crime stories about the work of police, the courts, the correctional system, criminal justice policies, crime prevention policies, and overall evaluations of the crime danger and statistical trends.

We selected these main points because they had predominated as the main themes in unstructured conversations about crime with a small panel of respondents. These conversations were part of a pretest conducted for this study in 1975. The bulk of FBI data came from monthly reports by the Chicago police department. No daily reports were available. Comparisons of media and police data had to be structured accordingly.

RESEARCH PROCEDURES: RESPONDENT ANALYSIS

The relationship between the supply of crime information and the awareness, perception, and use of this information was tested through a series of lengthy interviews. Ten interviews, averaging two hours in length, were completed with each member of the Evanston core panel. The other panels were interviewed nine times for periods ranging from a half hour or less for telephone interviews to two hours or more for personal and group meetings. All interviews were conducted between January 1976 and January 1977 and were spaced out at roughly six-week intervals. The schedule was varied at times to place interviews before or after important political events that were likely to affect media coverage patterns and respondent learning patterns. All core panel interviews were conducted in person and tape-recorded to permit a variety of analyses of the manner in which the respondents conceptualized and expressed problems beyond recording the substance of the responses. The taping method was chosen after three months of pretesting with taped and untaped interviews, which disclosed that taping did not inhibit conversations once rapport between interviewer and respondent had been established. Remarks by respondents support this conclusion.

Seven of the nine interviews with the larger panels were conducted by telephone. One interview, midway in the study, was a personal taped session; another, at the end, was a group interview conducted with groups of four to seven respondents at a public meeting place. In open-ended interviews, telephone responses are apt to be leaner than replies in a face-to-face setting. But they were found to be sufficiently rich for the purposes of the study to justify their use as a way to save expense. A small part of the information loss was recouped through the one personal taped interview.

The group interview was designed to explore attitudes that panel members had developed about the conduct of the research project and the project's impact on their opinions. Exploration in a group setting eases the difficulty of formulating ideas, which individuals often experience. It also reduces inhibitions to express ideas that might be threatening to the interviewer.[5]

Test Panel Selection

The following description details core panel procedures. Selection methods for the larger panels were basically the same, with only minor variations in such matters as the size of the pool from which respondents were selected, failure rate in contacting respondents, and refusal rates after contact had been made.

The Evanston core panel consisted of 21 respondents selected from a pool of 200 respondents who were randomly chosen from the Evanston list of registered voters. Contact with these 200 respondents represented an 80 percent success rate in reaching voters identified from the voting rosters that election officials had compiled 20 months earlier. Most of the unreachables, particularly university students, had moved out of the city. Of the 200 registrants who were contacted, 84 percent agreed to participate in the study, following the filter interview. Registered voters were used for the study on the assumption that this somewhat select pool would tap the more politically alert elements of the population whose perceptions were likely to be the most informed in the three communities. Compared to nonvoters, need for political information was likely to spur them to broader and more thorough media exposure.[6] In addition to the core panel, the 48 members of the larger Evanston panel were also selected from the pool. The remainder of the pool served as controls to test the degree of sensitization of panel members.

The core panel was drawn to represent a combination of interest in politics and ready availability of information. This combination taps the eagerness to be informed, as modified by the effort required to get information or use it in the face of competing demands on the respondent's time. A four-cell design was used to divide people into the following groups: (1) high interest, high availability; (2) low interest, high availability; (3) high interest, low availability; and (4) low interest, low availability. Assignments were made on the basis of responses to five questions for the interest score and four questions for the availability score.* The accuracy of initial assignments was retested repeatedly to correct initial mistakes or to adjust for subsequent changes in respondents' interest or availability scores.

In addition to the interest-availability criteria, an effort was made in the final selection process to reduce the coding task by choosing only people who were *Tribune* readers.† It was not possible to narrow television coding in the same manner. To correspond to respondents' television tastes, two local and three national telecasts had to be coded. Additionally, an attempt was made to select respondents with a wide spread of demographic and socioeconomic characteristics. Table 1.2 summarizes the demographic characteristics of all four panels. Table 1.3 depicts the types of respondents included in the core panel. Because Evanston is primarily a university town, socioeconomic and educational levels of registered voters are higher than would be true of a national sample. Mixing Evanstonians with panelists from Indianapolis and Lebanon dilutes these characteristics but does not obliterate them. The likely differences between the panels and less advantaged groups will be pointed out when relevant findings are discussed. Judging from responses by panel members representing lower socioeconomic and educational groups, these differences are matters of degree rather than substance.

---

*The interest variable was based on the following questions: 1. How much do you use newspapers for news about political issues and events? 2. How much do you use television for news about political events? 3. In general, how often do you discuss politics with others? 4. Overall, how interested are you in politics? 5. How far did you go in school? The availability variable was based on the following questions: 1. How often do you read a daily newspaper? 2. How often do you watch the news on television? 3. Do you subscribe to a newspaper, buy it at a newsstand, secure it in specified other ways? 4. How often do you watch television? Probes elicited reasons for the answers.

†Analysis of variance between *Tribune* readers and those using other papers showed no significant differences.

TABLE 1.2
Demographic Characteristics of the Four Panels
(in percentages; N = 164)

Age	Sex	Occupation	Education*
Under 30 = 27	Male = 51	Skilled workers = 20	Grade school = 17
30-40 = 24	Female = 49	Sales and service = 15	High school = 16
41-50 = 10		Professional = 13	Trade school = 24
51-60 = 20		Homemaker = 12	College = 43
61-70 = 10		Retired = 9	
71-80 = 7		Business = 8	
Over 80 = 1		Clerical = 6	
		Unskilled = 6	
		Students = 4	
		Miscellaneous = 4	
		Unemployed = 3	

*Each grouping signifies graduates. The trade school grouping includes people with partial college educations.

Source: Original research.

The original research design called for four panel members in each cell with a fifth one selected as replacement in anticipation of a 20 percent dropout rate. When one panel member expected to be transferred out of the Chicago area during the first trimester of the study, an additional substitute was recruited. Although the transfer did not materialize, the substitute was retained. Because there were no dropouts, contrary to the experience of other panel studies, all 21 respondents completed the project. The high retention rate appears to have been due to a combination of factors, chief among them that the panel members were paid for their efforts ($1 per day for diaries and $5 for each interview), that they were interviewed only by the principal investigator, permitting the establishment of good rapport, and that a series of regular reports and letters kept them aware of the significance of studying political learning and the importance of their contribution. Copies of all published findings were promised to them as well. In the regular panels where rapport between interviewers and respondents was less close, the dropout rate averaged 15 percent. Replacements were made from reserve lists only for people who had dropped out prior to the sixth interview.

Awareness Tests

Respondents were tested for awareness of news stories, for the complete-ness of recall of the news stories of which they became aware, and for their

TABLE 1.3
Demographic and Media Characteristics of the Core Panel

Age	Sex	Education*	Occupation
1. High-interest, high-availability group			
25	M	College	Research engineer
38	M	College	Administrator
45	M	College	Academic
74	M	College	Lawyer
75	M	Grade school	Blue-collar
2. High-interest, low-availability group			
28	F	College	Home/child care
28	F	College	Corporation executive
30	F	College	Job/home/child care
33	M	College	Government administrator
36	M	College	Editor
3. Low-interest, high-availability group			
25	M	College	Grocery clerk
46	F	High school	Dress shop owner
50	F	College	Homemaker
65	F	High school	Bookkeeper
78	F	High school	Homemaker
4. Low-interest, low-availability group			
23	M	High school	Hospital clerk
27	M	College	Retail sales
28	F	High school	Insurance clerk
36	F	High school	Nurse
56	F	3rd grade	Maid
62	M	College	Plant manager

*Each grouping signifies graduates. The trade school grouping includes people with partial college educations.

Source: Original research.

basic knowledge about a variety of current happenings and conditions. These tests ranged over all types of information. To assess current learning from the mass media, the respondents were told that the interviewers were interested in whatever news had come to their attention. To avoid influencing their answers, they were never told that news of any particular type, such as crime and justice news, was of particular interest. Interview questions provided few clues because they ranged over a large number of topics, as the research encompassed several areas of political learning. In fact, there were many more questions about the 1976 elections stories than about crime stories.

To test respondents' awareness of crime stories, three measures were used. One was interviewing, which tested respondents' awareness of specific crime stories and recall of details from these stories. During each interview core panel members were questioned about an array of 20 to 30 news stories that had been covered by the newspaper and/or television news programs to which they normally paid attention. Stories about subjects prominent in the news during the preceding month were included. Out of a total of 285 news stories for which recall was tested, 25 percent dealt with matters relating to crime and crime-fighting policies.

The second method was diary analysis, which ascertained on a daily basis the types of stories to which respondents paid attention. Diaries permitted comparison of the manner of recall of crime and noncrime stories that had come to respondents' attention and that were spontaneously remembered. A third measure was narrative self-assessment during background interviews. Here the respondents talked generally about their experiences and beliefs, about the type of information they had received from various media and nonmedia sources, and about the impact that information supplied by these sources had on their cognitions and feelings. The interviews covered experiences and lifestyle during childhood, adolescence, and adulthood. Respondents were asked to recall events in their lives that had seemed memorable when they occurred or seemed memorable in retrospect. They were also asked about their recollection of specific political and social events during their lifetime, such as wars, economic upheavals, and major political changes.

Perception Tests

From the information that comes to their attention, average individuals form images of reality, along with evaluations and feelings about the world that exists in their minds. These individual perceptions of crime and the criminal justice process were assessed through three different measures. The first of these consisted of interview questions that asked respondents about the details they remembered about particular crime stories that had come to their attention. The type of detail that was reported indicates what sorts of things are important to particular respondents. Likewise, diary stories about crimes were analyzed to detect the types of details that people selected. Third, general questions, unrelated to particular crime stories, were asked during interviews to check people's perceptions and conceptualizations of crime and the criminal justice process.

Answers to general questions indicated, for instance, that some respondents appraised crime stories in terms of self and family protection. Those details that were applicable to their own life situations were stored and processed into messages about protective behavior. Other respondents processed crime stories in a "societal sickness" context. They sought links between crime and such social problems as inadequate housing and unemployment. Still others ignored crime stories almost totally, considering them repetitious, uninteresting, and devoid of any behavioral clues. For them, crime, like the weather, had to be endured and was not worthy of attention.

From the answers that respondents gave to a variety of questions over an extended number of interviews, cognitive maps for individual respondents were constructed that could then be correlated with background and behavioral data. Because people do not perceive various aspects in their environment in isolation, it is important to reconstruct the totality of their mental images by aggregating their answers to individual questions. Cognitive mapping attempts this. A cognitive map represents perceptions of various aspects of a problem and provides insights into the dynamics of interaction among these aspects. Cognitive mapping was done to spot interrelations among such matters as perceptions of locations where crime occurs most often, mental profiles of the typical criminal and the typical victim, views about the causes of crime and potential remedies, and appraisals of the police, the courts, and the correctional system.

The data about crime and criminal justice procedures gathered through perception and awareness tests were compared to the content analysis data to assess their correspondence and the degree to which the media shape citizens' awareness and perception of crime. The data were also compared to crime data available from police records and to data from victimization and other crime occurrence studies. Similarly, the correlation between perceptual data and crime avoidance and protective behavior was appraised.[7]

Behavioral Tests

In addition to observing and evaluating panel members' perceptions of the crime scene, we also observed crime avoidance behavior and asked questions about such behavior. The observations and questions concerned protective devices that respondents used to guard themselves against crime, restraints in movement they had adopted to avoid exposure to crime, and their past experience with crime and criminals. While similar data have been gathered by other studies, such as Northwestern University's Reactions to Crime project, this study contributes fresh insights for the interpretation of these data because of more intensive and prolonged contact with respondents.

Interview Questions

The following questions were asked in interviews to shed light on awareness, perception, and use of crime information. For each question, there were unlimited probes to elicit more complete information and to ascertain the reasons for the respondent's answer. Furthermore, to increase the level of confidence in the reliability of the data, many questions were repeated in successive interviews, with the same wording or in an alternative form. To control for the impact of prior questions, repeat questions were always placed into contexts within the interview that differed from previous contexts. Broad open-ended questions were followed by more focused open-ended questions, designed to elicit a common data base for all respondents. Roughly 25 percent of the questions presented fixed alternatives.

As indicated earlier, a large number of questions were asked about the respondent's past and current lifestyle and experiences and about his or her perceptions and evaluations of ongoing events. Questions about the crime and justice system were part of this broader matrix (Appendix D contains coding information for these questions). These questions can be grouped under six headings:

I. Use and Appraisal of Mass Media

1. During the past month, how much attention did you pay to newspaper and television stories about crime?

2. What kinds of crime did you read or hear about most?

3. In general, do you feel that the newspapers report crime accurately? How about television, radio, news magazines, fiction stories?

4. In general, do you feel that newspapers give too much or too little coverage to crime stories, or is coverage about right?

5. What about stories about white-collar crime? Are they adequately covered?

6. Do you learn about crime mostly from mass media, personal knowledge, or from conversation with others?

7. Do you recall whether newspapers generally describe the kinds of injuries that victims suffer? What do you remember about injury description?

8. Some people say that the media teach people how to commit crimes by describing crimes in detail. Do you think that people learn how to commit crimes by watching television shows/reading newspaper accounts of crime/ reading crime fiction in books or magazines? Is it a serious problem? Why or why not? What, if anything, can/should be done about it?

II. Personal Experience and Concern with Crime

1. Have you or your friends or your family ever been a victim of crime? What happened?

2. Have you ever personally known a person accused of crime or convicted of crime? Tell me some of the details.

3. Are you personally concerned about becoming a victim of crime? If yes, how much?

4. Recently, there have been many stories about crime and illegal activities involving people in all walks of life. As a result of these, do you trust any of the following less than you did five years ago? Or are things pretty much the same? Doctors/lawyers/big business/repairmen/merchants/politicians/Congress/courts/ police/Greeks/Italians/Latinos/Swedes/blacks/teenagers/neighbors?

5. Do you do anything special to protect yourself against becoming a victim of crime? What is that?

6. Do you avoid going to certain neighborhoods or places because you think they are dangerous? Which ones do you consider dangerous? Which ones do you avoid?

7. What makes you think that place X, Y, Z, etc., is dangerous? Who told you that?

8. Do you think that most crimes occur outdoors or inside buildings? What kinds of outdoor locations are most dangerous? What kinds of indoor locations are most dangerous? Why?

9. Do you try to avoid these places? How? At what times?

III. Images of Crime, Criminals, and Causes of Crime

1. Do you have any ideas about what causes people to commit crimes? Which of these causes is most important? What, if anything, can be done about it?

2. If you had to describe the person most likely to commit a crime, how would you describe that person? (Probe for age, sex, occupation, national background, and so on if not supplied spontaneously.)

3. If you had to describe the person most likely to become a victim of crime, how would you describe that person? (Probe for age, sex, occupation, national background, and so on if not supplied spontaneously.)

4. Do you think that most crimes are committed by people acting alone, or are there usually several people involved? How many?

5. Do you think that in most crimes just one person gets hurt, or are there usually several victims? How many?

6. Do you think that most people who commit crimes already have a record of crime? Why is that?

7. I am going to mention a list of nonviolent and white-collar crimes. In each case, tell me how often it occurs, whether it happens more or less frequently than violent crimes, and who the most likely criminals and victims are. Extortion/forgery/counterfeiting/fraud/consumer deceit/embezzlement/bribery/kickbacks/corrupt deals/dealing in stolen property/weapons violations/escape from custody/parole violations/illegal wiretaps/prostitution/other sex offenses/drug offenses/gambling/tax cheating/welfare cheating/contributing to minor's delinquency/child abuse/drunken driving/vagrancy/disorderly conduct/perjury/false fire alarm/civil or criminal contempt of court.

IV. Coping with Crime: The Criminal Justice System

1. Do you feel crime is on the increase, decrease, or about the same in Evanston/Chicago compared to last year? Compared to five years ago? Why is that?

2. Do you think that the police are very successful or very unsuccessful in catching criminals? Why is that? What are the criteria for being "successful"?

3. People accused of crime often complain that the police violate their civil rights. Do you feel, in general, that these claims are justified? Why or why not? In what ways are civil rights most often claimed to be impaired?

4. In general, would you say that the police are doing a good job, fair job, or poor job in protecting the community? Explain.

5. Compared to five years ago, are they doing a better, worse, or stable job? Why or why not?

6. How about the correctional system — prisons, parole boards, etc.? Are they doing a fair, good, or poor job? Why or why not?

7. Compared to five years ago, are they doing a stable, worse, or better job? Why or why not?

8. What about the courts? Are they doing a poor job, fair job, or good job? Why or why not?

9. Compared to five years ago, are they doing a better, worse, or stable job? Explain.

10. Some people feel that the courts are far too lenient in imposing penalties. Others feel that penalties are too severe. Others think they are just about right. What do you think? How would you determine the kind of penalty that is right for a particular offense?

11. Do you think the federal/state/local/subdivisional government is doing all it can to reduce crime in the United States/state/city/subdivision? Do you think that citizens are doing all they can? What else could be done? What is your source of information?

12. Corruption in government is considered to be a serious problem. Tell me briefly what the problem is. Is it serious or not? Why do we have it? What can be done about it? What are your sources of information about the problem?

V. Public Protective Policies

1. Do you think that guns are used frequently to help criminals commit crimes? What other weapons are often used?

2. Are you in favor of gun control legislation? What kinds? Do you know any political leaders who favor gun control? What kind of control?

3. Do you have any idea why attempts to pass gun control legislation have been largely unsuccessful?

4. Some people are primarily concerned with doing everything possible to protect the legal rights of those accused of committing crimes. Others feel that it is more important to stop criminal activity, even at the risk of reducing the rights of the accused. Where would you place yourself on a seven-point scale when point 1 puts the rights of the accused first and point 7 puts the need to stop crime first? Where would you place Gerald Ford/Jimmy Carter/the Democratic party/the Republican party/most blacks/most whites?

5. Have you read or heard anything about programs that provide for public compensation for crime victims? What is that? What do you think about it? What else could be done?

6. Have you heard or read anything about programs to protect wives who are beaten by their husbands? What is that? What do you think about it? What else could be done?

7. Have you heard or read anything about protection of children from beatings by their parents? What is that? What do you think about it? Could anything else be done?

8. Have you heard or read anything about help for people who believe that businesspeople have cheated them? What is that? What do you think about it? Could anything else be done?

9. Have you heard or read anything about places that will help a person annoyed or injured by environmental pollution (noise, air, and so on)? What is that? What do you think about it? Could anything else be done about it?

Periodically, detailed questions were asked about specific crimes that had received major attention in the news. The chief examples are the Hearst kidnapping/bank robbery case and the Chowchilla bus hijacking case.*

VI. Images of Specific Crimes

1. Are you watching the stories about the Patty Hearst/Chowchilla bus hijacking case? How closely? On what medium?

2. If you had to tell a friend very quickly what it was all about, what would you say? Why do you pick these facts?

3. What outcome do you predict in the case? Do you think that is a good or a bad outcome, or partly good and partly bad? Why?

4. Do you think that the media are doing a good job in reporting this kind of story? Why or why not?

5. Are there any other crime stories that stand out in your mind for the last month? What are they? Why do you remember them?

PROCEDURES FOR DIARIES AND STORY RECALL CHECKS

Members of the core panel were asked to complete diaries for five days each week (Appendix E presents forms, instructions, and the codebook). Although five days was the norm, some members occasionally dropped below that level, skipping three or four days. Others occasionally recorded a full week. The diaries reported current happenings to which the respondent had been exposed through the mass media, through conversations, or through personal experience. Respondents were asked to record at least three current events stories per day, if they could, but to delay recording until several hours after exposure to the information to allow normal forgetting to take place. The delay, as reported by respondents, normally was four hours or more. The diary forms requested brief accounts about the main theme of the story, its source and length, and the respondent's reasons for interest in the story and her/his reactions to it.

Of the 21 panel members, 13 completed diaries on their own, while 5 reported diary information to an interviewer via telephone. Pretests had indicated that there was no substantial difference in quantity and quality between telephone and self-administered diaries. A check during the course of study, involving two respondents who alternated between self-administration and telephone collection, substantiated this finding. Three of the alternates were not asked to complete diaries for economy reasons. This saved the daily diary fee and the substantial costs incurred in diary coding.

The average number of diary stories per person was 533, with a range from a low of 351 to a high of 969. Diary completion generally was regular, except

---

*The Hearst case involved criminal activity by kidnapped heiress Patricia Hearst as a member of a terrorist organization, the Symbionese Liberation Army. The Chowchilla case involved hijacking a school bus and holding the children captive for ransom.

for periods of illness in the family and for vacations. At those times, most respondents claimed that they did not pay attention to news, either directly or indirectly, through conversation. Tests of information recall support the accuracy of this claim. Respondents who normally recalled several of the 20 to 30 prominent news stories about which they were routinely questioned in interviews showed sharply reduced recall scores for periods in which their daily routines had been interrupted.

Besides testing story memory, diary data also provide information on the media or personal sources from which diary stories originated. This information was collected to check a number of theories about the impact of various information sources. Particular interest was in discovering whether stories that were recalled well enough to appear in diaries came predominantly from print or electronic media or from conversation. If media sources were mixed, were there differences in the types of stories usually reported from a particular medium? As it turned out, this aspect of the research did not provide clear answers. Most people who had been exposed to a variety of information sources either listed multiple sources of information or failed to remember the precise source.

The story recall questions previously described checked the extent to which diary stories, as well as stories that had not appeared in a respondent's diaries, were remembered by various respondents. They were asked whether they remembered a story about a recently publicized event, such as "the story about the girl raped at the bus station," or "the story about charges of corruption in the governor's office." If the answer was "yes," the respondent was then asked to provide details about the story and about her or his reaction to it. Respondents were also asked to name the source of the story and to indicate why they thought they remembered or failed to remember it. Memory factors, along with data about conceptualization of stories, were then analyzed in light of the personal and social context data collected about individual respondents.

While the diaries and interview questions ascertained the substance of information that people noticed, absorbed, and recalled, a series of additional tests was initiated to determine information selection strategies and tactics employed by individual respondents. These tests involved respondents' marking of newspapers to indicate precisely what parts of various stories they had noticed and which stories they had ignored on a given day. The fact that these tests indicated that two thirds of the information was ignored supports the overall impression that respondents did not generally exaggerate their attentiveness to the media. News selection strategies were also discussed at length during group interviews. In the group situation, a wide array of behaviors is brought to the fore. This makes it easier for individuals to recall their own experiences and to appraise the full scope of their own behaviors.

DATA FROM RELATED STUDIES

For a number of the questions asked during interviews, there are data from other studies that are useful for comparison. Examples include the U.S. Department of Justice's study of *Public Opinion About Crime: The Attitudes of Victims and Nonvictims in Selected Cities,* which presents survey data from Chicago, New York, Los Angeles, Philadelphia, and Detroit. Similarly, the Reactions to Crime project at Northwestern University reports interview and content analysis data from Chicago, Philadelphia, and San Francisco. In addition, various public opinion polls conducted during the past 15 years have regularly included questions on crime and the criminal justice system. The FBI's Uniform Crime Reports and the Law Enforcement Assistance Administration's *Sourcebook of Criminal Justice Statistics* also contain valuable comparative information, as do many of the sources cited in the annotated bibliography at the end of this book.

To compare the attitudes of core panel members with the attitudes of a national sample of respondents, we secured advance copies of questionnaires used in the fall of 1976 by the Center for Political Studies of the Institute for Social Research at the University of Michigan for its regular preelection and postelection surveys. A series of questions from these surveys relating to perceptions of social problems was administered to the core panel. The results were then compared with the results obtained in the Center for Political Studies surveys. The fact that the patterns of responses in the two surveys are similar when one matches demographic groups increases confidence in the representativeness of our data. If this microcosm mirrors the opinion distribution of the national sample on one set of social policy questions, it seems reasonable to assume that the same is likely to be true for a set of related social policy questions.

NOTES

1. John W. C. Johnstone, Edward J. Slawski, and William W. Bowman, *The News People* (Urbana: University of Illinois Press, 1976), p. 224.

2. Data on the similarity of coverage in a cross section of 20 daily newspapers are discussed in Doris A. Graber, "Effect of Incumbency on Coverage Patterns in the 1972 Presidential Campaign," *Journalism Quarterly* 53 (Fall 1976): 499-508. Crime coverage similarities are discussed in Shari Cohen, "A Comparison of Crime Coverage in Detroit and Atlanta Newspapers," *Journalism Quarterly* 52 (1975): 726-30; E. Terrence Jones, "The Press as Metropolitan Monitor," *Public Opinion Quarterly* 40 (1976): 239-44; and John C. Meyer, Jr., "Newspaper Reporting of Crime and Justice: Analysis of an Assumed Difference," *Journalism Quarterly* 52 (1975): 731-34. Data collected for the Reactions to Crime project at Northwestern University during a comparable time period also support this conclusion. The papers were the *Philadelphia Evening Bulletin,* the *Philadelphia Inquirer,* the *Philadelphia Daily News,* the *San Francisco Examiner,* and the *San Francisco Chronicle,* in addition to the *Chicago Tribune,* the *Chicago Sun-Times,* and the *Chicago Daily News.*

3. Content analysis reliability tests are discussed in Ole R. Holsti, *Content Analysis for the Social Sciences and Humanities* (Reading, Mass.: Addison Wesley, 1969), pp. 135-42.

4. The argument that generalizable findings about human behavior can be made on the basis of intensive study of small numbers of individuals has been made persuasively by many scholars. Examples are Steven R. Brown, "Intensive Analysis in Political Research," *Political Methodology* 1, (1974): 1-25; Fred M. Kerlinger, "Q-Methodology in Behavioral Research," in *Science, Psychology, Communication*, ed. Steven R. Brown and Garry D. Brenner (New York: Teachers College Press), pp. 3-38; Robert E. Lane, *Political Ideology: Why the American Common Man Believes What He Does* (New York: Free Press, 1962), pp. 1-11; and Karl Lamb, *As Orange Goes: Twelve California Families and the Future of American Politics* (New York: Norton, 1975), pp. vii-xiii, 3-23.

5. The following sources provide information about various interviewing issues considered in the choice of the research design: David and Chava Nachmias, *Research Methods in the Social Sciences* (New York: St. Martin's Press, 1976), pp. 100-18; Robert Bogdan and Steven J. Taylor, *Introduction to Qualitative Research Methods* (New York: Wiley, 1975), pp. 104-24; and Mathew Hauck, "Group Interviewing," in *Handbook of Marketing Research*, vol. 2, ed. Robert Ferber, 2 (New York: McGraw-Hill, 1974), pp. 133-46.

6. David H. Weaver, "Political Issues and Voter Need for Orientation," in *The Agenda-Setting Function of the Press*, ed. Donald L. Shaw and Maxwell E. McCombs (St. Paul, Minn.: West, 1977), pp. 107-19.

7. The process of learning crime prevention behavior is discussed in George I. Balch and John A. Gardiner, "Getting People to Protect Themselves: Information, Facilitation, Regulatory, and Incentive Strategies," Midwest Political Science Association Paper, 1979.

Two

CRIME AND JUSTICE
NEWS IN PERSPECTIVE

Social scientists, as well as citizens in general, have complained a good deal in recent years about coverage of crime news. Crime news, it is claimed, is too plentiful in the press and on television. This is bad for society because it leads to exaggerated fear of crime and rising crime rates. There are also complaints that excessive emphasis on crime news debases the news process because crime displaces other, more desirable news content. Important political news may be slighted because the media routinely allot a large part of coverage to crime and the judicial process. Another major complaint is that crime news is distorted. It creates the impression that the most violent forms of street crime are the most prevalent. It also makes white-collar crime appear insignificant in numbers and consequences.

A CRIME NEWS GATEKEEPING MODEL

Underlying all these charges is the much debated question of what is, or ought to be, "news" and how news professionals do, or ought to, go about selecting the proper mix of a variety of news items for each paper or broadcast or for a series of papers and broadcasts. To answer this larger question, as well as to address the specific indictments, the data about crime and justice news were examined in light of a popular sociological model. This model, which explains the newsmaking process better than competing psychological and political models, has been fully described and applied in several recent analyses of newsmaking.[1]

According to this model, news is a product of socially determined notions of who and what are important. These notions, in turn, lead to organizational structures that routinize news collection by establishing regular "beats." News from these beats is allotted space and air time according to fairly regular patterns. Consequently, there is a steady stream of news of varying degrees of importance from these beats. Events occurring remote from these beats, by contrast, are often ignored, except when they are sensational in nature, or when a reporter's whim has suddenly cast them into the limelight of attention as a feature or special investigative report.

If this sociological model is a correct representation of the process of newsmaking, it should produce a number of distinctive coverage patterns:

1. There should be substantial similarity in the types of "news" covered by most media within the same society because most are subject to the same social pressures.

2. Similarity should be greatest among news sources of the same general type, such as daily or weekly papers or local or national television news, because the same technical and audience demands and intramedia competitive pressures shape their responses to social pressures.

3. One would also expect a high degree of stability in the component parts of the news stream because of intraorganizational pressures to use a fixed portion of the news that comes from regular beats. This news flow represents substantial financial investments that cannot be discarded lightly by the news organization. It also represents large investments in personnel resources that require the recognition of effort that comes from seeing one's stories published in one's print or broadcast medium.

4. Along with the uniformity in news topics, one may anticipate considerable diversity in news play, such as length of stories, headline size, page or broadcast placement, and the like. This diversity in prominence criteria would reflect individual differences in newspeople's preferences for stories, in their conceptions of the social role of news, and in their appraisals of the needs and desires of their particular audiences. Journalistic conventions sanction such differences in display as a way of diversifying the thrust and appearance of an essentially homogeneous product.

5. Turning to crime news specifically, the structure of the beat system would seem to preordain substantially more coverage of street crime, particularly the more violent and bizarre incidents, than coverage of more routine crime occurrences, including white-collar crime. Police headquarters, which dispense street crime news information, often in the form of news releases, stress the more sensational crime incidents. By contrast, news about white-collar crime is not routinely supplied through the police or any other regular beat.[2]

How well did the crime and justice news supply conform to this model in 1976 in the papers and television broadcasts included in this study?

FREQUENCY OF COVERAGE OF CRIME AND JUSTICE STORIES

To assess crime and justice news media coverage in relation to other news, we coded 19,068 stories from the Chicago *Tribune,* 335 from the *Sun-Times,* and 282 from the *Daily News.* From national network news, we coded 4,763 stories from ABC, 4,879 stories from CBS, and 4,561 stories from NBC. From local newscasts, we coded 4,592 CBS and 7,371 NBC stories.* Because most news stories cover more than one topic, triple topic coding was used because it gives a better picture of coverage realities than single topic coding (see Table 2.1). With up to three topics coded per story, this yielded 33,200 topics for

TABLE 2.1
Percentage of Distribution of Selected News Topics in the *Tribune,* Based on Coding of One Topic per Story and Three Topics per Story (N = 7,123 for first topics; 12,144 for three topics)

Crime Topics			Noncrime Topics		
	Single	Triple		Single	Triple
Individual crimes	11.8	16.5	Education	6.2	7.3
Judiciary	20.3	15.5	Congress	8.9	6.9
Police/security	12.9	12.7	Disaster/accident	7.8	5.9
Political terrorism	1.4	5.2	City government	6.7	5.2
Corrupt politics	1.9	4.0	Middle East	7.0	4.9
Drug crimes	0.7	1.8	State government	6.8	4.8
Business crimes	1.1	1.7	Political gossip	5.1	4.4
Gun control	0.3	0.5	Energy policy	1.1	2.7
	50.4	57.9		49.6	42.1

Note: Single topic coding yielded 3,592 crime topics and 3,531 noncrime topics in this topic array. Triple coding yielded 7,025 crime topics and 5,119 noncrime topics.

Source: Original research.

---

*The reason for the larger number of NBC local stories, compared to CBS, is the fact that the local broadcast was expanded to 90 minutes during the last three months of the study. The figures for the networks represent coding from April through December only. Spot checks indicate that addition of January through March data does not change the picture presented here. The array of topics covered by the *Indianapolis News, the Indianapolis Star,* and the *Lebanon Valley News* is quite similar to the Chicago papers. However, there are differences in the relative frequencies with which specific topics are presented in the three locations.

the *Tribune,* 581 for the *Sun-Times,* and 506 for the *Daily News.* Figures for the national networks were 7,962 for ABC, 8,193 for CBS, and 7,667 for NBC news. For the local newscasts, the figures were 7,597 for CBS and 12,274 for NBC. Table 2.1 illustrates the significant differences that result from single and triple coding.

The share of coverage reported for 11 of 16 topics in Table 2.1 changed by more than one percentage point when triple coding was used. The greatest changes occurred in crime topics, with individual crime and terrorism increasing by five and four percentage points, respectively, and stories about the judiciary declining by four percentage points. Overall, the table indicates that the share of crime topics rose by almost eight percentage points, compared to the noncrime topics when one moved from single to triple coding.

In Table 2.2, the data on topical coverage collected in 1976 have been arranged into four general groupings. Within these groupings, 67 separate subtopics coded originally have been condensed into 26 subtopics. Table 2.2 reveals that all news sources were strikingly similar in the proportion of news devoted to various topical areas, particularly when newspapers and local and national television are considered as two separate groups.* The pattern extended to individual subtopics as well as the subtopic groupings and was particularly pronounced within the television groups.

If percentage figures are rounded off and a leeway of one percentage point is allowed, the three national networks had identical frequencies of coverage for 25 of the 26 subtopics. Only foreign affairs coverage was out of line, with a two percentage point differential. For the local networks, only 3 of the 26 subtopics diverged, namely, business and labor subjects (three points), health and medicine (two points), and sports and entertainment (three points). This left 23 subtopics with nearly identical frequency of coverage. The *Sun-Times* and *Daily News,* like the national networks, had similar coverage for 25 of the 26 subtopics. Only environment and transportation were out of line with a two percentage point discrepancy. Differences in coverage patterns between the *Tribune* and the other papers were somewhat larger, but this may be due to the fact that the *Sun-Times* and *Daily News* were coded for one constructed week only, compared to 52 weeks of coding for the *Tribune.* The *Sun-Times* and *Daily News* and *Tribune* differed in six instances.†

---

*A comparison between the rank order of frequency of news topics for the ten highest ranked topics showed agreement between the *Tribune* and *Indianapolis Star* on nine out of ten topics. For the *Indianapolis News,* the figure was eight out of ten; for the *Lebanon Valley News,* it was four out of ten. The two Indianapolis papers shared eight out of ten topics with each other and four topics with the *Valley News.* Accordingly, it appears that Chicago and Indianapolis papers are quite similar in coverage, but the small town New Hampshire paper places its emphasis differently.

†A comparison of the frequency of mention of crime and noncrime topics based on the array of topics listed in Table 2.1 shows significant differences (.01) between *Tribune*

TABLE 2.2

Percentage of Frequency of Mention of Various Topics in the *Tribune*, *Sun-Times*, and *Daily News*, CBS and NBC Local News, and ABC, CBS, and NBC National News.

(N = 33,200 for the *Tribune*, 581 for the *Sun-Times*, 506 for the *Daily News*, 7,597 for CBS local, 12,274 for NBC local, 7,962 for ABC, 8,193 for CBS, 7,667 for NBC news)

	Tribune	Sun-Times	Daily News	CBS local	NBC local	ABC national	CBS national	NBC national
Crime and Justice								
Police/security	4.7	7.2	7.7	3.3	3.1	1.5	1.6	1.5
Judiciary	5.7	5.0	4.0	4.6	4.7	3.6	3.4	3.7
Corruption/terrorism	4.0	5.7	5.5	4.0	3.3	3.1	3.3	3.1
Individual crime	7.5	10.2	9.5	7.8	8.5	4.1	4.0	4.6
	21.9	28.1	26.7	19.7	19.6	12.3	12.3	12.9
Government/Politics								
Presidency	2.7	0.9	1.8	2.3	1.9	4.5	4.2	4.2
Congress	2.5	4.1	3.0	1.7	1.2	3.7	4.4	4.1
Bureaucracy	1.9	1.9	1.6	1.9	2.0	4.9	4.5	4.4
Foreign affairs	9.8	9.8	10.3	4.6	5.2	16.5	17.1	15.0
Domestic policy	12.6	13.1	13.8	5.6	4.5	6.6	7.6	7.4
Elections	7.6	10.0	11.5	6.8	6.2	15.7	15.2	15.2
State government	1.8	1.4	0.8	2.7	2.2	0.6	0.9	0.8
City government	1.9	0.3	1.2	4.3	3.2	0.7	0.5	0.5
Miscellaneous	0.6	0.7	0.0	0.9	1.0	0.7	0.6	0.4
	41.4	42.2	44.0	30.9	27.4	53.9	55.0	52.0

Economics/Social Issues								
State of economy	2.4	2.1	2.4	1.1	1.0	1.7	1.7	1.9
Business/labor	5.9	6.4	4.9	6.6	10.2	7.8	6.8	6.8
Minorities/women	2.7	2.9	3.8	2.1	2.0	2.7	2.9	2.4
Environment/transportation	3.2	4.1	1.8	9.1	9.1	3.5	4.0	4.0
Disaster/accident	2.2	1.9	2.4	3.8	5.0	3.2	2.8	3.3
Health/medicine	2.5	2.4	1.6	3.3	4.6	2.1	2.8	3.2
Education/media/religion	4.4	2.2	2.8	4.0	4.0	2.8	3.0	2.5
Leadership style	1.2	1.5	1.4	0.2	0.2	0.8	0.7	0.6
Miscellaneous	1.7	0.7	0.6	1.3	1.2	1.8	1.4	1.5
	26.2	24.2	21.7	31.5	37.3	26.4	25.1	26.2
Human Interest/Hobbies*								
General human interest	2.9	1.9	3.4	6.0	6.8	1.8	1.8	2.3
Celebrities	3.6	1.4	2.0	2.2	2.1	1.4	1.5	1.7
Political gossip	1.6	0.5	1.2	1.4	1.4	1.4	1.1	1.4
Sports/entertainment	2.6	1.7	1.4	8.3	5.3	2.9	2.1	3.4
	10.7	5.5	8.0	17.9	15.6	7.5	6.5	8.8

Note: *Sun-Times* and *Daily News* data are based on sample coding of one constructed week for each paper. NBC local news is based on full-hour broadcast, others on half-hour. National news data are based on nine months of coding, April-December 1976.

*When stories of this type appeared in special sections (for example, People, Leisure, Food), they were not coded individually. Rather, the entire section was counted as one story. This depresses the Human Interest/Hobbies story count.

Source: Original research.

Looking at the relative frequency of mention of individual topic areas, it was found that crime and justice topics averaged 25 percent of all offerings in the newspapers, 20 percent of all offerings on local television, and 13 percent of all offerings on national television.[3] The corresponding figures for individual crime were 9 percent for newspapers, 8 percent for local television, and 4 percent for national television. In the *Tribune,* a comparatively prolific source of crime stories, the coverage of individual crimes just about matched election coverage. Individual crime coverage was topped by only two other topic areas: foreign affairs, which included U.S. foreign policy and events throughout the entire world, and domestic policy, a category that lumped together the bulk of public policy. Individual crime received nearly three times as much attention as the presidency or the Congress or the state of the economy, which included unemployment and inflation. It received nearly four times as much coverage as state government or city government.

For national television, which had the smallest component of individual crime news, it was on a par with the presidency and Congress. It was more than twice as plentiful as news about the state of the economy. It was outranked by news about foreign affairs and news about elections by a ratio of 1 to 4, and by news about business and labor and about domestic policy by a ratio of 1 to 2. On the local television scene, individual crime news ranked on a par with news about business and labor. It was outranked only by news about the environment and transportation, which includes weather reports. It received double the coverage bestowed on city government and triple the coverage for state government. Figure 2.1 compares coverage of these and other selected topics for the press and local and national television. The noncrime topics were selected for their substantive diversity and as a numerical match to the crime stories, which include all crimes mentioned in the news.

The diet of crime presented by print and television news was supplemented by crime television dramas. In 1976, prime time television featured 20 shows weekly in which crime and law enforcement were the main themes. A total of 63 program hours per week were devoted to these shows, which took up 33 percent of the total program time. The figures for television specials were quite similar. In addition to Westerns and shows centered on crime and justice subjects, a large number of other types of entertainment programs, including shows designed for children, were rich in crime and law enforcement episodes. In fact, nearly half (49 percent) of all the violence shown on the screen occurred in these shows. While the portrayals were notoriously unrealistic, when compared to crime news or official data of various types, they were believable enough to

---

coverage and that of each of the three national networks. Differences were also significant between the local and national news. There were no significant differences between the *Tribune* and local television news, between the local television news programs, or among the three national television news programs. Chi square statistics were used.

FIGURE 2.1
Percentage of Frequency of Mention of Selected Topics in the *Tribune*, CBS Local News, and ABC National News
(N = 14,798 for the *Tribune*, 3,141 for CBS Local News, and 4,565 for ABC National News)

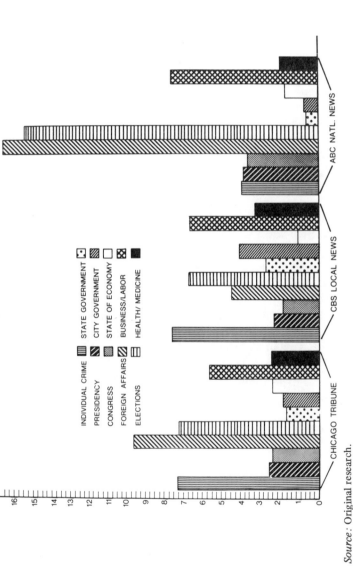

Source: Original research.

be accepted as valid images of crime and the justice process by large numbers of audience members.[4]

Given these facts, can one say that the coverage of crime news was and is disproportionately large as charged by numerous critics? This is a difficult question that cannot be answered without qualifications that set forth the norms underlying the judgment. These norms fall into three principal categories. The first bases judgments on a hierarchy of social significance. If one believes that matters other than crime — for example, the presidency, the state of the economy, or environmental questions — are socially more significant, and that relative social significance and the corresponding social needs of the audience should determine relative space allocations, then crime coverage is too high. It is also too high when one considers that contemporary public opinion polls rate the importance of crime substantially below inflation, unemployment, and energy as an urgent problem facing the country. Its prevalence in the news bestows an unwarranted importance on it that deflects attention from noncrime issues.[5] It may also unduly enhance the public's fear of crime and the socially harmful consequences of that fear. It maximizes the chances that crime-prone individuals will be exposed to stories that may stimulate criminal behavior.[6]

One can also judge according to a hierarchy of audience preferences. Audiences, it is argued, are little concerned with the social and civic significance of news. They want news that is timely, conflictual or humanly touching, occurring comparatively close to home, and with a readily discernible immediate impact on the reader's or viewer's life. Crime news ranks highly in all these aspects. Judged by audience preference criteria, which are intrinsically as well as commercially important to the journalistic profession, crime news is not excessive.[7]

The third judgmental category might be called the modified mirror of society concept. According to this concept, news should mirror society so that events selected for coverage are placed into a realistically balanced context. Social news about white citizens should, accordingly, be matched by social news about black citizens; news about U.S. misdeeds abroad should be matched by corresponding news about misdeeds by other great powers; violent crimes should be depicted in proportion to their frequency in the total crime context, including nonviolent crime. Judged by these criteria (which run counter to many journalistic conventions), the news about violent crime, as Tables 2.6 through 2.9 show, is quite excessive.

PROMINENCE OF COVERAGE OF CRIME AND JUSTICE STORIES

The amount of attention that news stories receive is affected not only by the frequency of mention but also by the prominence given to them within a news offering, such as one newspaper issue or one news broadcast. To assess this coverage dimension, relative placement of crime and justice stories within papers and newscasts was examined, along with story length, headline presence and size, and use of pictures, film, or graphics. The findings for the *Tribune* and NBC local television are presented in Table 2.3, and are representative of the findings for the other media. The table is based on eight crime topics (individual crime, judiciary, police/security, political terrorism, drug crimes, corrupt politics, business crimes, and gun control) and eight noncrime topics (Congress, city government, state government, Middle East problems, education policy, energy policy, disasters/accidents, and political gossip). It includes better than one third of all stories coded for the *Tribune* and NBC local news.

Table 2.3 indicates that crime stories were displayed slightly less prominently than other stories. But the difference was slight and not even consistent for all prominence features. For all practical purposes, the two types of topics received similar coverage.* We can therefore conclude that crime-related subjects ranked above average in frequency of mention, compared to most other topics listed in Table 2.2, but they did not receive preference in display.[8] Claims made regarding excessive attention must therefore rest solely on frequency of mention. One can also say for the news sources examined here that news professionals did not use their freedom to determine prominence criteria to downplay stories about crime and the criminal justice process. They chose a middle course instead.

To test whether individual media varied in the prominence of display accorded to various topics, as the sociological model suggests, news sources were compared with respect to page and section placement of various topics, length of story, headline size, and picture allotment. Table 2.4 presents the data, using length of story as surrogate for all prominence criteria, and focusing on the proportion of stories in each subtopic area that received prominent treatment. This permits comparison of treatment of "important" stories, considered significant enough to merit the most extensive type of coverage. The table confirms the hypothesis. Prominence criteria are indeed quite diverse within and among news source groupings. For example, the networks, which had shown such close correspondence in topic distribution in national newscasts, show wide divergence in air time allotted to similar topics. Only Congress and Middle East stories received very similar top coverage. On 10 of the 16 topics included in the table, coverage differences were substantial (3 to 17 percentage points.)

On local television newscasts, only Middle East story treatment was similar in air time exposure. For all other topics, stations varied considerably in top coverage (3 to 19 percentage points). Comparisons between and among the

---

*For local and national television, differences between crime and noncrime stories were significant (.01) only for the use of film on local programs. For the *Tribune*, the two types of stories differed significantly (.01) in section placement, headline size, and use of pictures. There were no significant differences in page placement and story length. However, there were substantial differences (.01) when media groups were compared to each other. Chi square statistics were used.

TABLE 2.3
Comparative Prominence of Crime and Selected Noncrime Stories
(N = 3,592 crime and 3,531 noncrime press stories and 1,262 crime and 1,283 noncrime NBC local TV news stories; percent of stories that share most prominent and least prominent positions)

	Crime Stories		Noncrime Stories	
	Press	TV	Press	TV
Section[a]				
Most prominent	60.3		62.3	
Least prominent	19.0		16.4	
Page[b]				
Most prominent	18.4		16.3	
Least prominent	37.5		34.1	
Headline[c]				
Most prominent	4.8	40.8	4.8	36.6
Least prominent	57.6	59.2	57.5	43.6
Pictures[d]				
Presence	18.9	6.0	28.1	29.2
Absence	81.1	0.0	71.9	20.3
Story length[e]				
Most prominent	4.6	21.8	5.9	18.0
Least prominent	25.5	57.9	26.0	60.6

[a]Most prominent = section 1; least prominent = sections 3-15.
[b]Most prominent = page 1; least prominent = pp. 6ff.
[c]For press, most prominent = 7 or more column inches, height times length; least prominent = 2 or less column inches, height times length. For TV, most prominent = presence of verbal or written headline; least prominent equals absence of headline.
[d]For press, presence means any size picture, absence = no picture. For TV, presence means use of graphics or film for 75 percent or more stories in individual crime and noncrime subcategories. Absence means graphics or film used for 50 percent or less of subcategory stories.
[e]For press, most prominent = 20 column inches or more; least prominent equals 5 column inches or less. For TV, most prominent = more than 120 seconds; least prominent = less than 60 seconds.

Source: Original research.

TABLE 2.4
Percentage of Comparative Length of Crime and Selected Noncrime Stories in Eight News Sources (N = 7,123 for *Tribune*, 238 for *Sun-Times*, 204 for *Daily News*, 1,601 for CBS local news, 2,545 for NBC local news, and, for network news, 1,668 for ABC, 1,773 for CBS, 1,594 for NBC)

	Tribune	Sun-Times	Daily News	CBS local	NBC local	ABC national	CBS national	NBC national
Crime Stories								
Individual crimes	3.0	44.4	7.7	5.6	18.1	2.8	1.5	4.2
Judiciary	4.7	15.4	11.8	4.6	12.6	1.2	1.9	4.0
Police/security	5.8	17.2	15.4	11.6	30.2	4.5	5.9	0.0
Political terrorism	9.6	—*	—*	14.5	9.0	0.0	6.0	3.3
Corrupt politics	2.2	0.0*	0.0*	8.0	15.9	0.0	0.0	4.7
Drug crimes	5.9	0.0*	—*	18.8	27.3	0.0	0.0	16.7
Business crimes	6.0	50.0*	—*	26.2	41.9	8.3	4.2	0.0
Gun control	0.0	—*	—*	0.0	20.0	—*	0.0*	0.0
Noncrime Stories								
Education	4.8	0.0*	0.0	6.1	33.6	2.2	4.1	15.6
Congress	5.6	0.0	14.2	0.0	2.6	3.5	3.5	2.6
Disaster/accident	4.3	20.0	8.3	3.8	10.8	1.3	2.9	4.3
City government	6.9	0.0*	0.0	17.8	36.5	0.0	16.7	7.5
Middle East	5.8	10.0	0.0	0.0	1.2	1.6	1.9	2.1
State government	4.5	0.0	50.0	8.7	25.6	3.4	7.6	0.0
Political gossip	11.3	0.0*	100.0*	11.3	7.7	3.7	0.0	3.7
Energy policy	6.3	0.0*	—*	8.4	26.3	11.5	10.2	15.9

Note: The figures indicate the percentage of stories in each topic area that received most prominent treatment. For newspapers, most prominent equals more than 20 column inches. For television, most prominent equals more than 120 seconds of air time. Figures based on N's that are too small to be meaningful also have asterisks.
Source: Original research.

*Dashes mean that no stories were recorded in the subtopic area.

newspapers are too unreliable for the limited number of topics included in the table. However, a comparison of all topics for the three papers shows trends toward diversity in news play quite in line with those displayed by the television networks. These findings are also corroborated by the newspaper data from Northwestern University's Reactions to Crime project.[9]

In practical terms, this means that data comparing prominence of crime and noncrime stories overall are deceptive. They conceal the fact that particular papers or broadcasts may give exceptional prominence to some crime topics while slighting others to an exceptional degree. In fact, we found that this is a common pattern. Among news sources that play up crime stories, the most sensational treatment generally was accorded to violent individual crimes that had occurred locally. These are the very kinds of crimes that frighten media audiences most and leave the strongest imprint on people's memories. The general finding, that crime stories do not receive preference in display, must therefore be modified to indicate that some news sources do indeed give preference to certain crime topics, with possibly profound consequences.

FLUCTUATIONS IN NEWS COVERAGE TRENDS: IS THERE A GRESHAM'S LAW?

If the sociological model of newsmaking is valid, then one would expect a high degree of regularity in the component parts of the news stream. Table 2.5 indicates that this is indeed the case. Semimonthly fluctuations showed great stability in the percentage of total news devoted to crime and justice, as well as to government and politics, economic and social issues, and human interest and hobbies stories. Table 2.5 presents the means, the standard deviations, and coefficients of variation. It shows very narrow dispersions around the mean in the majority of instances. The proportions of news devoted to economic and social issues and government and politics were most constant; those allotted to crime and justice and to human interest and hobbies were most flexible.

Semimonthly Z scores for each topic group only rarely reached or exceeded two standard deviations. Out of a total of 576 semimonthly scores for the four topic groups, only 21 (3.6 percent) amounted to two or more standard deviations. Of these, crime and justice and human interest/hobbies news had six each, while government and politics news had five and economic and social issues had four. The bulk of the fluctuations (16 out of 21) represented upward rather than downward deviations, demonstrating that it is easier to increase regular allotments of space and time than to cut them.

Does the high degree of regularity in the component parts of the news stream mean that the news mix is largely impervious to demands for time and space that may arise from the ebb and flow of major political news? More specifically, is crime and justice news a "filler" that contracts as political news

TABLE 2.5
Percentage of Semimonthly Fluctuations in News Coverage Trends: Means, Standard Deviations, Coefficients of Variation
(N = 19,068 *Tribune* stories, 4,592 CBS local news stories, 7,371 NBC local news stories, 4,763 ABC national news stories, 4,879 CBS national news stories, 4,561 NBC national news stories)

	Tribune	CBS Local	NBC Local	ABC National	CBS National	NBC National
Crime and Justice						
Mean	18.88%	18.75%	19.71%	9.00%	9.44%	9.83%
S.D.	1.96	3.91	4.22	3.79	2.98	2.41
Var.	0.10	0.21	0.21	0.42	0.32	0.25
Government/Politics						
Mean	48.50	29.92	26.33	63.33	64.78	60.72
S.D.	3.81	5.40	4.09	6.71	6.61	7.54
Var.	0.08	0.18	0.16	0.11	0.10	0.12
Economics/Social Issues						
Mean	19.08	31.25	37.75	20.78	19.94	21.39
S.D.	3.27	5.06	3.91	3.97	4.12	4.78
Var.	0.17	0.16	0.10	0.19	0.21	0.22
Human Interest/Hobbies						
Mean	13.58	20.00	16.00	6.83	6.06	8.39
S.D.	2.43	3.42	2.47	3.35	2.88	3.52
Var.	0.18	0.12	0.15	0.49	0.48	0.42

Source: Original research.

expands? To answer these questions, semimonthly fluctuations in news about politics and about crime and justice in the *Tribune* were plotted (see Figure 2.2). While fluctuations in news flow are narrow, Figure 2.2 does show that peaks in political news are usually matched by valleys in crime and justice, and vice versa. This mirror image is slightly more pronounced in the match between these two topic areas than in matches between other topic areas. Hence there is some evidence to support the conclusion that justice system news does indeed contract to make way for socially more significant news. Gresham's law is not an iron one.

To check out the possibility that crime and justice news might be the dog that wags the political news tail, rather than the reverse, the semimonthly variations of election news and news about individual crime were examined. Election news had well-defined expansion points in 1976. It was bound to rise

FIGURE 2.2

Semimonthly Fluctuations in News about Politics, the Justice System, Crime, and Elections in the *Tribune*

(N = 9,207 for politics stories, 3,511 for justice system stories, 2,205 for elections stories, 909 for crime stories)

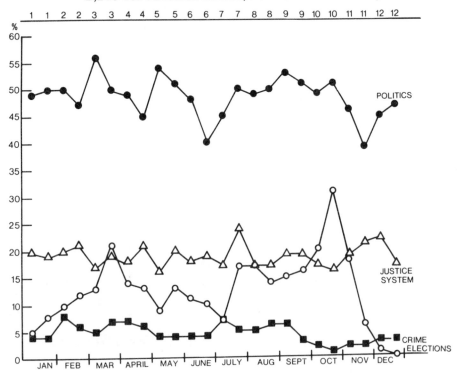

Source: Original research.

at times of primary elections, political conventions, the presidential debates, and during the final election week. The supply of news about individual crimes was apt to be quite stable throughout the year. Hence a pattern that showed election news expanding at the high points of the election contest and crime news contracting would indicate that crime news was the dependent variable.

Figure 2.2 shows that election news was allowed to peak at the crucial times, and that its bulges were reflected in bulges in the politics category. In turn, as already noted, the fluctuations in politics news were complemented by accommodations in justice system news. The fluctuations in the news about individual crime were extremely small and correlations with election news fluctuations were weak. This means that justice system news as a group gave way, to a moderate degree, to politics news, but the adjustments were not primarily made in news about individual crime. Rather, most of the adjustments occurred in news about the judiciary and news about the police. Moreover, upward and downward compensatory bulges were generally followed by bulges in the opposite direction. Given the ample stream of news, expansion, which is dictated by pressures to use fixed amounts of news from regular beats, is no problem at all. The outcome of this balancing process is a total news flow that, over time, remains constant in each group. The patterns of semimonthly fluctuations in various news components presented by local and national television were similar to those of the *Tribune* shown in Figure 2.2.

DISTORTIONS IN CRIME NEWS COVERAGE

Like questions about appropriate levels of coverage, questions about distortions in the presentation of various crime news elements must be answered within a framework that sets forth the standards by which distortion is judged. The appraisal of the appropriateness of balance between street and white-collar crime news presented here rests on two assumptions: (1) that white-collar crimes, particularly many business crimes involving threats to public health and safety, are of equal or greater social significance than violent crimes against individuals; and (2) that the modified mirror image concept, described earlier, represents a valid guide for appraising fairness of coverage. Applied to crime and justice news, this means that serious white-collar crime should be given coverage that is roughly proportionate to serious violent crime against individuals.[10] If these assumptions are granted (they are debatable), then crime and justice news is badly distorted like its severest critics claim.

Tables 2.6 through 2.9 tell the story. They also present further support for the sociological model of newsmaking. As predicted from the model, news about violent crimes, which is readily available from police beats, is far more plentiful than crime news, which is not as readily available from these beats.[11] Table 2.6 indicates the frequency of mention of various types of crimes in eight news

TABLE 2.6
Percentage of Frequency of Mention of Various Types of Crimes
(N = 3,545 for *Tribune*, 92 for *Sun-Times*, 76 for *Daily News*, 815 for CBS local TV news, 1,501 for NBC local TV news, 568 for ABC national TV news, 599 for CBS national TV news, 587 for NBC national TV news)

	Tribune	Sun-Times	Daily News	Local		National		
				CBS	NBC	ABC	CBS	NBC
Street crimes	56.5	51.0	52.6	49.9	46.8	46.8	43.0	47.0
Terrorism	17.7	17.3	15.7	12.5	24.2	22.8	23.0	16.6
Corruption	13.6	18.4	21.0	21.7	13.2	20.5	22.3	24.0
Drug offenses	6.1	6.5	5.2	4.5	4.7	3.3	3.8	3.7
Business crimes	5.9	6.5	5.2	11.2	10.8	6.3	7.6	8.5

Note: *Sun-Times* and *Daily News* data are based on sample coding of one constructed week for each paper. National news data are based on nine months of coding, April-December 1976. CBS local news is based on 60-minute broadcasts. NBC local news is based on 60- and 90-minute broadcasts. National news is based on 30-minute broadcasts.

Source: Original research.

sources.* It shows that street crimes received the most plentiful coverage by far. But the figures for white-collar crime, which are recorded under the headings of "corruption" and "business crime," are by no means insignificant. They range from a low of 20 percent of the total crime coverage in the *Tribune* to a high of 33 percent on CBS local and NBC national news. Overall, street crime constituted slightly less than half of all crime discussed on television and slightly more than half of all crime discussed in the newspapers.† It was dominant, but not to the degree that critics of crime news coverage would lead one to believe.

It is not clear whether this substantial focus on white-collar crimes is a recent phenomenon, linked to Watergate and Vietnam war cynicism about government and business, or whether it is typical of media emphasis during other years as well. However, because there seems to be some evidence that exposure of one form of corruption tends to lead to exposure of other forms, one would suspect that the emphasis on government corruption in particular would be unusually heavy in the years after Watergate.[12] Likewise, in a year that provided the nation with a ringside seat at the trial of several members of the extremist Symbionese Liberation Army, and that featured a number of airline hijackings and bombings linked to political causes, the number of crime stories covering terrorism is probably above normal.

Table 2.7 presents data on the prominence of display of various types of crime stories in the *Tribune*. It sheds light on ways in which news-play factors enhance or diminish the relative prominence bestowed on white-collar crime stories by sheer frequency of mention. The table shows that, contrary to general beliefs, white-collar crime stories received basically the same display as street crime stories in prominent page and section placement, headline size, story length, and pictorial coverage. However, that does not necessarily mean that they have the same impact as street crime stories, even if one ignores, for the moment, that they are mentioned less frequently. When the emotional effect

---

*The significance of coverage differences among individual media and groups of media were computed, using chi square and .05 significance as the cutoff point. On that basis, there were no significant differences among the three newspapers. The three networks differed significantly (.05) only on terrorism. The two local networks differed significantly (.01) on terrorism and corruption. There were significant differences (.01 but .05 for business crime) between all *Tribune* and network coverage topics, except for terrorism in the case of NBC, which showed no significant differences. Similarly, *Tribune* and local television news coverage differed significantly (.01, but .05 for drugs) for all topics except for corruption in the case of NBC, which showed no significant differences. Comparisons between local and national TV broadcasts showed significant differences (.01) for street crime, corruption, and business crime, but no significant differences for terrorism and drug offenses. Patterns of comparison for stories about the judiciary showed local network coverage significantly different from the *Tribune* and the networks. For police and security stories, all media differed significantly among each other.

†For the relation of street crime news to news about the judiciary and about police and security matters, see Table 2.2.

TABLE 2.7

Percentage of Prominence of Display of Various Types of Crime Stories in the *Tribune*

(N = 2,006 for street crimes, 628 for terrorism, 481 for corruption, 57 for drug offenses, 212 for business crimes)

	Page 1	Section 1	Picture Present	Large Headline*	Long Story*
Street crimes	18.7	66.2	19.5	4.5	3.0
Terrorism	14.5	73.3	18.8	7.0	9.6
Corruption	20.0	61.6	23.7	6.9	2.2
Drug offenses	14.2	45.1	14.7	4.1	5.9
Business crimes	20.8	69.1	13.2	4.7	6.0

*Large headling = seven or more column inches, height by length. Long story = 20 column inches or more.

Source: Original research.

of subject matter is added to other prominence factors, the balance in favor of street crime impact is overwhelming.*

Table 2.8 tells a similar story of slighting of white-collar crime to a lesser degree than might be expected. It presents the rank order of frequency of mention of the 12 crimes that head the list when all *Tribune* stories are ranked for the year. Seven street crimes make it into the list and two capture top spots. But two white-collar crimes — consumer fraud and bribery and kickbacks — also rank highly, attaining third and sixth place, respectively.

COMPARISON OF POLICE AND MEDIA DATA

The accuracy of police crime statistics is open to question.[13] Many crimes are not reported to the police. Even those that are reported may be inaccurately recorded. Changes in classifications of crimes or variations in reporting periods or districts may obscure trends. Nonetheless, police data are the major source for media crime stories and thus are the standard by which the accuracy of media reporting must be judged. When one compares the media rankings of crime to

*Comparison between prominence features used by the *Tribune* and local and national television news shows significant differences (.01, using chi square statistics) for most pairs. In 53 comparisons, only 4 fell below the .01 level of significance to .05, and 10 were not significant at all. Most of the latter occurred in intramedia group comparisons and in comparisons between the *Tribune* and network national news.

TABLE 2.8
Rank Order and Frequency of Mention of Street and White-Collar
Crime in the *Tribune*
(12 ranks only = 77 percent of crime topics; N = 2,619 topics)

Street Crime			White-Collar Crime		
Rank		Percent	Rank		Percent
1	Murder	24.2	3	Consumer fraud	5.9
2	Robbery	12.9	6	Bribery/kickbacks	4.6
4	Assault	5.8	10	Drug offenses	2.8
5	Kidnapping	5.1	11	Tax cheating	2.3
7	Arson	4.5	12	Extortion	2.1
8	Rape	3.4			
9	Larceny/theft	3.4			

Source: Original research.

police and court records, the match is poor. Table 2.9 presents such a comparison for street crime, matching the coverage of crimes recorded in the official Chicago police record with coverage of corresponding crimes in the *Tribune*.

Murder, the most sensational crime, constitutes 0.2 percent of all crimes recorded in the police index. In the *Tribune,* it constitutes 26.2 percent of all crime mentions. By contrast, nonviolent crimes like theft and car theft constitute 47 percent of all crimes on the police index, but only 4 percent of all crimes mentioned in the *Tribune*. While police and *Tribune* figures are not precisely comparable because *Tribune* crime coverage reaches beyond the Chicago area included in the police reports, and while there are slight discrepancies in the dates for which coverage is reported, the trends demonstrated by the data are accurate. An exaggerated picture is presented of the incidence of the most violent kinds of crime, while the incidence of lesser crimes is minimized.

Table 2.9 also shows that the *Tribune* devotes 48 percent of its coverage to nonindex crimes. In the Chicago police crime summaries, nonindex crimes constitute 31 percent of the total. Nonindex crimes, which include most white-collar crimes, thus receive a proportionately heavier emphasis in the *Tribune* than in police records. This constitutes tacit recognition that such crimes are important and of sufficient interest to the public to warrant media emphasis proportionately greater than the emphasis in public records. Table 2.9 also reveals that, except for murder, only a tiny portion of crime reported by the police is publicized by the media. The data for the other media that were content-analyzed for this study show similar gatekeeping practices.[14]

TABLE 2.9
Comparative Frequency of Mention of Index Crimes by Chicago Police Official Record and by *Tribune*, 1976
(N = 1,377 for *Tribune;* 212,270 for police)

Police Index Crimes			Tribune Index Crimes		
	N	Percent		N	Percent
Murder	820	0.2	Murder	689	26.2
Rape	1,172	0.4	Rape	88	3.4
Robbery	17,489	5.7	Robbery	283	10.8
Assault	11,001	3.6	Assault	152	5.8
Burglary	38,369	12.4	Burglary	56	2.1
Theft	111,008	36.0	Theft	90	3.4
Auto theft	32,421	10.5	Auto theft	19	0.7
	212,270	68.8		1,377	52.4

Note: Tribune coverage dates start and end one week later than police crime report dates. Police dates are January 8, 1976 to January 5, 1977. *Tribune* data include crimes outside the Chicago area and therefore are not strictly comparable to Chicago police data. All differences between police and media data are significant at the .01 level, using chi square.

Source: Original research.

Table 2.10 presents the ranking and proportionate frequency of coverage that the *Tribune* gave to all types of crime. Because comparable detailed police figures could not be obtained for Chicago, and since *Tribune* crime coverage extends beyond Chicago, the national rankings are indicated, based on FBI 1976 data. Obviously, there is no mirror image, not even a distorted mirror. Of the ten most frequently mentioned crimes in the *Tribune,* only two — larceny and drug offenses — rank among the top ten in the FBI list. Five of the ten most frequently recorded crimes on the FBI roster rank below the 20 mark in the *Tribune* frequency list. Liquor law violations, which the FBI ranks first, number 37 for the *Tribune.*

SUMMARY AND CONCLUSIONS

The data presented thus far are consistent with the sociological model of newsmaking and support most, but not all, charges made by critics of crime news coverage.

Crime news receives ample coverage and display compared to other types of news. By certain social significance criteria, it is excessive. However, if current notions about audience preferences are accurate — and readership and viewer

TABLE 2.10
Comparative Rankings of Frequency of Mention of All Types of Crime by the FBI and the *Tribune*, 1976 (proportionate frequency of coverage for the *Tribune* only; N = 9,608,500 for the FBI; 2,619 for the *Tribune*)

Crime	Tribune Rank	Tribune Percent	FBI Rank
Murder	1	26.2	21
Robbery	2	10.8	13
Consumer fraud	3	5.9	10
Assault	4	5.8	8
Kidnapping	5	5.1	
Bribery/kickback	6	4.6	
Arson	7	4.5	22
Rape	8	3.4	20
Larceny/theft	9	3.4	2
Drug offenses	10	2.8	5
Tax cheating	11	2.3	
Burglary	12	2.1	6
Extortion	13	2.1	
Weapons violations	14	1.6	11
Official misconduct	15	1.5	
Corruption	16	1.3	
Perjury	17	1.2	
Forgery	18	1.2	18
Custody escape	19	1.1	
Contempt of court	20	1.1	7
Lesser assault	21	0.8	9
Vandalism	22	0.8	19
Sex offenses	23	0.7	12
Vehicle theft	24	0.7	17
Prostitution	25	0.7	14
Fencing stolen property	26	0.6	
Disorderly conduct	27	0.6	4
Gambling	28	0.5	15
Illegal wiretap	29	0.4	
Piracy	30	0.4	
Embezzlement	31	0.4	23
Obstruct justice	32	0.3	
Welfare cheating	33	0.3	
Child abuse	34	0.3	16
Contributing to minor's delinquency	35	0.2	
Drunken driving	36	0.2	3
Liquor law violations	37	0.1	1
Parole violation	38	0.08	
Miscellaneous		3.6	

Note: FBI designations have been recoded to conform to the *Tribune* designations used in this study. Where this proved impossible because the FBI aggregated crime groups differently, FBI figures have been added to the "miscellaneous" category. FBI data are for offenses charged after arrest, rather than offenses reported to the police.

Source: Original research.

41

data seem to support them – then ample coverage of crime news can be justified as satisfying a strong consumer demand.

Crime news does not, apparently, prevent political news from expanding at times of major political activity, such as elections. However, when contractions take place to compensate for increased political coverage, they are followed by expansions so that the total news flow for various news categories remains constant over time.

Crime news does distort the realities of crime commission by disproportionate emphasis on street crime as compared to white-collar crime. It also presents a distorted image of the relative incidence of various types of street crimes by exaggerating murder, rape, and assault and underrepresenting robbery, burglary, and theft.

There is substantial similarity in the types of news presented by various newspapers and television sources and substantial stability in the frequency with which these news areas are covered. This type of stability is a natural concomitant of a news system that shares notions about newsworthiness of institutions and events and develops an organizational structure to provide regular coverage for the preselected institutions and events.

The beat system encourages coverage of crime news readily available from regular police sources and discourages coverage that is off the beat. The finding that street crime news receives the lion's share of coverage conforms to this expected pattern. However, white-collar crimes do receive substantial attention, possibly because they are made available from different beats, such as prosecuting agencies, grand juries, or court dockets.

Finally, the display features of news vary widely among the sources examined here. This finding, when coupled with the finding of striking similarity in topics covered and in frequency of coverage, underlines the limits of the beat system. Beats determine the sources of most news and ensure a steady, constant stream of regular coverage. But once the news is in the pipeline, the constraints of newsmaking attenuate. Individual choices emerge and are encouraged to meet the needs of specific audiences and the whims of news personnel. As a result, crime stories come in many different shapes – from front page lead to back page filler. Prominence features bear heavily on their impact but are modified by salience of the subject matter to the audience. A salient story snippet, if noticed, can be more potent than a lengthy feature to which the audience does not relate.

NOTES

1. Bernard Roshco, *Newsmaking* (Chicago: University of Chicago Press, 1975); Leon V. Sigal, *Reporters and Officials: The Organization and Politics of Newsmaking* (Lexington, Mass.: Heath, 1973); Edward Jay Epstein, *News from Nowhere: Television and the News* (New York: Vintage Books, 1974); and Mark Fishman, *Manufacturing the News* (Austin, Texas: University of Texas Press, 1980). For a discussion of the merits of

various models of newsmaking, see Paul M. Hirsch, "Occupational, Organizational and Institutional Models in Communication Research: Towards an Integrated Framework," in *Strategies for Communication Research,* ed. Paul M. Hirsch, Peter V. Miller, and F. Gerald Kline (Beverly Hills, Calif.: Sage, 1977), pp. 13-42. For additional discussions of the criteria that media use to select crime news for coverage, see Bob Roshier, "The Selection of Crime News by the Press," in *The Manufacture of News: Social Problems, Deviance, and the Mass Media,* ed. Stanley Cohen and Jock Young (London: Constable, 1973), pp. 55-72. Also see Alfred Friendly and Ronald L. Goldfarb, *Crime and Publicity: The Image of News and the Administration of Justice* (New York: Twentieth Century Fund, 1967), pp. 60-65; and E. Terrence Jones, "The Press as Metropolitan Monitor," *Public Opinion Quarterly* 40 (1976): 239-44.

2. Police wires to the press are discussed in Mark Fishman, "Crime Waves as Ideology," Society for the Study of Social Problems Paper, 1977.

3. Complementary data can be found in Jones, "The Press as Metropolitan Monitor"; Shari Cohen, "A Comparison of Crime Coverage in Detroit and Atlanta Newspapers," *Journalism Quarterly* 52 (1975): 726-30; and John C. Meyer, Jr., "Newspaper Reporting of Crime and Justice: Analysis of an Assumed Difference," *Journalism Quarterly* 52 (1975): 731-34. For a contradictory view, see Emery L. Sasser and John T. Russell, "The Fallacy of News Judgment," *Journalism Quarterly* 49 (1972): 280-84.

4. Joseph R. Dominick, "Crime and Law Enforcement in the Mass Media," in *Deviance and Mass Media,* ed. Charles Winick (Beverly Hills, Calif.: Sage, 1978), pp. 105-27. Also see George Gerbner et al., "The Demonstration of Power: Violence Profile No. 10," *Journal of Communication* 29 (Summer 1979): 177-96; and John H. Culver and Kenton L. Knight, "Evaluating TV Impressions of Law Enforcement Roles," in *Evaluating Alternative Law-Enforcement Policies,* ed. Ralph Baker and Fred A. Meyer, Jr. (Lexington, Mass.: Heath, 1979), pp. 201-12.

5. See, for example, "Crime and Its Impact: An Assessment," President's Commission on Law Enforcement and Administration of Justice (Washington, D.C.: U.S. Government Printing Office, 1967), pp. 85-109, and sources cited there. Also David G. Clark and William B. Blankenburg, "Trends in Violent Content in Selected Mass Media," in *Television and Social Behavior: Media Content and Control,* ed. George A. Comstock and Ali A. Rubinstein, vol. 1 (Washington, D.C.: U.S. Department of Health, Education, and Welfare, 1972), pp. 188-243; and Jack B. Haskins, "The Effects of Violence in the Printed Media," in *Mass Media and Violence,* ed. David Lange, Robert Baker, and Sandra Ball (Washington, D.C.: U.S. Government Printing Office, 1969), pp. 493-502.

6. Haskins, "The Effects of Violence in the Printed Media." For a brief, lucid discussion of the effects of fear of crime, see Wesley G. Skogan, "Public Policy and the Fear of Crime in Large American Cities," Midwest Political Science Association Paper, 1976.

7. Charles Swanson, "What They Read in 130 Daily Newspapers," *Journalism Quarterly* 32 (1955): 411-21.

8. The impact of various display characteristics is discussed in Richard W. Budd, "Attention Score: A Device for Measuring News 'Play'," *Journalism Quarterly* 41 (1964): 259-62. Additional information on differential treatment of crime news by the mass media can be found in Jones, "The Press as Metropolitan Monitor"; Cohen, "A Comparison of Crime Coverage in Detroit and Atlanta Newspapers"; and Meyer, "Newspaper Reporting of Crime and Justice."

9. *The Reactions to Crime Papers,* vol. 5, chaps. 4 and 5.

10. Crime stereotypes and their deviation from factual data are discussed in Austin Turk, "The Mythology of Crime in America," *Criminology* 8 (1971): 397-411. Also see Richard Quinney, *The Social Reality of Crime* (Boston: Little, Brown, 1970), pp. 15-25; and Roshier, "The Selection of Crime News by the Press."

11. See Fishman, "Crime Waves as Ideology"; and Roshier, "The Selection of Crime News by the Press."

12. For data on the contagion effects of crime news, see David and Kay Payne, "Newspapers and Crime in Detroit," *Journalism Quarterly* 47 (1970): 233-35.

13. Thorsten Sellin and Marvin Wolfgang, *The Measurement of Delinquency* (New York: Wiley, 1964). Richard F. Sparks, Hazel G. Glenn, and David J. Dodd, *Surveying Victims: A Study of the Measurement of Criminal Victimization, Perceptions of Crime and Attitudes Toward Criminal Justice* (London: Wiley, 1977).

14. For discussions of the criteria that media use to select crime news for coverage, see Roshier, "The Selection of Crime News by the Press." Also see Friendly and Goldfarb, *Crime and Publicity;* and Jones, "The Press as Metropolitan Monitor." Jones weighted crimes by prominence as well as frequency of attention in St. Louis newspapers. Crimes against persons, such as murder and robbery, received about 35 times as much attention as crimes against property. Also see George E. Antunes and Patricia A. Hurley, "The Representation of Criminal Events in Houston's Two Daily Newspapers," *Journalism Quarterly* 54 (1977): 756-60.

Three

MEDIA AND PUBLIC IMAGES OF CRIMINALS AND VICTIMS

The focus now shifts to the substantive content of crime news. To avoid excessive repetition of data, we shall depict three facets simultaneously. We shall present and compare both media and respondent images of crime and the criminal justice process, and, at the same time, assess the degree of distortion present in these images. The point of departure for assessing distortions will be the criticism leveled by radical criminologists against the media's handling of crime and justice news.

Before discussing specific images, we shall briefly present some general characteristics of crime story coverage that indicate major and minor areas of emphasis and the general quality of coverage. We shall also supply information about the amount of attention panel members paid to crime story coverage to indicate the relationship between information supply and information use.

GENERAL CHARACTERISTICS OF CRIME STORIES

Figure 3.1 indicates that the bulk of crime stories (44 percent) uses either the court system, the correctional system, or the police as its main thrust (courts 31.9 percent, police 10.3 percent, corrections 2.2 percent). As one might expect from news presentations, most of these stories are descriptive, rather than analytical, reporting current happenings. One seldom finds interpretive analyses that place criminal justice system information into historical, sociological, or political perspective. Equally rare are explicit evaluations of the performance

FIGURE 3.1
The Major Thrust of Crime Stories in the *Tribune* (in percent)
(N = 2,769)

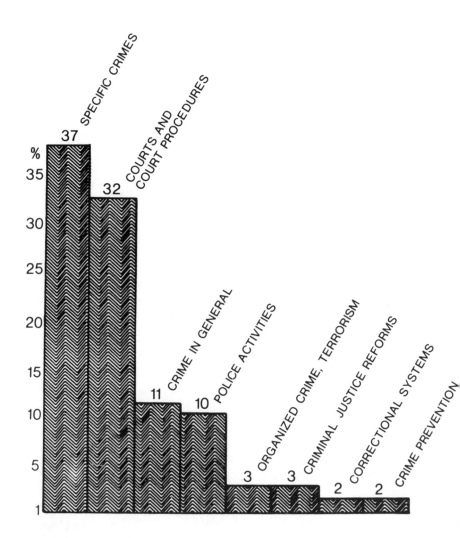

Source: Original research.

of the system in light of the demands made on it. However, there is a sprinkling of stories (4.3 percent) about various types of proposed reforms of the criminal justice system and various crime prevention measures. There also are comparatively frequent reports on crime and crime trends in general. These make up 10.9 percent of all crime coverage.

The remainder of the stories, well over a third (40.3 percent), deal with specific individual crimes or crimes directed by syndicates or terrorist groups.[1] Most of these crime stories read like police blotter reports, peopled by remote, impersonal, motiveless figures. One rarely encounters flesh-and-blood human beings who are involved in the drama of crime and victimization. The human conditions surrounding the crime are usually skipped, except when the crime is a freakish one or involves an unlikely victim or a socially prominent person.*

When an ordinary man is accused of killing his wife and burning the house to hide the crime, this is only a routine matter, covered inconspicuously and insipidly. Figure 3.2 diagrams a typical crime scenario, taken from a *Tribune* story of July 19, 1976. The story contains the stock elements, and little else: name, age, and occupation of the victim, place of crime, the name, age, and occupation of the suspect or suspects, a few facts about the crime, and the work done by the police.

Table 3.1 provides additional information from three newspapers about the amount of detail reported in crime stories about various facets of crime. Ample detail on any facet — defined as three or more sentences on it — is the exception rather than the rule. It is found in less than a third of the stories. Table 3.2 demonstrates that this paucity of detail cannot be attributed to large numbers of repeat stories that could be expected to omit details covered earlier. The bulk of stories are either completely new or represent major new facts, amounting to an essentially fresh story. If they sound like copies from the police blotter, the explanation is that this is what they are. Reporters rarely stray from what their police contacts supply.[2]

ATTENTIVENESS TO CRIME AND JUSTICE STORIES

How much attention do people pay to crime and justice system information? The answers are important because media images are not automatically transferred to media audiences. Rather, transmission requires that the audience become

---

*When New York mass murderer David Berkowitz ("Son of Sam") was arrested in 1977, the *New York Post* carried 16 stories and 36 photographs, using 10 full pages. The *New York Daily News* ran a special edition, with 14 stories and 17 photos. The *New York Times* devoted 2 full pages to the story. CBS and ABC spent two and a half hours and NBC spent two. Story content was sensational. Audience attention to the news rose dramatically and newspaper circulations jumped.

FIGURE 3.2
Typical *Chicago Tribune* Crime Story, July 19, 1976

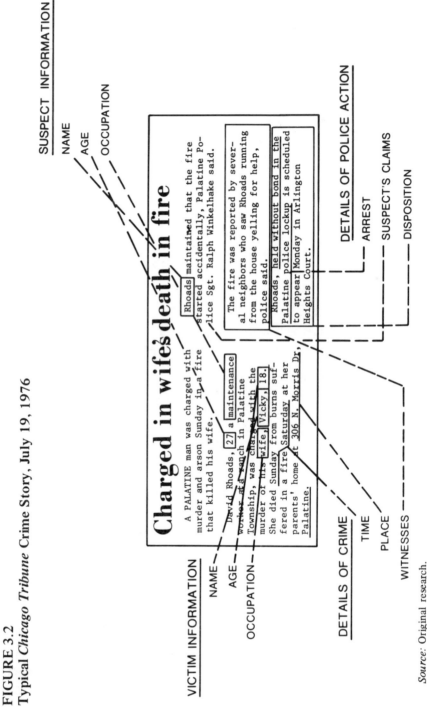

Source: Original research.

TABLE 3.1
Percentage of *Tribune, Sun-Times,* and *Daily News* Stories
Containing Three or More Sentences about Various
Aspects of Crimes
(N = 1,946 for the *Tribune,* 36 for the *Sun-Times,*
33 for the *Daily News*)

News Topic	Tribune	Sun-Times	Daily News
Extent of injuries	2.2	0.0	8.8
Crime execution details	29.5	27.8	5.9
Criminal(s) apprehension	22.2	33.3	26.5
Pretrial legal procedures	13.8	25.0	20.6
Trial procedures/sentence	16.8	11.1	11.8

Source: Original research.

aware of the media image and then internalize and/or transform it in full or in part.

We approached the question of attention to media crime stories both directly and indirectly, and asked for chief sources of information as well as for the amount of attention given to the information supply. Directly, we inquired on two occasions whether panel members learned about crime mostly from the mass media, personal knowledge, or conversation. Ninety-five percent of the answers rated the mass media as the primary source. However, 38 percent cited other sources as well. Only 14 percent of the panel members had had any personal involvement with crime through victimization of family members, self,

TABLE 3.2
Degree of Novelty of Crime Stories Published in the *Tribune, Sun-Times,* and *Daily News*
(N = 1,946 for the *Tribune,* 36 for the *Sun-Times,*
33 for the *Daily News*)

Degree of Novelty	Tribune	Sun-Times	Daily News
Completely new	53.7	52.8	41.1
Major update	34.9	30.6	44.1
Old	8.4	2.8	5.9
Undetermined	3.0	13.9	5.9

Source: Original research.

or close friends. An even smaller percentage had ever known a person accused of crime. None had ever been formally accused of crime, though several acknowledged committing minor offenses.

While the respondents used the media as prime sources for factual data about crime and criminal justice matters, they used them less frequently as sources for evaluations. For instance, when assessing crime danger at various sites, 57 percent named the mass media as the source of their knowledge, while the rest cited word of mouth. Reliance on media was even less for evaluation of crime-fighting activities. Only 24 percent of the panel members cited the media as origins of these evaluations. Personal experience and personal evaluations were mentioned as chief sources by 57 percent. The remaining 19 percent named conversations or professional sources. Recent studies of media effects have shown that such variability in media impact is quite common. Whenever dependence on the media is reduced because alternative credible sources of information and judgment are available, media influence declines. Generally, these alternative sources are personal experiences or judgments that have been distilled over long periods of time from information provided by media and interpersonal sources.[3]

The fact that the media are prime information sources does not mean that all media information is absorbed. To the contrary, when panel members were repeatedly asked how much attention they paid to media crime information, 50 percent of the panel members indicated that they paid only little attention, 48 percent claimed to give a lot of attention, and 2 percent claimed that they paid no attention at all. A check of their general reading habits showed that, on an average, 66 percent of the stories in a newspaper that had been "read" were ignored. Sixteen percent of the stories were partly read with an average of two thirds of the story omitted, and a mere 18 percent were fully read.

Inattention was largely due to competing claims on the respondents' time and not to distrust of the media. Between one half to three fourths of the respondents generally judged both press and television coverage of crime stories as accurate. Complaints about distortion of crime news were rare. However, there were complaints about sensationalism and lack of detail.

Data on story recall confirm that a large number of crime stories were ignored or quickly forgotten. Only 24 percent of the members of the core panel could recall the bulk of crime stories (85 percent or more) to which they had been exposed during the four to six weeks preceding each interview. Nevertheless, the overall recall rate of crime stories was somewhat better than recall of other types of stories when recall rates for selected crime and noncrime topics were compared. Using the list of topics in Table 2.1, stories about six crime subjects – individual crimes, the judiciary, political terrorism, drug crimes, business crimes, and gun control – were recalled better than stories about four noncrime subjects – education, Congress, the Middle East, and state government.

Stories about energy, accidents, political gossip, and city government paralleled the recall rates of the crime stories.* In tests of actual reading of news materials, individual crime stories ranked second, behind 1976 election stories. Overall, crime and justice topics constituted 15 percent of the news topics that were actually read on an average day, with half of them dealing with individual crime. A higher degree of involvement with crime stories was also demonstrated by the fact that people reported more reactions to crime than to noncrime stories, and that they related crime stories more often to their past or current personal behavior.

Examination of stories reported by core panel members in their diaries discloses that individual crimes represented the single largest category. Overall, crime topics constituted 16 percent of the 15,419 topics mentioned in the diaries. Table 3.3 rank-orders diary stories according to the frequency of mention of selected crime and noncrime topics. Assigning point values to each story equal to its rank, crime stories came up with the winning low scores, with 29 percent fewer points than noncrime stories. The matching data for press and television coverage are roughly similar in rankings to the diary data. This supports the claims of agenda-setting theorists who argue that the mass media influence the array of topics to which media audiences pay attention.†

In contrast to diary and specific story recall, spontaneous general recall for crime stories was low. During various interviews, an average of 35 percent of the panel could not spontaneously recall any crime stories when asked generally what stories they remembered, rather than specifically whether they remembered story X or Y.

Despite inattention and substantial forgetting, the subjects developed a broad knowledge base from the media information available to them. It consisted of specific information about particular crimes, such as the Patty Hearst case and the Chowchilla kidnapping case. Every respondent could give a brief, yet reasonably complete account of the gist of events presented in the media about these crimes. People also acquired some general notions about trends in crime rates, specifics of crime commission, and general characteristics of criminals and victims.[4] Because the media supply few analytical stories about the crime problem, this indicates that people as a group are able to make generalizations from specific data and that they construct their own stereotypical

---

*The recall rate for each panel member was measured by scoring recall in interview recall tests as high if it reached 50 percent or more of the stories in a particular category. Recall of less than 50 percent was scored as low. The overall recall rate of a given topic was judged by subtracting the low scores from the high scores.

†The similarity should not be overemphasized, however. The significance of relationships between diary and press and television coverage of particular topics was computed, using chi square. Out of 48 relationships, 26 were significant at the .01 level and 10 at the .05 level, but 12 were not significant.

TABLE 3.3
Rank Order of Frequency of Diary, Press, and TV Mentions of
Crime and Selected Noncrime Topics
(N = 4,287 for diary mentions, 12,144 for press mentions,
4,333 for TV mentions)

Crime Topics	Noncrime Topics	Diaries	Press	TV
1. Individual crimes		18.4	16.5*	16.2*
2. Judiciary		10.8*	15.5	12.1*
	3. Disasters/accidents	10.7	5.9	12.5
	4. Political gossip	8.4	4.4	3.6
	5. City government	7.3	5.2	8.5
6. Political terrorism		5.9*	5.2*	8.4
	7. Education	5.7	7.3*	7.4*
8. Corrupt politics		5.6	4.0*	4.6*
	9. Middle East	5.2*	4.9*	2.9
	10. Congress	5.1	6.9	3.1
11. Police/security		4.5	12.7	7.8
	12. State government	4.5*	4.8*	5.6
13. Business crimes		2.9	1.7	3.8
	14. Energy policy	2.5*	2.7*	1.8
15. Drug offenses		1.3*	1.8*	1.7*
16. Gun control		0.3*	0.5*	0.2*

*Differences are not significant at the .05 level. For drug offenses, only relations between diary and television and press and television are insignificant. For gun control, only diary and press and diary and television relationships are insignificant.

Source: Original research.

images. What they know and the deductions and inferences that spring from this knowledge (evidently) are not limited to what the media supply.

Beyond descriptive generalizations, panel members were also able to speculate about causes of crime and possible ways to reduce the crime rate. Although media crime stories supply relatively little information about crime causes (only 5 percent of all stories discuss causes and only 3 percent mention remedies), all panel members could cite at least one cause of crime and a majority could cite multiple causes. Most panel members could also suggest remedies to reduce crime and crime-related problems. Similar to public opinion poll data, the percentage of "no" and "not sure" answers was lower for these types of questions than for most other public policy questions.*

---

*See the Polls section of the *Public Opinion Quarterly*.

Knowledge about crimes was not limited to violent offenses. Subjects were reasonably well versed about various types of white-collar crimes as well. When presented with a list of the most common white-collar crimes and asked for their comparative seriousness and frequency, 85 percent out of a total of 2,760 answers voiced judgments.* Most panel members likewise had opinions about the relative frequency of commission of white-collar crimes compared to violent offenses. A somewhat higher percentage gave don't-know answers when quizzed about likely criminals and victims for these types of crimes.

Panel members also expressed ample views about the police, the courts, and the correctional system. They were superficially familiar with recruiting and training policies for policemen and prison personnel, with custodial and rehabilitation policies in prisons, with court procedures like plea bargaining, immunity grants, and suspended sentences, with the bail and parole system, and with fluctuations in the crime rate and the rates of recidivism. They also had opinions about the promptness and efficiency with which the police and courts generally operate, and about trends in the quality of performance of these institutions.

While information levels about various crimes, criminals, victims, and the law enforcement system were high (though not always accurate), information levels about various public programs designed to help victims of crime were spotty and generally low. The potential boost that crime-fighting evaluations might receive from this knowledge was therefore diminished. Panelists were asked whether they had heard or read anything about programs that provide for public compensation for crime victims, protection of women who are beaten by their spouses, protection of children who are physically abused by their parents, assistance to people who have been cheated by merchants, and assistance to people endangered or injured by environmental pollution. Eighty-six percent knew one or more organizations that would assist them if they felt defrauded by businesspeople. Sixty-two percent were aware of antipollution programs that might protect them from health and property hazards. But only 43 percent had heard of programs to compensate crime victims, only 14 percent knew where to turn for aid for abused children, and barely 10 percent had heard about protection for battered wives. Interestingly, the rank order of knowledge levels parallels the age of these types of programs, suggesting that considerable time may be required to acquaint the public with new social services. The rank order also parallels the frequency of the acts against which average people think they might need protection.

MEDIA AND AUDIENCE IMAGES OF CRIME AND THE JUSTICE PROCESS

Radical criminologists and other critics contend that the mass media in the United States disseminate the false views of their corporate owners about the

---

*A list of possible answers was provided. This probably increased the number of answers beyond the results on a more open-ended question.

nature and causes of crime. These views, which presumably are widely accepted by the public, rest on the notion that crime springs from character deficiencies in lower-class individuals, particularly nonwhites, rather than from social causes.[5] The media also depict violence against isolated individuals as far more serious than violence against masses of people who are harmed because the business world produces defective goods, polluted air, unsafe housing, or dangerous working conditions. The effectiveness of the criminal justice system is improperly judged by the media and the public in terms of apprehension and punishment of criminals, rather than primarily in terms of reforming society and eliminating the social causes of crime.

To investigate the validity of these claims, four image areas will be examined. First, we will focus on the descriptions of criminals and victims to determine whether they are depicted and perceived as flawed in character, nonwhite, and linked predominantly to the lower classes. Second, we will investigate the role that white-collar and corporate crimes play in crime news and in the perceptions of crime news audiences. This is to determine whether violence against individuals is emphasized and white-collar crime and economic and social crime deemphasized, as radical criminologists and others claim.

Chapter 4 will look at the way in which causes of crime and the ways to control crime are depicted. What emphasis, if any, is placed on socioeconomic factors as causes of crime? Do the recommended remedies for the escalating crime problem include major socioeconomic changes? Chapter 4 also examines whether the police, the courts, and the correctional system are appraised by the media and people in terms of suppression of crime symptoms or in terms of reform of society. Are the various arms of the criminal justice system depicted as tools of repression by which the established elites seek to continue their dominance, or are they pictured primarily as social servants who are working for the public's welfare?

CRIMINALS, VICTIMS, AND SITES OF CRIME

If one wants to assess whether people in the United States think of criminals as coming from a particular social class, one must generally look at inferential social indicators of class, as the U.S. public does not ordinarily speak in class terms. Such inferential indicators are the criminal's or victim's race and occupation and the neighborhood in which the crime occurred. Minority racial status, unemployment, unskilled or low-skilled blue-collar jobs, and inner-city neighborhoods and slum areas can be construed as code words for "lower class." Using this construction, one can say that the press does not depict criminals and victims largely as nonwhite, poor, and lower class, but the panelists do.

This conclusion is based on content analysis of explicit mentions of racial and ethnic origins of criminals and victims by the *Tribune,* and on coding specific mentions of the location of crime according to the ethnic composition and economic status popularly ascribed to the neighborhood in question.[6] Information about the panelists' images of criminals and victims was obtained through direct as well as indirect questions designed to avoid receiving stock answers about the demographics and geography of crime. For instance, we asked for identification of "dangerous" neighborhoods and then recoded the list according to the dominant ethnic composition. The panel data presented below are based on composite scores derived from successive interviews. They are reported in numbers of replies, omitting don't-know answers. Tables based on fewer than 100 replies come from core panel data only, unless specified otherwise. When larger numbers of replies are reported, the data come from all four panels.

Table 3.4 presents the explicit racial, age, and sex designations for criminals and victims supplied by the panel members, when asked about the characteristics of typical criminals and victims, and corresponding characteristics excerpted from *Tribune* crime stories. FBI statistics have been added for comparison, based on data for arrested suspects.

The table indicates that panel members who identified criminals demographically viewed crime largely as the work of young males, black or belonging to other minority races. The *Tribune,* in turn, identified 70 percent of the criminals as white, past 25, and somewhat better balanced sexually than was true of the panel's images. However, if one considers that most panel members suspected that nearly all crimes in which no ethnic information was given were committed by blacks, then panel estimates are a fairly close match for the media data. Adding the unidentified criminals to the list of those identified as black by the *Tribune* raises the *Tribune* total for crimes committed by blacks to 61.6 percent.[7] It should be emphasized, however, that these types of mental calculations, which most respondents admitted, receive no support from the actual *Tribune* stories.

Victims, too, were seen as more heavily black by the panelists than by the *Tribune,* but the discrepancies between media and panel data were smaller. Age and sex data for victims differed widely. The panel pictured victims as considerably older, and hence more vulnerable, than did the *Tribune.* It also saw two thirds of the victims as female, a direct reversal of *Tribune* proportions, which depicted two thirds of the victims as male. FBI data are a fairly good match for *Tribune* data except for age categories, where differences may be due to the fact that FBI data exclude a number of nonviolent crimes that are included in *Tribune* coverage. Likewise, National Victimization Survey data parallel the images conveyed by the *Tribune.*

Comparisons between media data and perceptual data become more difficult when occupational characteristics are considered. If the unemployed, unskilled, homemakers, and students are counted as "poor" – obviously an overly broad grouping – 26.5 percent of all occupational listings of criminals in the *Tribune*

TABLE 3.4
Criminals' and Victims' Racial, Age, and Sex Designations: *Tribune* and Panel; FBI Data on Criminals Only (in percentages)
(For criminals: *Tribune* N = 489 for race, 766 for age, 1,498 for sex; Panel N = 67 for race, 148 for age, 133 for sex; FBI N = 7,383,960 for race, 7,912,348 for age, 6,957,080 for sex. Blank and mixed responses omitted. For victims: *Tribune* N = 466 for race, 588 for age, 720 for sex; Panel N = 46 for race, 89 for age, 100 for sex. Blank and mixed responses omitted)

	Criminals			Victims	
	Panel	*Tribune*	*FBI*	*Panel*	*Tribune*
Race					
Black	61.4	21.6	25.3	41.3	23.6
White	7.4	70.3	72.3	54.3	67.0
Latino	4.4	4.9	–	–	5.2
Other	23.8	3.2	2.4	4.3	4.3
Age					
Under 25	47.6	29.6	56.8	20.2	43.0
25-35	43.6	31.2	20.1	33.7	18.3
Over 35	8.8	39.1	23.1	46.0	38.6
Sex					
Female	2.0	14.4	15.9	65.0	37.3
Male	98.0	85.5	84.0	35.0	62.6

Note: FBI statistics are based on 1976 nationwide reports on arrested suspects only. The array of crimes on which these reports are based is more limited than the array presented in *Tribune* coverage.

Source: Original research.

involved poor people. This leaves three out of four criminals in the middle and upper economic strata. The panel data run in the opposite direction. Whenever criminals' occupational status was mentioned, it was either unemployed, unskilled, or poor, and little else. Table 3.5 provides the data. Lower-class members of the panel were indistinguishable from middle- and upper-class members in these characterizations. Most of them blamed society, rather than the individual, for the poverty-crime sequence.

The difficulties that panel members had in specifying occupations could not be blamed on media deficiencies. Fifty-one percent of all stories reporting crimes included information regarding the suspects' occupations. Evidently, this information went largely unnoticed or failed to leave images in its wake. When panelists were asked to describe the typical criminal in terms of sex, age, race, and occupation, one third of the answers about occupation made reference to emotional status and drug use instead. Criminals were described as emotionally disturbed and often hooked on drugs, with the implication that these were character defects. The newspaper data rarely contained comments about the emotional status of criminals. In fact, most *Tribune* criminals are pasteboard, one-dimensional characters, bereft of motives and emotions. Likewise, reference to drug use was rare in the *Tribune* except when it was pertinent to the crime.[8] However, the *Tribune* did indicate in 4 percent of the stories that repeat offenders were involved. The panelists mentioned this information only in connection with appraisals of the criminal justice system.

TABLE 3.5
Percentage of Criminals' Occupational Designation:
Tribune and Panel
(*Tribune* N = 1,083; Panel N = 160)

Tribune		Panel	
Bureaucrat	29.9	Unemployed	52.5
Professional	16.6	Poor	27.5
Business manager	15.4	Uneducated	11.8
Unemployed	10.6	Unskilled labor	5.0
Skilled labor	8.4	Slum dweller	3.0
Students	8.4		
Unskilled labor	6.6		
Clerical/sales	2.8		
Homemaker	0.9		

Source: Original research.

In the views of the panelists, crime is not an interclass phenomenon where the poor prey on the rich. Rather, it is a self-destructive battle where the poor prey on the poor and those whose lifestyles make them especially vulnerable. As Table 3.6 shows, 33 percent of the victims were identified in terms of poverty criteria; 49 percent were identified in terms of vulnerability because of location, naivete, physical weakness, or addiction. Only 17 percent were pictured as well-to-do.

Again, *Tribune* data are quite different. As Table 3.7 indicates, nearly two thirds of the victims were in the middle- and upper-income groups, even when generous assignments were made to the list of "poor" by including students and homemakers. While panel members had made little reference to victims' occupations, 41 percent of the *Tribune* stories about individual crimes contained

TABLE 3.6
Victims' Lifestyle Characteristics: Panel
(N = 69; in percentages)

Loners/isolated	27.5	Drug users/alcoholics	8.6
Poor	21.7	Uneducated/unskilled	7.2
Trusting/careless	10.1	Middle Class	7.2
Rich	10.1	Slum dweller	4.3
		Children	2.8

Source: Original research.

victim occupational data. As was true for data about criminals, inattention, rather than unavailability of information, explains the panelists' inability to characterize victims along occupational lines.

Might the differences between the panels' images and *Tribune* images spring from the fact that the *Tribune* data included criminals and victims of street as well as white-collar and other crimes, while the respondents had mainly street crimes in mind when the subject of crime was discussed? Probing the panelists' images of white-collar criminals and victims supplied the answer. There were, indeed, substantial differences in their images linked to these different types of crimes. For white-collar criminals, better than half of the panelists (54.6 percent) were able to supply a list of occupational categories. As Table 3.8 shows, this list was fairly similar to the *Tribune*'s occupational designations for white-collar crime, with "poor" groups making up 6.1 percent of the panels' list and 6.2 percent of the *Tribune*'s.* (*Tribune* occupational data for street

TABLE 3.7
Victims' Occupations: *Tribune*
(N = 759; in percentages)

Students*	16.7	Unemployed	10.8
Business manager	14.4	Unskilled labor	9.2
Professional	14.2	Clerical/sales	5.7
Bureaucrat	14.0	Homemaker	3.4
Skilled labor	11.1		

*The high number of student victims is explained by multiple stories about the Chowchilla school bus kidnapping case.

Source: Original research.

---

*Fraud was blamed largely on business managers, bribery and kickbacks on politicians and managers, wiretaps on bureaucrats, and embezzlement on clerical and sales personnel.

TABLE 3.8
White-Collar Criminals' Occupational Designation: *Tribune*
and Panel
(*Tribune* street crime data added; N = 113 for panel, 477 for *Tribune*
white-collar crime, 606 for *Tribune* street crime; in percentages)

Panel		Tribune	White-Collar	Street*
Business manager	32.7	Business manager	24.3	8.4
Politicians/bureaucrats	30.0	Bureaucrat	41.7	20.7
Clerical/sales	15.9	Clerical/sales	1.4	3.9
Professional	13.2	Professional	20.7	13.3
Unemployed	5.3	Unemployed	3.3	16.3
Skilled labor	1.7	Skilled labor	5.4	10.8
Homemaker	0.8	Homemaker	0.2	1.4
Unskilled labor	—	Unskilled labor	2.5	9.9
Students	—	Students	0.2	14.8

*Note that only 42.4 percent of the occupational designations fall into the poverty group even after white-collar criminals have been removed.

Source: Original research.

criminals have been added for comparison.) However, the panelists also supplied a number of social-psychological characteristics that were not mentioned by the press. These indicated that even white-collar criminals often are considered economically disadvantaged. Table 3.9 shows that the ratio of poor to well-to-do criminals was three to one. Educational and character defects make up 45 percent of the list.

The data in Table 3.10 on victims of white-collar crime are similar to the data on white-collar criminals. The panelists were able to supply a list of victims' occupations that roughly matched the *Tribune* data. The poorer classes — unemployed, students, and homemakers — constituted 32 percent of the panelists' group of victims and 49 percent of the *Tribune* sample.

In response to questions about social-psychological characteristics, the panelists depicted the bulk of victims in terms of their economic status, 53 percent as middle or upper class and 12 percent as poor. Another 24 percent of the replies indicated mental instability, previous criminal involvement, often in organized crime, or unusual vulnerability because of working conditions (see Table 3.11).

Judging from comments made during the interviews, the notion that victims are weaker than ordinary people, or that their exposure to crime is exceptionally great, appears to be one defense mechanism for coping with the fear of crime. To those who do not consider themselves in the vulnerable categories, it means that crime happens to others, not to them.[9]

TABLE 3.9
Social-Psychological Characteristics of White-Collar
Criminals: Panel
(N = 204; in percentages)

Economic Traits	
Poor	35.7
Middle income	10.7
Rich	0.4
Character Traits	
Criminal tendencies	19.6
Unstable	14.2
Weak	3.9
Drug/alcohol addict	2.8
Education	
Educated	9.3
Uneducated	4.4

Source: Original research.

TABLE 3.10
White-Collar Crime Victims' Occupational Designation:
Tribune and Panel
(*Tribune* street crime data added; N = 98 for panel, 51 for *Tribune*
white-collar crime, 708 for *Tribune* street crime; in percentages)

Panel		*Tribune*		*White-Collar*	*Street**
Business manager	28.5	Business manager	39.2		12.7
Unemployed/retired	26.5	Unemployed/retired	37.2		8.8
Clerical/sales	16.3	Clerical sales	—		6.2
Skilled labor	14.2	Skilled labor	1.9		11.8
Politician/bureaucrat	6.1	Bureaucrats*	3.9		14.8
Professional	3.0	Professional	5.8		14.8
Homemaker	3.0	Homemaker	1.9		3.5
Student	2.0	Student	9.8		17.2
Unskilled labor	—	Unskilled labor	—		9.8

*Bureaucrats include police, fire-fighters, and similar public employment categories.

Source: Original research.

60

Racial tags were comparatively rare in connection with white-collar crimes. The *Tribune* data for both white-collar criminals and victims are listed in Table 3.12.* Crime and victimization, judging from the data, are obviously a white affair. There were too few responses among the panelists to venture a guess at the trends.

TABLE 3.11
Social-Psychological Characteristics of White-Collar Crime Victims: Panel
(N = 34; in percentages)

Economic Traits	
Poor	11.7
Middle income	8.9
Rich	44.1
Character Traits	
Criminal tendencies	17.6
Unstable	8.8
Exposure	
Vulnerable location	8.8

Source: Original research.

TABLE 3.12
White-Collar Criminals' and Victims' Racial Designations: *Tribune*
(street crime data added for comparison; N = 212 for *Tribune* white-collar criminals and 637 for street criminals; N = 14 for *Tribune* white-collar victims and 452 for street crime victims; in percentages)

	Criminals			Victims	
	White-Collar	*Street*		*White-Collar*	*Street*
Black	6.6	26.5	Black	14.2	23.8
White	85.8	65.1	White	78.5	66.5
Latino	5.1	4.8	Latino	–	5.3
Other	2.3	4.2	Other	7.1	4.2

Source: Original research.

*Racial breakdowns for white-collar crime are unavailable from official sources. Table 3.4 contains comparative official and panel figures for street crime.

An examination of sites of crime also shows that black and poor neighborhoods are emphasized as sites of crime and victimization. Roughly 40 percent of the crime locations mentioned in the *Tribune* and 60 percent of the crime locations mentioned by the panelists were in inner-city slum areas (see Table 3.13).

TABLE 3.13

Sites of Crime and Victimizations: *Tribune* and Panel
(N = 1,644 *Tribune*, 300 Panel; in percentages)

	Panel	*Tribune* Specifics	*Tribune* General	
Slums/black neighborhoods	29.3	–	Inner city	39.9
Home/low income housing	26.3	26.3	Outer city	38.9
Alleys/street at night	16.6	15.7	Suburb	17.3
Public buildings/parking lots	9.6	20.4	Nonurban	4.0
Parks/campuses	7.0	3.1		
Bars/nightclubs	5.3	3.2		
Public transportation	3.6	9.1		
Miscellaneous	2.0	0.7		
Banks	–	11.3		
Stores/factories	–	9.7		

Source: Original research.

Although panelists depicted both criminals and victims as predominantly poor and uneducated and living in deprived neighborhoods, it was clear from listening to their answers that any explicit notion of class was absent from their conceptualizations of criminals and victims. Rather, there was a notion that individuals in certain life situations — which happen to occur more often among the poor — have a greater opportunity to commit law infractions. Given these opportunities, human frailties, which are apparent at all economic levels, then lead to crime and victimization. The absence of explicit class concerns was particularly striking when respondents discussed crime in their own way. For example, when the panelists were asked to describe briefly a particular crime to a friend who had not heard about it, social class specuations were totally absent.* Five aspects of the crime were most commonly discussed: the criminal's and victim's past lives, details about their current lives, details about the criminal's or victim's personality, details about the crime, and details about

---

*Diary data also were devoid of references to social class status.

various aspects of police and court procedures. Table 3.14 indicates the proportionate amount of attention given to each aspect.

TABLE 3.14
Percentage of Commentary Devoted to Various Aspects of Crime
(N = 136)

Crime details	55.8
Past life of criminal/victim	27.2
Present life of criminal/victim	8.8
Police/court procedures	6.6
Personality of criminal/victim	1.4

Source: Original research.

In a number of criminal cases, when wealthy defendants were involved, such as the case of Patricia Hearst, respondents were asked whether they expected the defendants to receive a light sentence or no punishment at all because of the influence enjoyed by the defendants' families. On an average, two thirds of the respondents felt that justice would be fair regardless of the defendants' economic status. The remainder felt that, because of the quality of lawyers that rich defendants have available, punishment would be light. Only a few of the generally more cynical respondents mentioned the possibility of bribery.

PERCEPTIONS OF WHITE-COLLAR CRIME

Although, as Tables 2.6, 2.7, and 2.8 show, white-collar crime was well and prominently covered by the media, it assumed a secondary role to street crime in the audience's comments.[10] When the panelists were asked about what crimes they heard of or read about most, with a chance to name several, they limited themselves almost completely to street crimes (see Table 3.15). Similarly, in the core panel's diaries, 72 percent of all crime stories dealt with violent crimes and only 29 percent with corruption and other white-collar crimes (see Table 3.16).

Spontaneous complaints about the adequacy of white-collar crime coverage were few when panelists were asked about the quality of crime reporting in general. However, in response to a specific question about the adequacy of white-collar crime coverage, half of the answers indicated that there was too little emphasis. One fourth of the replies stated that emphasis was about right, and the remaining fourth indicated that white-collar crime, like most other crimes, was covered too heavily.

TABLE 3.15
Crimes Most Heard of or Read about: Panel
(N = 280; in percentages; *Tribune* ranks added for comparison)

Tribune *Rank*	*Panel* *Rank*		
(1)	1.	Murder	29.2
(2)	2.	Robbery/burglary	23.5
(4)	3.	Assault	14.6
(8)	4.	Rape	13.2
(5)	5.	Kidnapping	10.0
(10)	6.	Drug offenses	4.6
(7)	7.	Arson	2.5
(22)	8.	Vandalism	2.1

Source: Original Research.

TABLE 3.16
Crime Distribution in Diary Stories: Panel
(N = 1,678; in percentages)

Violent Crime		White-Collar Crimes	
Street crime	54.4	Corruption	15.6
Terrorism	17.5	Business crime	8.5
		Drug offenses	3.9

Source: Original research.

From the fact that the panelists did not mention white-collar crime very much when asked about crime and crime coverage, one might conclude that they consider it a rare occurrence or that it is not very salient to them. Nothing could be further from the truth. People perceived white-collar crimes as common and serious, albeit generally less serious than street crime. When the panelists were asked to rate a list of 15 white-collar crimes as "serious," "moderately serious," or "not serious," 48 percent of the ratings were "serious," 38 percent were "moderately serious," and only 13 percent were "not serious." Table 3.17 rank-orders crimes in the order of seriousness, awarding two points for ratings of "serious," one point for "moderately serious," and no points for "not serious." The average ratings for individual crimes, using the same point scheme, are also noted.

TABLE 3.17
Rank Order of Seriousness Rating of White-Collar Crime: Panel
(average rating for individual crimes in parentheses; N = 2,214)

1.	Child abuse	(1.7)
2.	Drunken driving	(1.6)
3.	Corruption	(1.6)
4.	Consumer fraud	(1.5)
5.	Weapons violations	(1.5)
6.	Drug offenses	(1.5)
7.	Fencing stolen goods	(1.4)
8.	Tax cheating	(1.3)
9.	Perjury	(1.2)
10.	Embezzlement	(1.2)
11.	Illegal wiretaps	(1.2)
12.	Extortion	(1.2)
13.	Forgery/counterfeit	(1.2)
14.	Gambling offenses	(0.9)
15.	Prostitution	(0.9)

*Ratings: not serious = 0; moderately serious = 1; very serious = 2. Point scores were divided by total number of responses.)

Source: Original research.

When asked about the basis of seriousness ratings, 35 percent of the replies mentioned sheer frequency. Twenty-six percent noted the severity of injury to society, and another 8 percent remarked that a given white-collar crime might well lead to other serious crimes (see Table 3.18). If the latter two are considered as concerns about societal impact, one third of the answers referred to societal impact. The remainder of the answers related primarily to individual human concerns about the impact of white-collar crime on strangers and on the respondent and his or her family and friends.

TABLE 3.18
Criteria for Judging Seriousness of White-Collar Crime: Panel
(N = 115; in percentages)

Crime frequency	34.7	Impact on self/family	9.5
Societal consequences	33.8	Other	4.3
Impact on victim	16.4	Don't know	0.9

Source: Original research.

One further bit of evidence that white-collar crime is personally salient to respondents is the fact that 86 percent of the panelists were aware of programs designed to protect them in case of consumer fraud. This compares with 43 percent who were aware of programs compensating victims of violent crime. There is substantial evidence that saliency and attentiveness are correlated regardless of the frequency of publication of the salient story or the prominence bestowed on it.[11]

The core panel was also given a list of 25 white-collar crimes and requested to indicate how frequently they occurred. Sixty-five percent of the answers rated crimes on the list as "common" or "fairly common." Only 31 percent of the answers labeled them as "rare"; the remainder indicated lack of knowledge. Table 3.19 presents the rank order of white-collar crimes perceived by a majority of the respondents as occurring commonly and the smaller list of crimes considered rare by the majority. The perceptions depicted in the table are not an accurate reflection of the frequency of these offenses as reported in police reports, victimization studies, or media stories. Nonetheless the table indicates that most white-collar offenses are perceived as staples on the crime list.

In fact, when core panel members compared white-collar crimes as a group with street crimes as a group, 16 percent of their comments indicated that white-collar crimes were more frequent, 39 percent that they were the same, and 46 percent that they occurred less often. Individual white-collar offenses considered as common or more common than most street crimes by a majority of the panelists were all crimes from rank 1 through 7 in Table 3.19, along with parole violations. These were deemed everyday occurrences. It should be noted that the list of white-collar crimes to which the respondents referred was based only on actions defined as "illegal" by the current social system. This excludes a number of individual and corporate behaviors that radical criminologists generally include in their lists of white-collar crimes but that the public does not perceive as such. Selling addictive substances or stimulating demand for unnecessary services are examples of undesirable behaviors that are not generally included in a list of white-collar crimes.

SUMMARY AND CONCLUSIONS

How well does the evidence presented thus far match the charges of radical criminologists? The answer is mixed, indicating that their indictment is too sweeping but that it nonetheless contains a great deal of truth. Most importantly, radical criminologists are wrong in assuming that the public is a mere blotter for media images, absorbing them in rough outline. As shown, there are substantial differences between media and public images, with the public, more often than the media, captured by the stereotypes that radical criminologists deem false.

TABLE 3.19
Rank Order of Frequency Ratings of White-Collar Crime: Panel
(N = 525; note a number of tied rankings; *Tribune* rankings added for comparison)

		Panel Rank	Tribune Rank
Frequent[a]			
1.	Drug offenses[b]	1	(3)
2.	Drunken driving[b]	2	(22)
3.	Fencing stolen goods[b]	3	(14)
4.	Weapons violations[b]	3	(6)
5.	Prostitution[b]	3	(13)
6.	Welfare cheating[b]	3	(19)
7.	Consumer fraud[b]	4	(1)
8.	Bribery/kickbacks	4	(2)
9.	Gambling offenses	4	(16)
10.	Tax cheating	5	(4)
11.	Corruption	6	(7)
12.	Disorderly conduct	6	(15)
13.	Parole violations[b]	7	(24)
14.	Nonprostitution sex offenses	7	(12)
15.	Child abuse	8	(20)
16.	Perjury	8	(8)
17.	Liquor law offenses	9	(23)
18.	Extortion	10	(5)
19.	Forgery/counterfeiting	10	(9)
Rare			
20.	Contempt of court	11	(11)
21.	Custody escape	12	(10)
22.	Illegal wiretaps	13	(17)
23.	Contributing to minor's delinquency	14	(21)
24.	Embezzlement	15	(18)
25.	False fire alarms	15	(−)

[a]Crimes listed in the "Frequent" column were perceived by a majority of panelists as occurring commonly; crimes listed in the "Rare" column were considered rare by a majority of the panelists.
[b]Considered more common than street crimes.

Source: Original research.

Specifically, it is the public, rather than the media, that perceives both criminals and victims as largely flawed in character, nonwhite, and lower class.[12] It is the public, rather than the media, that thinks of crime almost exclusively in terms of street rather than white-collar crime. These are the two types of images that, in the views of radical criminologists, most closely represent the stereotypes that capitalist ruling classes like to perpetuate. Inasmuch as the media do not closely hold to this stereotypical line, they are not the capitalist mouthpieces that radical criminologists charge them to be.[13]

While crime and justice news does not conform to the Marxist conceptions of "truth," neither does it conform to the stereotypes of capitalist ideology that Marxists postulate. Rather, like much of U.S. ideology and politics, it represents a medley of conflicting views and motivations. It also reflects a desire to stick with the existing system and patch up its faults, without totally ignoring the possibility for development in new and different directions.

NOTES

1. An overview of comparable data is presented in Joseph R. Dominick, "Crime and Law Enforcement in the Mass Media," in *Deviance and Mass Media,* ed. Charles Winick (Beverly Hills, Calif.: Sage, 1978), pp. 105-27.

2. Sanford Sherizen, "Social Creation of Crime News: All the News Fitted to Print," in *Deviance and Mass Media,* pp. 203-24.

3. Harold G. Zucker, "The Variable Nature of News Media Influence," in *Communication Yearbook 2,* ed. Brent D. Ruben (New Brunswick, N.J.: Transaction Books, 1978), pp. 225-40; Chaim H. Eyal, "The Impact of Issue Choices on the Agenda-Setting Effect," Midwest Association for Public Opinion Research Paper, 1979; and Tom R. Tyler, "Drawing Inferences from Experiences: The Effect of Crime Victimization Experiences Upon Crime-Related Attitudes and Behaviors" (Ph.D. diss., University of California, Los Angeles, 1978).

4. Comparative data for larger samples of populations in the Chicago area in 1972 are included in U.S. Department of Justice, *Public Opinions About Crime: The Attitudes of Victims and Nonvictims in Selected Cities* (Washington, D.C.: Law Enforcement Assistance Administration, 1977), pp. 295-309.

5. Brief expositions of the views of radical criminologists as well as counterarguments are presented in Austin T. Turk, "Prospects and Pitfalls for Radical Criminology"; and Mary Marzotto, Tony Platt, and Annika Snare, "A Reply to Turk," in *Crime and Social Justice* 4 (Fall-Winter 1975): 41-45. Also see Suzie Dod, Tony Platt, Herman Schwendinger, Greg Shank, and Paul Takagi, "Editorial: The Politics of Street Crime," *Crime and Social Justice* 5 (Spring-Summer 1976): 1-4; Richard Quinney, *The Social Reality of Crime* (Boston: Little, Brown, 1970), pp. 15-25, for a theoretical basis for the contentions of radical criminologists; as well as Richard Quinney, *Critique of Legal Order: Crime Control in a Capitalist Society* (Boston: Little, Brown, 1974). A brief rejoinder to the basic assumptions underlying the radical critique is presented in Ernest Van den Haag, "No Excuse for Crime," in "Crime and Justice in America, 1776-1976," ed. Graeme R. Newman, *Annals of the American Academy of Political and Social Science* 423 (January 1976): 133-41.

6. Crime stereotypes and their deviation from factual data are discussed in Austin Turk, "The Mythology of Crime in America," *Criminology* 8 (February 1971): 397-411.

7. For recent data on comparative crime rates for blacks and whites presented in context, see John A. Davis, "Blacks, Crime, and American Culture," in "Crime and Justice

in America, 1776-1976," pp. 89-98.

8. A perceptive analysis of the impressions conveyed by media images of criminals and victims is contained in Drew Humphries, "Newspapers and Crime Ideology: An Exploratory Analysis," Society for the Study of Social Problems Paper, 1977.

9. In the same escapist vein, people do not generally identify their own neighborhoods as "dangerous." See, for example, John E. Conklin, *The Impact of Crime* (New York: Macmillan, 1975), p. 81.

10. The impact of white-collar crime is discussed in the President's Commission on Law Enforcement and Administration of Justice, *Task Force Report, Crime and Its Impact: An Assessment* (Washington, D.C.: U.S. Government Printing Office, 1976), pp. 102-9.

11. Charles Atkin, "Instrumental Utilities and Information Seeking," in *New Models for Mass Communication Research,* ed. Peter Clarke (Beverly Hills, Calif.: Sage, 1973), pp. 205-39. Also see Jay G. Blumler and Elihu Katz, *The Uses of Mass Communications: Current Perspectives on Gratification Research* (Beverly Hills, Calif.: Sage, 1974).

12. It has been argued that the lack of detail about the human aspects of crime implicitly conveys the images that the public perceives. See Humphries, "Newspapers and Crime Ideology."

13. A contrary view, claiming that the media ignore the social causes of looting and stereotype looters, is presented in Andrew Karmen, "How Much Heat? How Much Light? Coverage of New York City's Blackout and Looting in the Print Media," in *Deviance and Mass Media,* pp. 179-200. In the same volume, pp. 203-24, Sanford Sherizen argues in "Social Creation of Crime News: All the News Fitted to Print," that lower echelon police officials cooperate with crime beat reporters to depict crimes in ways that benefit the police. Crime news thus is an ideological construct – the officials' version of crime.

Four

MEDIA AND PUBLIC IMAGES ABOUT CRIME FIGHTING

THE CAUSES AND CURES OF CRIME

What images do the media and their audiences hold about the causes of crime and ways to cope with crime? Looking at the media picture first, one is struck by the scantiness of information. Only 4 percent of the stories mentioned causes of crime, only 1 percent noted more than one cause, and only four tenths of 1 percent mentioned three or more causes. Among the causes that were mentioned (see Table 4.1), one fifth dealt with deficiencies of the political system in general, alerting the reader to possible needs for major changes. If one assumes that poverty and economic stress are consequences of a defective socioeconomic system, the figure rises to 28 percent. However, this assumption must be supplied by the reader; it was not made explicit in the stories. Racism, sexism, imperialism, and other crime causes stressed by radical criminologists were totally absent from the list.

The largest share of the blame for crime was placed on the criminal justice system. Better than one third of the *Tribune* stories indicated that the criminal justice system encourages crime by dealing improperly with criminals. Excessive leniency by all branches of the system was the most common complaint. Personal deficiencies, alcohol and drug addiction, and poor home life conditions, including lack of moral training, accounted for another 28 percent of the causes. Depending on the reader's predilections, these "personal" deficiencies could be blamed on the social system. But the linkage had to be supplied by the reader; it was not made explicit by the *Tribune* stories.

TABLE 4.1
Causes of Crime: *Tribune* and Panel
(N = 158 for *Tribune;* 343 for Panel; in percentages)

	Tribune	*Panel*
Criminal justice system deficiencies	37.1	10.7
Political system deficiencies	20.1	–
Home life deficiencies	15.0	12.5
Alcoholism/drug addiction/instability	9.4	14.5
Poverty/economic stress/unemployment	7.5	34.6
Miscellaneous	5.0	2.0
Materialism/greed/human vices	3.1	8.4
Media violence images	1.8	2.9
Peer group pressure/boredom/thrill	–	13.9

Source: Original research

Discussion of the immediate motives that led to crime further enhances the impression that personal rather than social causes are paramount.* Table 4.2 shows that almost two thirds of all mentions of motives referred to personal quarrels of various types or to character traits that produce violence. In prior years, this figure would probably have been even higher. The high percentage of political motivations for 1976 is an abnormality due to the heavy emphasis placed on the Symbionese Liberation Army in connection with the Hearst case and on a number of politically motivated airplane hijackings and bombings.

TABLE 4.2
Motives for Crime: *Tribune*
(N = 477; in percentages)

Personal (quarrels, greed, and the like)	65.2
Political differences	24.5
Racial/ethnic differences	6.3
Labor strife	3.6
National security needs	0.4

Source: Original research.

---

*14.6 percent of the stories had information on motivation. Of these, 0.7 percent had two motives and 0.1 percent had three or more.

Only 3 percent of the crime stories contained explicit discussions of remedies for crime. Societal changes were hardly mentioned (1 percent). Eight percent of the stories dealt with social programs for high-crime populations, 24 percent emphasized penalties, and the remainder dealt primarily with precautions and protective devices that might prevent crimes from being committed. Additional information about remedies suggested by *Tribune* stories can be gleaned from looking at the causes of crime and considering the elimination of these causes as cures. *Tribune* stories dealing with general reforms of the criminal justice system (see Table 4.6) provide further clues. The bulk of recommendations in these stories deals with fixing up institutional deficiencies such as improving gun control laws, death penalty laws, immunity grants, and laws relating to freedom of the press in reporting criminal cases. There was no mention of changing the social system to improve criminal justice.

The panelists' assessment of the causes of crime and possible remedies was gauged through a series of direct questions, as well as several questions that asked about reasons for increase in crime and ways to cope with it. Table 4.1 presents the combined replies. Better than a third of the answers named poverty and economic stresses as causes of crime, followed by human weaknesses and vices, home life deficiencies, and alcoholism and drug addiction. Furthermore, when asked to name the most important causes of crime, poverty and economic stress received the largest number of votes. It is obvious from these answers that the panelists stress the significance of social causation of crime. Compared to Gallup poll ratings ten years earlier, the proportion of answers mentioning social causes has tripled.[1] However, the bulk of the blame for crime (49 percent) was still placed on personal factors. And, whatever the deficiencies of the economic system may be, the transcripts of interviews indicate that few respondents have lost faith in the ability of the present political system to remedy its economic ills without a major restructuring of society.

That most, though by no means all, remedies for coping with rampant crime are sought within the system was also demonstrated by an analysis of replies to questions about crime remedies in general and about governmental changes that would reduce crime. As Table 4.3 indicates, better than half of the suggested remedies are reforms of the criminal justice system. Economic and educational reforms were proposed in less than one third of the replies.[2]

The data on causes and cures for white-collar crime are too scanty for both the *Tribune* and the panels to assess trends with confidence. What evidence there is suggests that white-collar crime is predominantly blamed on human weaknesses and easy opportunities to gratify greed and indulge in carelessness. For instance, in reply to questions about causes of corruption in government, 70 percent of the answers referred to human failings, such as lust for power, lack of ethics, and general character weaknesses. Twenty-six percent of the answers mentioned opportunity, with the implication that easy access to wealth is corrupting. Four percent cited need, saying that public officials were underpaid.

TABLE 4.3
Remedies for Crime: Panel
(N = 329; in percentages)

Criminal justice reforms/toughen system	54.4
Economic and educational reforms	29.7
Gun/drug control tightening	8.2
Family life improvements	5.4
Media violence reduction	1.2
Miscellaneous	0.9

Source: Original research.

Unlike the heavy stress on formal penalties for violent crime, only 11 percent of the answers stressed formal penalties as a way to cope with white-collar crime. Rather, the stress was on publicity to shame the criminals (37 percent), internal checking to prevent malfeasance (26 percent), and political pressures, electoral or otherwise (26 percent). The obvious underlying assumption is that white-collar crime is born from bad impulses of individuals, which can be curbed through pressures and prevention at the individual level.

SUMMARY AND CONCLUSIONS ABOUT CAUSES AND CURES OF CRIME

In summary, one can say that radical criminologists are correct, in part, in claiming inattention to social causes of crime and failure to stress socioeconomic reform or revolution as a way to cope with escalating crime. Here the media conform most closely to the picture that radical criminologists have drawn. Curable deficiencies in the existing criminal justice system and personality defects in individuals are depicted by the media as the main causes of rampant crime. Social causes play a subordinate, though by no means nonexistent, role. Suggested remedies are sparse and do not generally include social reforms. Given the fact that the U.S. news media see themselves primarily as reporters of events, rather than as crusaders for social change, the infrequent probing of causes and almost total neglect of remedies are not surprising. The media do not explicitly advocate any particular social system, be it the existing one or a totally different one. Implicitly, through accepting the assumptions on which the existing system is based, and through silence about most alternatives, they do, however, support it.

Radical criminologists are less accurate when they claim that the public lacks concern for social causes of crime and for social remedies. Social and economic factors were regularly mentioned by panel members as causes of crime, and social and economic reforms were advocated, albeit within the existing political structures. As discussed earlier, these views were heavily attributed to personal experiences and evaluations, as well as conversations with lay and professional sources.

Many panelists also exhibited far stronger human concerns about criminals and victims than was reflected in the media stories. They talked a great deal about what might have been done at the individual level to keep a particular criminal from the path of crime or to keep a victim out of the reach of crime. In the media, these types of concerns only come to the fore in the most sensational types of crimes or when prominent criminals or victims are involved. If a prominent figure — doctor, lawyer, merchant, and, yes, crime syndicate chief — is murdered, it is announced in big headlines on the front pages. For the average black or white murder victim, a few lines on back pages suffice. De-emphasis of human concerns in the media is a discouraging sign for those who hope for a more humanistic and socialistic approach to crime and justice problems. Such an approach is not likely to flourish in the absence of human concerns at the individual level, which encompass all criminals and victims, however ordinary they may be. While public attitudes are encouraging on that score, media practices are apt to be a countervailing influence.

THE ROLE OF THE CRIMINAL JUSTICE SYSTEM

Media appraisals of the criminal justice system, like appraisals of causes of crime, are rare. Barely over 1 percent of all crime stories contained explicit evaluations of the courts, the correctional system, or the police (courts = 1.3 percent, police = 1.1 percent, corrections = 1.2 percent). Court system evaluations received the most prominent coverage among the few stories dealing with evaluation of the criminal justice system, with 54 percent appearing on the first three pages. This was slightly above the average 46 percent figure for crime stories in general. For correction system evaluations, the figure was just above average, 47 percent, and police stories trailed with 27 percent. In section placement, evaluation stories did considerably worse than other crime stories. Against an average of 61 percent of crime stories appearing in the first section, only 43 percent of the police evaluation stories, 34 percent of the correction system evaluations, and 26 percent of the court evaluation stories appeared in the front section. This yields an average of 34 percent, slightly over half the comparable overall figure. Substantively, the evaluations were heavily negative, with the courts and the correctional system faring worst. The police fared reasonably well.[3] Table 4.4 tells the story.

The bulk of media evaluations was implicit, rather than explicit, conveyed through mentions of the ability of the system to apprehend criminals, to convict and punish them when apprehended, and to return them to society as reformed

TABLE 4.4
Evaluations of the Police, the Courts, and the
Correctional System: *Tribune*
(N = 30 for police, 35 for court, and 32 for correctional system;
in percentages)

	Improving	Stable	Declining	Mixed
Police	23.3	36.6	20.0	20.2
Courts	2.8	14.2	40.0	42.8
Correctional system	0.0	15.6	25.0	59.3

Source: Original research.

individuals unlikely to repeat their crimes. *Tribune* stories did not question the basic notions of what constitutes criminal behavior or the validity of the belief that correction hinges on proper treatment of individual offenders rather than on reform of society.

A closer look at implicit indicators shows that 46 percent of the crime stories provided data about apprehension of suspects. Of these, 41 percent indicated that no arrests had been made. In the remaining cases, arrests were reported. In two thirds of the arrest cases, all suspects had been apprehended. In the rest, some suspects remained at large. Judging by the criteria enunciated by the panel members (reported below), they deemed a 59 percent arrest rate as good performance. The media scorecard for police performance in apprehending criminals is thus favorable.

Penalties are also an important indicator by which the effectiveness of the criminal justice process is judged. Panel members were highly critical of this phase of criminal justice policy, which makes it important to look at media information about penalties. Only 11 percent of the crime stories covered the topic explicitly. Of these, the death penalty was reported for 12 percent of the murder cases. Additionally, long prison sentences, in excess of 11 years, were reported for 75 percent of the kidnapping cases, 40 percent of the rape cases, 38 percent of the robbery cases, 29 percent of the murders, and 17 percent of the manslaughter cases. All other reported penalties involved prison sentences of ten years or less. Table 4.5 provides data on sentencing reported in media crime stories. It shows that in nearly half of the stories dealing with the topic, there was no penalty at all, or it was delayed and uncertain.

The subject of penalties was discussed in other contexts as well. A fourth of the stories dealing with crime prevention (2.7 percent of the total) pointed to shortcomings in sentencing and penalties as a factor in criminal activities. Likewise, nearly half of the general discussions of criminal justice policies (4 percent of total stories) dealt with penalties and the correctional system. This included

TABLE 4.5
Sentences in Crime Cases Reported in the Press
(N = 309; in percentages)

Prison	34.9
Release without penalty	24.2
Further legal steps pending	21.6
Fine and prison	6.7
Death	4.2
Mental institution commitment	4.2
Fine only	3.8

Source: Original research

discussion of the death penalty, sentencing in general, granting immunity, plea bargaining, continuances, parole, and decriminalization of various victimless offenses.

Yet another implicit assessment of justice system performance is represented by crime rate fluctuations. Although increasing crime and criminal apprehension rates may flow from more comprehensive reporting and better police work, rather than actual increase in crime, most observers draw different conclusions. They equate increasing crime rates with poor performance by the criminal justice system. Stable or declining rates, in turn, signify satisfactory or good performance. Sixty percent of the small number of stories that assessed crime rates (1.6 percent of the total) indicated that crime was increasing and the remainder depicted crime rates as stable or decreasing or a mixture of the three. Again, these stories were displayed less prominently than other crime stories. Only 28 percent appeared on the first three pages, compared to the average rate for crime stories of 46 percent; and 47 percent were covered in the first section of the paper, compared to 61 percent for other crime stories.

Tribune stories about the possibilities for policy changes indicate the areas in which the press explicitly characterizes the criminal justice system as particularly weak. These stories constituted 4 percent of all stories dealing with crime and stressed court and correctional system deficiencies primarily. As Table 4.6 shows, various aspects of prison management of convicts and changes in the criminal laws to make penalties more certain and harsher were most often pictured as needed reforms (44 percent of mentions). The need for the death penalty was an especially strong focus of attention. Another 17 percent of the comments dealt with tightening of various court procedures, such as immunity grants, repeated continuances, and plea bargaining. The remainder covered gun control (12 percent), better protection of crime victims (5 percent), decriminalization of certain drug offenses and prostitution (5 percent), and discussions of the scope of the free press in relation to the criminal justice process. The stories about decriminalization and freedom of the press generally took a liberal stance. But there was no exposition at all of the views of radicals, either left or right, concerning basic changes in the criminal justice system and in society in general.

A small portion of crime stories (3 percent) discussed civil rights violations by criminal justice agencies. Violations were alleged in 59 percent of the cases involved. In the remainder, the case was pictured as mixed or occasionally favorable, indicating that law enforcement agencies had actually protected civil rights. The mere fact that such stories are sparse is another indication that the topic of repression by the criminal justice system is not a major concern of media gatekeepers.

A summary of the evidence on media evaluations of the crime and justice system presents a motley picture. Specific evaluations of police, courts, and correctional institutions showed a mixture of positive and negative comments, with negative ones predominating for the correctional system and the courts. There is no evidence to prove or disprove claims that the greater negativism expressed toward courts and correctional institutions reflects tense relations between media personnel and often secretive and uncooperative news sources. The explanation that a sweetheart relationship exists between police and news-people because they need each other as story sources and publicity channels is equally unsubstantiated. Implicit media evaluations gave a predominantly negative picture for crime rate trends and provided some grist for the mills of those who believe that sentences are too light. On the other hand, the data on apprehension rates were favorable in light of the public's standards.

How do media appraisals of the crime and justice system square with the public's view?[4] Panel members' answers to multiple questions tell the story. Questioning about the police opened with: "In general, would you say that the police are doing a good job, fair job, or poor job in protecting the community?" After the initial judgment had been rendered, the interviewer probed for

TABLE 4.6
Areas of Criminal Justice Policy Change Requirements: *Tribune* (N = 260; in percentages)

Death penalty	18.8	Continuance grants	5.3
Press freedom	17.6	Victim protection	4.6
Harsher criminal laws	12.3	Parole management	3.8
Gun control	11.5	Plea bargaining	3.4
Immunity grants	7.3	Fixed sentences	2.3
Convict management	6.5	Polygraph use	0.7
Decriminalizations (drugs, prostitution)	5.3	Other	0.4

Source: Original research.

underlying reasons. To put the replies into a time perspective, subjects were then asked: "Compared to five years ago, are they doing a better or worse job, or just about the same?" Again, reasons for the answers were solicited.

Fifty-seven percent of the panel members gave the police a "good" rating; the rest rated it as "fair." There were no "poor" ratings. However, many respondents qualified their judgment by indicating that performance varied in different parts of the city and suburbs and with respect to different crimes. Racial distinctions were also noted, with service to the white community rated superior. When asked for reasons for "fair" ratings, the difficulty of the problems facing the police, insufficient manpower, and lack of public cooperation were cited, along with lack of skills and dedication and the poor caliber of police personnel. A typical comment often was prefaced by "considering the tough problems they face," or "given community attitudes," followed by a favorable evaluation. This leaves the impression that a large proportion of those who gave the police less than top ratings put the blame on the criminal justice system in general and the difficulty of its mission rather than the particular institution. A few respondents indicated that their judgment was based on media appraisals, but most claimed to have judged independently. The fact that some respondents had been crime victims or greatly feared that they might be victimized did not seem to affect their answers.

Because apprehending criminals is widely considered to be the most important function of the police, the subjects were requested to rate the success of the police in catching criminals. Forty-eight percent of the panel saw the police as very successful, 14 percent made the opposite judgment, and the remainder gave answers qualified according to various crimes. In general, the rate of solving murders was deemed much better than solution for other crimes.* Again, the bulk of reasons given for negative assessments was difficulty of catching criminals and insufficient manpower rather than police deficiencies. In line with the notion that apprehending criminals is a difficult task, the standards that were used to make favorable ratings were relatively low. People who judged the apprehension success rate as good estimated it as ranging from less than 10 percent to a top level of 75 percent. Eighty percent of the group that considered apprehension rates as "good" had estimated them to be below 50 percent.

In view of the widely publicized images of police-hating publics in the late 1960s and early 1970s, the favorable ratings may seem surprising. However, they actually present a continuation of the approval rates registered in polls conducted in the late 1960s.[5] Interviews suggest several reasons for approval of the police. Unlike the courts and correctional institutions, which seem remote, forbidding, and unpredictable, many people regard the police as a source of aid

---

*For 1976, the FBI reported the following arrest rates: murder = 79 percent, aggravated assault = 63 percent, forcible rape = 52 percent, robbery = 27 percent, burglary = 17 percent, larceny-theft = 19 percent, and motor vehicle theft = 14 percent.

in various emergencies, including catching and safekeeping of criminals. People can understand and relate to the job performed by police. By contrast, they are mystified by the ways of the courts and correctional system and hold them responsible for returning unreformed criminals to society.

Because the publicized complaints during the periods of internal turmoil had depicted public perceptions of the police as "pigs" who violated citizens' civil rights, often for political reasons, the panelists were asked a direct question to test the current status of that reputation. Only 29 percent of the panel members felt that the complaints of civil rights violations were justified and based on incidents of physical brutality, failure to inform accused persons of their rights, illegal searches, and insensitivity to the needs of crime victims. There were no claims that these acts were politically motivated. The nearest thing to a claim of repression was the charge, voiced by 20 percent of the panelists, that police often fail to inform accused persons of their rights and deprive them of the opportunity to defend themselves properly.

If these figures represent a change in appraisal by a few of the panel members, it may spring from the view that police performance has improved. Thirty-one percent of the sample indicated that they believed that the police were doing a better job than they had done five years previously. Better training and better technology were given as reasons for the changes. However, 62 percent of the group thought that performance was about the same, and the remaining 7 percent rated it as worse or could give no judgment. Lack of improvement or deterioration was blamed on increased difficulty of the job because of surging crime rates rather than on personal or organizational deficiencies of the police.

While the police received fairly favorable ratings, the correctional system did not. Sixty-five percent of the respondents rated its performance as "poor," 15 percent rated it as "good," and the remaining 20 percent gave it a "fair" rating. The reasons for the generally poor ratings were expressed in terms of three criteria: expected results, staff, and facilities. Over half of the sample expressed disappointment with the failure to rehabilitate criminals, as shown by high rates of recidivism. Twenty-five percent of the respondents also deemed prison staffs and management poor, 14 percent mentioned poor facilities, and 14 percent mentioned mixed-up purposes of the institution. As one respondent expressed it:

> If they are going to rehabilitate criminals, it's doing a lousy job. If it's merely a place to store them, to keep them off the street, they are doing a better than average job, as long as they keep them. If the purpose of the correctional system is to punish, revenge, they don't do as well as they used to because it's becoming more plush and convenient. The punishment isn't what it used to be. I think the correctional system is all mixed up as to its purposes.

Half of the respondents felt that the performance of the correctional system had remained unchanged during the past five years, 30 percent thought that it was worse, and 20 percent thought that it was better. Overcrowding, rather than personnel or organizational deficiencies, was given most frequently as the reason for failure to improve over the past five years. Overcrowding was also seen as a reason for unduly brief prison sentences, dismissals of cases without penalties, and leniency in granting paroles. In the words of one respondent: "The jails are full to the brim. They can't let any more criminals in, and they've got to let some out. That's why really bad criminals are thrown back out on the street; psychotics, murderers, rapists, they all get out."

The court system received poor marks as well, though not quite as poor as the correctional system. Forty-two percent of the respondents evaluated it as "poor," 11 percent called it "good," and the remaining 47 percent gave it "fair" ratings. Table 4.7 provides comparative figures for the courts, the police, the correctional system, as well as for crime-fighting efforts at various government levels and by the general public. In each instance, individuals were only moderately consistent in their negative or positive orientations. Apparently judgments were specific rather than general expressions of cynicism or system support.

Poor ratings for the courts were based on the quantity and quality of the judges, on legal procedures, and on the inadequacy of penalties. Forty-eight percent of the complaints mentioned the corruptibility and laziness and insufficient number of judges, excessive judicial leniency, and abusive treatment of accused persons. Legal procedures, such as long delays or judgments based on technicalities, were scored by 15 percent, and 37 percent of the panel members

TABLE 4.7
Comparative Performance Ratings for Crime-Fighting Activities
(N = 168; in percentages)

	Good	Fair	Poor
Police	57	43	0
Courts	11	47	42
Correctional system	15	20	65
Federal government	29	5	66
State government*	24	10	66
City government*	29	19	52
Suburban government*	43	24	33
General public	10	5	85

*Figures are for Illinois state government, Chicago city government, and suburban government in Evanston, Illinois.

Source: Original research.

complained about inadequate sentencing and an overly lenient parole system. As one respondent put it somewhat extremely, "Society gets no protection at all from the courts. All the marbles are on the criminals' side." Another complained:

> There's something wrong with the sentencing. I don't go along with all the legal technicalities, guys getting off because of a legal technicality. They've still committed the crime. If they do apprehend a guy for mugging or raping or something like that, it's a two-time loser that's been in and out of jail on bail a couple of times. To me, I always want to say, "What's that guy doing out of jail?"

Comparing court performance in 1976 with that in the early 1970s, the sense of deterioration was great. Fifty-nine percent of the panel members felt that courts were performing worse than five years earlier. Eighteen percent judged performance as better; the remaining 23 percent considered it stable. Overloading of the court system was perceived as the chief reason for failure to improve and for deterioration. While some of the blame was thus placed on circumstances judged as largely beyond the control of the institution, the major share was put on personnel and procedural deficiencies. However, there were few explicit suggestions that criminal justice institutions should be reorganized to cope with current workload levels, or that procedures should be streamlined.

Because panel members had frequently mentioned overlight penalties as one of the reasons for poor performance by the criminal justice system, they were asked for their views on the appropriateness of sentences, as well as standards by which judges might determine appropriateness. Sixty-five percent of the respondents deemed all sentences generally too light; 20 percent thought that some, but not all, were too light; and 5 percent thought that sentences were too severe. Only 10 percent thought that sentences were about right. Panel members had difficulty in articulating standards by which sentences might be applied or judged. Criteria for sentencing that were mentioned were the percentage of cases in which sentences were below the legal maximum for a given crime, the percentage of cases in which sentences for repeaters were substantially harsher than sentences for first offenders, and comparisons of the severity of current sentences with sentences for similar offenses in the past. It was also suggested that crimes with serious social consequences should receive far heavier penalties than crimes with lesser consequences, and that the death penalty should be used more often for the most vicious crimes.

Answers to general questions about causes and remedies for crime corroborated the perceptual trends that have been outlined. Judicial leniency was mentioned prominently as a reason for spiraling crime rates, with the implication that stiffer sentences and greater certainty of punishment would at best reduce recidivism and discourage first offenders. At the very least, it would keep criminals away from their potential victims for a longer span of time. Overall, 12 percent of all causes of crime (N = 255) were linked to failures of the criminal justice system.

Because the criminal justice system operates at various levels of government, respondents were asked for their perceptions of the adequacy of performance at each of these levels and for possible corrective measures. Levels included were the federal, state, urban, and suburban. Except for the suburban level, "poor" performance levels were registered by over half of the answers (see Table 4.7). Many of the answers explaining these ratings and indicating ways to improve performance provided additional confirmation that the criminal justice system is perceived as weak and that several areas are in particular need of reform. Table 4.8 presents a list.

The table shows that, along with stress on the deficiencies of the criminal justice system, many respondents believe that economic and social causes deter efficient crime fighting. This emphasis on the need to correct social and economic causes of crime was strongest of all in response to a question regarding steps that citizens could take to aid the fight against crime. Eighty-five percent of the recommendations suggested that citizens should work for programs designed to reduce economic and educational deficiencies among the crime-prone population. Fourteen percent of the recommendations called for better crime reporting by citizens and for more participation in stopping illegal activities. One percent called for better home security measures. Overall, 86 percent of the panel members believed that citizens were lax in aiding the fight against crime.[6]

While there is thus a modicum of concern with the social implications of criminal justice reform, it is clear from the interviews that most respondents perceived these social reforms as occurring within the established system, rather than thinking in terms of revolutionary changes.

TABLE 4.8
Frequency of Mention of Reforms to Improve Crime Fighting
at Various Government Levels
(N = 110; in percentages)

Harsher, more certain penalties, including death	33.6
Correction of economic and educational deficiencies	20.9
Reform of the court system	19.0
Reform of police law enforcement	9.0
Decriminalization of drug use	5.4
Reform of prison system/rehabilitation efforts	4.5
Tighter gun control laws	4.5
Reduction in media emphasis on crime	2.7

Source: Original research.

SUMMARY AND CONCLUSIONS ABOUT THE ROLE
OF THE CRIMINAL JUSTICE SYSTEM

What general observations and conclusions can be drawn from the analysis of images and evaluations of the criminal justice system? In the first place, it is worthy of note that the mass media supply a large amount of data about specific crimes. These data convey the impression that criminals threaten a legitimate social system and its institutions. But there is little explicit analytical or evaluative information to help citizens put the data into perspective. There are few yardsticks for gauging the seriousness of the problem or the efficacy of corrective measures. Specific evaluations of the police, the courts, and the correctional system are particularly sparse. Nonetheless, the public manages to use the factual information supplied about individual crimes to draw its own conclusions.

The public's evaluations of the criminal justice system are largely negative. Eighty-one percent of the respondents saw crime as rising, particularly in suburban areas, and deemed the criminal justice system incapable of coping adequately with these increased responsibilities. Next to deficiencies in the criminal justice system, a major part of the blame for crime-fighting failures was put on general socioeconomic conditions, such as population shifts, heavy unemployment, or alcoholism and drug abuse, beyond the control of the criminal justice system, as presently constituted.

To protect themselves from the hazards of rampant crime, panel members talked primarily in terms of self-protection and psychological and physical restraints on the would-be offender. When the focus was on personal danger and protection, there was little mention of broader societal changes that might reduce street and white-collar crime and alter the current emphasis on punishment as a means to cope with violations of the established legal order. As protective measures, people mentioned keeping away from certain locations, traveling in pairs, increasing police vigilance, punishing convicted criminals severely enough to discourage crime, and keeping them in prison, away from potential victims.

The strong feeling that crime must be controlled through isolating criminals from society made the panelists approve of police crime-fighting activities. It also made them disapprove of the leniency of courts in sentencing offenders and the laxity of the correctional system in retaining and rehabilitating them. The criminal justice system was therefore seen as an ineffective servant of the public, but not as a repressor of the poor and disadvantaged. While court and correctional personnel received substantial criticism, the deficiencies of the system were also blamed heavily on circumstances presumably beyond its control, particularly on excessive workloads.

Overall trust in the criminal justice system appears to be eroding. When asked to compare levels of trust in various public institutions at the present time with levels remembered from five years ago, 43 percent of the subjects voiced less trust in the police and 62 percent trusted the courts less. Because 57 percent also trusted politicians less and 62 percent trusted Congress less, erosion of trust in the criminal justice system obviously is not unique. But that does not lessen the seriousness of this state of affairs in a democratic society.

Public appraisals of the crime and justice system are apparently based on the factual conditions reported in the media, and not on media evaluations, which tend to be overlooked, forgotten, or ignored. Therefore any media-related changes in public perceptions hinge on changes in factual reporting. Such changes can easily be made, without impairing accuracy, because newspeople routinely exercise substantial discretion in selecting particular stories and story angles for publication. Evaluations of the criminal justice system might improve, for example, if fewer crime stories were reported, reducing the impression that crime is rampant. The image of the system could also be improved by reporting more facts about apprehension and conviction of criminals, and by featuring incidents when penalties were swift, certain, and substantial.

Crime incidents and facts about the criminal justice system could also be put into a more realistic, less sensational perspective that would give people greater insight into the reasons for difficulties and efforts to improve deficiencies. But the major burden for improved evaluations of the criminal justice system falls on the system itself because the blemishes in its image are largely a reflection of sordid reality. Major changes in institutional practices are required to alter the facts underlying mass media reporting and the perceptions and experiences of the public. Unlike changes in reporting practices, these institutional changes will be difficult to achieve. Hence, for the foreseeable future, the public's esteem for the criminal justice system is likely to remain at a low ebb, regardless of the publicity that the system receives.

NOTES

1. President's Commission on Law Enforcement and Administration of Justice, *Task Force Report, Crime and Its Impact: An Assessment* (Washington, D.C.: U.S. Government Printing Office, 1967), p. 89. Also see Hazel Erskine, "Causes of Crime," *Public Opinion Quarterly* 38 (1974): 288-98.

2. For similar recommendations, see Erskine, "Causes of Crime." Nearly half of the comments of the panelists concerning recidivism (48.2 percent) cited the judicial leniency and adverse prison conditions as chief causes. Gratification from crime and social reintegration problems are mentioned by 31 percent of the responses. The remaining 20.6 percent of responses list personal problems.

3. For more complete recent data on police evaluations, see Ralph Baker, Fred Meyer, Jr., A. M. Corbett, and Dorothy Rudoni, "Citizen Evaluation of Police Services," American Political Science Association Paper, 1977. Also see the same authors' "Public Opinion on Police Services, Implications for Public Policy," Midwest Association for Public Opinion Research Paper, 1977. Comparative data from 13 large cities are analyzed in Wesley G. Skogan, "Citizen Satisfaction with Police Services," *Evaluating Alternative Law-Enforcement Policies,* ed. Ralph Baker and Fred Meyer, Jr. (Lexington, Mass.: Heath, 1979), pp. 29-42.

4. In a 13-city study, variations in favorability of evaluations were primarily linked to individual background factors (46 percent). See Skogan, "Citizen Satisfaction."

5. President's Commission on Law Enforcement and Administration of Justice, *Task Force Report, Crime and Its Impact: An Assessment.*

6. The significance of citizen participation in crime fighting is discussed in Stephen L. Percy, "Citizen Coproduction of Community Safety," in *Evaluating Alternative Law-Enforcement Policies*, pp. 125-34.

Five

INDIVIDUAL AND INTERGROUP VARIATIONS IN COGNITIVE MAPS

The discussion thus far has shown that panel members' images of the crime and justice process differed in many substantial ways from the images found in the media. There are several plausible explanations. Some panelists did not pay attention to the media because they were preoccupied with other things. Those attentive to the media generally may have ignored some particular issue because it lacked interest for them. These explanations are plainly incomplete, though, because there obviously were attentive, interested panelists whose images nonetheless differed from media images. In these cases, we must look to the effect of previous belief systems on information-processing. Alternately (or jointly), there may be competing and conflicting sources of information, such as direct personal experiences and deductive reasoning, interpersonal contacts, or political and religious beliefs.

Panelists' images do not only diverge from media images, though. There is also image diversity among the panelists themselves. This occurs because the combination of factors that affect attention to media content, as well as its perception, interpretation, and acceptance varies from time to time and from individual to individual. Such individual differences will be examined through a series of individual and group cognitive maps of the crime and justice process developed from the panel data. Individual cognitive maps depict an individual's cognitions on a large number of dimensions; group cognitive maps depict the cognitions of several individials on a more limited number of dimensions. While the tables that follow present group cognitive maps only, a portion of the discussion will deal with cognitive maps of selected individuals.

Conceptual configurations in subject matter presented in the diaries will be examined first. The patterns will indicate what combinations of topics leap to the fore in short-term recall of stories heard from media or personal contacts earlier in the day or night. Next, corresponding information from the story recall tests obtained during interviews will be considered. Compared to diary stories, these recall stories tap longer range memories of stories selected by the interviewer, rather than the respondent, from the pool of information available from the respondent's ordinary media sources during the previous month.

To the information from diary and recall cognitive maps, add information from a series of individual cognitive maps constructed from interview data. These will sample the large amounts of information from the interviews that are suitable for cognitive mapping of various types. Finally, briefly examine some differences between the cognitive maps of panel members located in the distinctive social settings represented by a suburban college town, inner-city living in a middle-sized community, and the comparative isolation of a small New England community.

Except for the intercity comparisons, which are based on responses from members of the three regular panels, the data are taken from 18 members of the Evanston core panel. To preserve anonymity each of them is identified by a letter, rather than name. Panelists are clustered to facilitate comparison between groups with demographic or behavioral characteristics known to affect media use. The main divisions are by sex and age groups and between groups distinguished by level of interest in current affairs and opportunity to gratify information needs through the mass media or interpersonal contacts. The small number of respondents for whom in-depth interview and diary data are available makes it impossible to expand group comparisons to other characteristics.

DIARY COGNITIVE MAPS

Table 5.1 displays the relationships among selected topics in individual diaries.* The table has been divided into male and female respondents to illustrate sex-linked differences in the types of stories that people remembered well and distinctly enough, after a lapse of time, to choose them for their diaries. Age-linked differences are made apparent by arraying the respondents in each group according to ascending age.

The table shows that consumption patterns correlate with sex patterns with seven of the nine women falling into the low-interest group compared to three of the nine men. Five of the women, compared to three of the men, also rank low in ready access to news. Reflecting cultural pressures which provide fewer

---

*These topics constituted roughly 35 percent of the topics mentioned in diaries. The range is from 28 to 51 percent.

TABLE 5.1
Individual Cognitive Maps of Diary Topics
(in percentages; N = 4,442 diary topics; distribution of *Tribune* topics added for comparison, N = 12,144)

	Women									Men									
	Age 40 and Under						Age over 40			Age 40 and Under						Age over 40			
	A[b]	B	C[b]	D	E[a]	F[a]	G	H[a]	I[a]	A	B[a]	C[c]	D	E[b]	F[c]	G[c]	H[c]	I[c]	Tribune
Individual crimes	17	44	26	18	29	11	30	27	14	22	13	15	13	13	13	11	3	14	16
Judiciary	17	5	15	11	12	11	11	8	10	5	10	10	14	9	10	18	14	9	15
Police security	4	2	4	7	4	4	6	6	2	2	0	7	0	5	7	8	1	3	13
Political terrorism	13	5	8	9	10	5	4	5	4	7	11	5	12	6	3	5	5	3	5
Corrupt politics	9	3	3	4	2	6	2	1	5	9	3	6	6	10	8	5	4	4	4
Drug crimes	1	1	1	4	1	2	1	2	0	3	1	2	1	1	1	1	0	1	2
Business crimes	3	2	1	2	1	6	0	1	1	4	3	3	4	3	0	3	0	2	2
Gun control	0	0	0	1	0	1	0	1	0	1	1	1	0	0	0	0	0	0	1
Total crime stories	64	62	58	56	59	46	55	55	36	53	42	49	50	47	50	51	27	36	58
Education	3	4	4	9	2	7	6	5	14	3	6	10	8	5	6	6	4	4	7
Congress	4	1	4	2	2	3	1	5	5	1	2	6	3	3	2	7	8	14	7
Disaster/accidents	11	16	9	13	15	7	23	9	5	18	16	9	15	12	11	8	6	5	66
City government	5	6	7	5	8	10	4	6	18	7	13	7	8	12	7	8	12	4	5
Middle East	5	1	6	4	4	6	2	2	1	3	2	4	2	2	9	5	20	13	5
State government	2	3	5	4	4	7	3	5	7	4	6	5	2	4	3	5	6	6	5
Political gossip	5	7	7	5	5	11	4	12	14	8	9	6	10	11	8	5	4	12	4
Energy policy	1	0	0	2	0	3	2	1	1	3	3	3	3	5	3	4	13	6	3
Individual N's for crime and noncrime stories	197	176	293	158	294	389	247	374	293	202	178	363	115	323	327	423	207	469	

Note: Superscript letters indicate news consumption behavior characteristics as judged by interest in news and ready access to news sources. Absence of letter indicates respondents with low interest and low news availability. The meaning of the classification is defined more fully in Chapter 1. Further respondent descriptions can be found in Table 1.3.

[a]Respondents with low interest and high-news availability.
[b]Respondents with high interest and low-news availability.
[c]Respondents with high interest and high-news availability.

Source: Original research.

opportunities for women, compared to men, to benefit from interest in current affairs, none of the women ranked high on both interest and media availability scales. By contrast, five of the men attained such rankings.

The data further suggest that news consumption patterns have an impact on the type of information that is recalled. As Table 5.2 shows, the percentage of diary stories devoted to the crime and justice system in general, as well as to individual crime, is lowest for groups with ready access to news. This leads to the conclusion that the high priority that panelists give to crime and justice news in their diaries becomes diluted for people exposed to more ample amounts of news. The information diet of people with news access problems thus is heavily concentrated on news about crime and assorted disasters.

The chief impression conveyed by the table is that diary patterns are quite similar in rank orders of emphasis and actual magnitude. Differences are age and sex linked and largely represent lifestyle diversities. Only three categories — individual crime, the judiciary, and disasters — show repeated deviations from the mean at a rate greater than five percentage points, plus or minus. For the topics selected here, younger people 40 years old or less, paid more attention to crime and justice stories than older people of the same sex over 40. Looking at individual respondents who, within sex groups, are arrayed according to ascending age, the pattern of declining interest as age increases is clearly apparent. Women as a group had a higher proportion of crime and justice stories in their diaries than did men. The respective average figures are 60 and 50 percent for women under and over 40 and 49 and 38 percent for men under and over 40: Ms. B. and G, the two black respondents were at the top of the scale. The corresponding figure for *Tribune* coverage of crime and justice stories compared to the matching group of noncrime stories is 58 percent.

TABLE 5.2
Percentage of All Crime and Justice and Individual Crime Topics in the Diaries of Diverse Interest/Availability Groups
(N = 4,442 diary topics)

News Availability	Interest in News			
	Low		High	
Low	All crime/justice	56.5	All crime/justice	56.3
	Individual crime	25.4	Individual crime	18.6
High	All crime/justice	47.6	All crime/justice	42.6
	Individual crime	18.8	Individual crime	11.2

Source: Original research.

For the respondents, the figures reflect perceived vulnerability to crime. Members of the under-40 group in the panel reported more often that they felt compelled by work and social pressures to expose themselves to crime by traveling in locations perceived as dangerous. Despite the higher victimization rate of men reported by official statistics, male panelists considered themselves generally less attractive as crime targets than female panelists and more capable of warding off potential attackers. Women expressed greater need for information about crime to detect possibly dangerous locations that they might avoid and warn loved ones, especially children and adolescents, to shun.

Looking at the major points of attention (10 percent or more of diary entries) in individual diaries, it appears that individual crime, the matter of greatest personal concern, ranked at or near the top for all except Mr. H., an elderly lawyer, who does not watch television and carefully selects his news to meet his personal and professional interests. His top areas of diary attention, selected regardless of story frequency patterns in the print media, were the Middle East, the judicial system, energy, and matters concerning Chicago politics. Besides stories about individual crimes, the average diary focused prominently on stories about the judiciary and about various natural and man-made disasters and, to a lesser extent, on stories about the private lives of politicians.

Among the women, only Ms. F. and Ms. I. showed substantial concern with major political trends outside the crime area. Both of them are widows, past age 40, who indicated during interviews that they had left surveillance of political happenings largely to their husbands during their lifetimes. Following the deaths of their husbands, they had felt the need to become their own information gatherers. Three of the four widows in the panels reported similar changes in information-gathering patterns, which set them apart from the search patterns pursued by other women, including currently married women in professional careers.

Ms. F. presents another interesting case study. She was robbed and held at gunpoint in her home at the midpoint of the study. This traumatic experience decreased the proportion of crime stories included in her diaries. However, it did not alter her recall of newspaper crime stories when questioned during interviews. While Ms. F. avoided focusing on crime in her diary, respondents B. and G., who were black women living in high-crime neighborhoods, had the highest emphasis on individual crime stories among the women. Ms. E. and Ms. H., who worked but did not live in high-crime areas, followed closely behind, as did Ms. C., who had been robbed and battered some years earlier. The difference between Ms. F., who slighted crime stories, and the others who stressed them, appeared to be that she felt that there was no protection against the type of assault she had suffered in a high-status neighborhood. The others felt that, despite their vulnerability, protective measures were possible based on knowledge about the current crime situation.[1] The fact that Ms. F's victimization was very recent may also have given her a temporarily exaggerated incentive to avoid stirring up painful memories.

While street crime had been the area of highest diary coverage for all but one of the women, it missed first place for four of the nine men. Interestingly, these were either single men, with no family obligations or, in one case, a married man whose family was exceptionally well shielded from crime danger. The men, as a group, showed the typical male pattern of higher interest in major political concerns outside the crime area. Five out of the nine paid substantial attention to either local politics, the Middle East, education, or Congress. In every case, the subjects stressed in the men's diaries were matters of personal or social, rather than primarily occupational, interest. This emphasis reflects their feeling that diaries ought to mirror matters of personal concern.

STORY RECALL COGNITIVE MAPS

Table 5.3 presents data on story recall. It repeats the pattern of age- and sex-linked differences, tied to lifestyle. During the interviews, each respondent had been asked to relate details about specifically identified stories that matched the categories listed in the table. An average of ten stories from each category was used throughout the study. In addition, respondents were occasionally asked during interviews to recall spontaneously stories that they remembered from the weeks preceding the interviews.

Table 5.3 is based on average recall of these ten stories in each of eight crime and eight noncrime story categories. The table was computed by awarding one point when no facts of the story were recalled, two points when one statement of facts was remembered, three points for two statements, and four points for three or more factual statements. The table also lists the percentage of stories for which a particular respondent had no recall at all and the percentage of stories for which the respondent reported no reaction to a remembered story. Lack of reaction generally implies that the respondent did not become involved with the story. When reactions occur, this indicates that the respondent went beyond awareness of the story to impute some personal meanings to it.

The mean recall for the crime and noncrime story groups listed in Table 5.3 was almost identical for each of the respondents. Women, who generally feel little social pressure to retain information, showed higher forgetting averages for crime and noncrime stories than did men. Older people remembered more than younger people of the same sex.* Women under and over 40 had totally forgotten an average of 36.5 and 27.4 percent of all stories requested during recall tests. The corresponding figures for men under and over 40 were 26.3 and 17.3 percent. Similarly, women 40 years and under showed the highest "no reaction" rates (47.5 percent of all stories), followed by women over 40 (41.2 percent)

---

*For crime story recall, women 40 and under averaged 2.0. Women over 40 averaged 2.2. Men averaged 2.6 in the 40-and-under group and 2.9 for the over-40 group.

TABLE 5.3
Individual Cognitive Maps of Story Recall Topics
(in point averages;[a] N = 1,888 recall story topics)

	Women									Men								
	Age 40 and under				Age over 40					Age 40 and under				Age over 40				
	A[b]	B	C[b]	D	E[a]	F[a]	G	H[a]	I[a]	A	B[a]	C[c]	D	E[b]	F[c]	G[c]	H[c]	I[c]
Individual crimes	1.8	2.3	2.7	2.3	2.4	2.7	2.1	2.5	2.4	2.5	2.3	3.4	2.3	2.3	3.3	2.9	2.6	2.6
Judiciary	2.4	1.6	2.7	1.9	2.2	2.5	1.6	2.6	2.0	2.1	1.8	3.4	2.4	3.1	2.7	3.4	3.4	2.1
Police/security	1.5	1.8	2.4	1.6	1.5	2.1	1.4	2.4	1.8	2.0	1.3	3.5	1.6	3.3	3.3	3.6	3.3	2.9
Political terrorism	2.2	1.5	2.7	2.2	2.3	3.0	1.9	2.6	1.8	2.1	1.7	3.7	2.6	2.7	2.9	2.8	3.2	2.1
Corrupt politics	2.4	1.3	2.0	2.1	2.0	2.6	1.5	2.4	2.1	1.8	1.8	3.5	2.1	2.8	3.0	3.6	3.0	2.3
Drug crimes	1.0	1.0	2.5	2.3	2.0	3.0	2.0	1.0	4.0	2.5	2.0	3.5	2.0	2.0	3.0	3.0	0.0	4.0
Business crimes	2.2	1.3	2.0	2.0	2.0	3.0	2.0	2.9	2.3	1.3	2.0	3.4	1.7	2.8	2.3	3.5	1.8	1.8
Gun control	2.0	0.0	3.0	0.0	2.0	0.0	1.0	0.0	0.0	3.0	0.0	4.0	0.0	0.0	0.0	4.0	0.0	2.0
Mean crime stories	1.9	1.5	2.5	2.1	2.1	2.7	1.7	2.2	2.3	2.2	1.8	3.6	2.1	2.7	2.9	3.4	2.9	2.5
Education	1.5	1.8	2.8	1.9	1.6	2.8	1.6	2.1	2.3	1.5	1.9	3.5	1.9	2.8	2.9	3.3	2.7	1.9
Congress	1.9	1.3	2.5	2.2	1.1	2.7	1.4	1.9	2.3	1.6	1.2	3.6	1.9	2.6	3.1	3.4	3.1	2.3
Disaster/accidents	2.5	1.9	2.2	2.1	2.9	2.9	2.1	2.5	2.8	2.6	2.3	3.5	1.9	2.5	3.3	3.0	2.9	3.1
City government	2.6	1.8	2.7	2.3	2.0	2.7	1.4	2.3	2.4	1.5	2.0	3.3	2.2	2.5	3.3	3.9	3.0	2.6
Middle East	1.8	1.3	2.2	1.9	1.9	2.5	1.9	1.8	1.7	1.6	1.4	3.3	2.0	2.0	3.2	3.6	3.5	2.4
State government	1.3	1.3	1.3	1.7	1.4	3.2	1.6	2.7	1.8	1.5	1.3	3.4	1.7	2.1	1.5	2.8	1.8	2.0
Political gossip	2.4	2.3	2.9	2.9	3.2	3.1	1.6	2.7	3.4	2.9	2.5	3.7	2.7	3.6	3.4	3.4	3.5	3.0
Energy policy	2.2	1.2	2.8	2.0	1.5	2.8	2.0	2.0	2.4	2.2	2.7	4.0	2.4	3.2	3.6	4.0	3.6	3.0
Mean Noncrime stories	2.0	1.6	2.4	2.1	2.0	2.8	1.7	2.3	2.4	1.9	1.9	3.5	2.1	2.7	3.0	3.4	3.0	2.5

continued

TABLE 5.3, continued

<table>
<thead>
<tr><th rowspan="3"></th><th colspan="9">Women</th><th colspan="9">Men</th></tr>
<tr><th colspan="5">Age 40 and under</th><th colspan="4">Age over 40</th><th colspan="5">Age 40 and under</th><th colspan="4">Age over 40</th></tr>
<tr><th>A[b]</th><th>B</th><th>C[b]</th><th>D</th><th>E[a]</th><th>F[a]</th><th>G</th><th>H[a]</th><th>I[a]</th><th>A</th><th>B[a]</th><th>C[c]</th><th>D</th><th>E[b]</th><th>F[c]</th><th>G[c]</th><th>H[c]</th><th>I[c]</th></tr>
</thead>
<tbody>
<tr><td>Individual N's</td><td>110</td><td>106</td><td>83</td><td>111</td><td>116</td><td>111</td><td>113</td><td>121</td><td>102</td><td>102</td><td>109</td><td>108</td><td>105</td><td>112</td><td>109</td><td>107</td><td>73</td><td>90</td></tr>
<tr><td>Fully forgotten stories[e]</td><td>40</td><td>51</td><td>24</td><td>31</td><td>35</td><td>17</td><td>43</td><td>20</td><td>22</td><td>42</td><td>39</td><td>5</td><td>40</td><td>21</td><td>11</td><td>10</td><td>21</td><td>21</td></tr>
<tr><td>No-impact stories[e]</td><td>53</td><td>58</td><td>35</td><td>44</td><td>53</td><td>27</td><td>58</td><td>36</td><td>32</td><td>58</td><td>52</td><td>16</td><td>52</td><td>30</td><td>27</td><td>22</td><td>15</td><td>28</td></tr>
</tbody>
</table>

Note: For explanation of superscript letters a-c, see the legend for Table 5.1.

[d]No recall = one point; one fact recall = two points; two facts recall = 3 points; three or more facts recall = four points.

[e]Percent of all recall stories that the respondent does not remember at all and percent of all recall stories for which the respondent reports no reaction at all.

Source: Original research.

and men under 40 (39.1 percent). Men over 40 gave "no reaction" responses to only 21.6 percent of all stories. These figures point to the fact, corroborated by other studies, that the cognitive maps of males and of older people are richer in detail about current happenings than those of females and younger people. People who are interested in news and have ready access to it retain more information than those with lesser interest and more precarious access.

Patterns for remembering different story topics varied considerably among individuals, but for two thirds of the respondents, retention scores were highest for political gossip. On the whole, noncrime subjects were more frequently well remembered by both women and men, young and old, than were crime and justice topics. Nonetheless, the highest number of low retention scores was recorded for certain noncrime topics, particularly stories about state government activities and stories about the Middle East. Because respondents who ranked low in interest in current events scored lowest in retention of news items, this suggests that interest in state government and Middle East stories was particularly low.

The interviews indicate that low recall of a particular topic was generally associated either with its intrinsic unattractiveness of a topic or with saturation boredom. The latter means that media audiences who are not vitally interested in a particular topic tire rather quickly of repeat exposures, even when new details are disclosed. For stories of high interest, the saturation point comes much later. The fatigue factor may even insulate people from different stories of similar type. For instance, saturation boredom with stories about the Hearst case cast a pall over interest in the Chowchilla kidnapping case. A number of people ignored the Chowchilla story in whole or in part, saying they were fed up with sensational crime stories.

INTERVIEW COGNITIVE MAPS

Table 5.4 presents an array of individual cognitive maps of various factors that influence learning from the mass media about crime and justice. The information depicted in Table 5.4 for Ms. A., the youngest woman, and Mr. I., the oldest man, in the group will be discussed as examples of the insights provided by a combination of cognitive mapping with unmapped data from the and in-depth interviews.

Ms. A. is a homemaker in her late twenties, married to a professional man. She has two preschool children whose care she finds very taxing. If she has free time when the children are sleeping, she is generally too tired to pay much attention to either the newspaper or television. However, she does discuss current affairs with her husband and with friends on social occasions. She is a college graduate, interested primarily in education, fine arts, and sports. She received a "middle third" rating on the news-interest/access score because she

TABLE 5.4

Individual Cognitive Maps of General and Specific Learning Factors
(N = 2,130 responses to multiple questions asked about each factor)

| | Women | | | | | | | | | | | | | | | | | | Men | | | | | | | | | | | | | | | | | |
| | Age 40 and Under | | | | | | | | | Age Over 40 | | | | | | | | | Age 40 and Under | | | | | | | | | Age Over 40 | | | | | | | | |
	A	B	C	D	E	F	G	H	I	A	B	C	D	E	F	G	H	I	A	B	C	D	E	F	G	H	I	A	B	C	D	E	F	G	H	I
Combination of news interest/access[a]	M	L	M	L	M	M	L	M	M	L	M	M	M	M	M	L	M	M	L	M	L	L	M	M	H	L	M	M	M	H	L	M	H	H	H	H
Conservatism-liberalism[b]	M	H	M	M	H	L	L	L	M	M	M	M	H	M	H	M	L	M	M	M	H	M	M	M	M	H	M	M	L	M	M	M	M	M	L	M
Civil rights scale[c]	H	L	M	M	M	H	M	M	M	H	L	M	M	M	H	M	M	M	H	L	M	M	M	H	M	M	H	H	M	H	L	H	M	M	L	M
Media dependence for crime information	L	L	L	L	L	M	L	L	M	L	L	L	L	L	M	L	M	M	L	M	L	L	L	L	L	L	H	M	L	L	L	L	L	L	M	H
Satisfaction with crime coverage	L	L	H	H	M	M	L	L	H	M	M	M	M	M	M	M	M	H	M	H	H	H	L	M	L	H	H	M	H	L	L	L	L	H	H	M
Attention to media crime coverage	H	M	H	M	M	H	L	M	M	M	L	L	L	M	H	L	M	M	M	L	H	H	H	M	L	L	M	M	L	L	H	H	M	L	M	M
Know Hearst/Chowchilla cases	H	M	M	L	M	H	L	M	L	M	L	L	L	M	H	L	L	M	L	L	H	M	H	M	L	M	M	M	M	L	M	M	M	L	M	M
Know crime control steps	H	M	M	L	M	H	L	M	M	M	M	M	L	M	H	L	M	M	H	H	L	H	H	M	L	M	M	M	M	L	M	M	M	M	M	M
Estimate crime increases	M	H	M	L	M	H	M	L	L	L	H	M	L	M	H	M	L	L	M	L	L	M	M	M	M	L	M	M	M	M	M	M	M	L	M	M
Trust in government and people[d]	L	M	H	H	L	L	L	L	M	L	M	M	H	L	M	L	L	L	L	L	M	L	M	L	L	H	L	M	H	M	L	L	L	L	L	H
Seriousness of extortion	L	M	H	H	M	H	L	H	H	L	M	H	H	M	H	H	H	L	L	L	M	L	L	L	L	M	M	H	H	H	M	M	M	M	M	H
Forgery/counterfeit	L	H	H	H	H	H	H	M	M	M	H	H	H	H	H	H	M	H	M	H	H	H	M	M	M	L	H	M	L	H	H	M	L	L	L	H
Consumer fraud	L	H	M	H	H	H	M	H	H	H	H	M	H	H	H	H	M	H	H	H	H	H	H	H	H	H	H	H	M	H	H	H	M	H	L	H
Embezzlement	M	H	M	H	L	H	H	M	M	H	M	M	H	H	H	H	H	H	L	L	L	H	H	H	M	M	H	H	H	H	H	H	M	H	L	M
Bribery/kickbacks	L	H	M	H	H	H	H	H	H	M	M	M	H	H	H	H	M	H	H	M	H	H	H	M	M	H	H	L	H	L	H	H	L	M	L	H
Corruption	L	H	H	H	H	H	H	H	H	L	M	M	M	H	H	H	H	L	M	H	H	H	H	M	M	L	H	H	M	L	H	H	M	H	M	H
Fencing stolen goods	H	H	H	H	H	H	H	H	M	H	H	H	H	H	H	H	M	M	H	H	H	H	M	M	H	M	M	H	H	H	H	M	H	H	M	H
Weapons violations	H	H	H	H	H	H	H	M	L	H	H	H	H	H	H	M	L	L	H	H	H	M	H	M	H	H	H	H	H	H	H	H	H	H	M	H

96

Custody escape	M	L	M	M	L	M	H	H	M	L	L	H	H	L	M	M
Parole violations	H	H	M	L	H	M	H	M	H	M	L	H	M	L	M	M
Illegal wiretaps	L	M	M	L	M	L	M	M	L	L	M	L	L	M	M	M
Prostitution	M	H	H	M	H	M	H	M	H	H	M	H	M	M	H	H
Other sex offenses	M	L	L	M	L	M	H	H	M	L	M	L	L	L	M	M
Drug offenses	H	H	H	L	H	H	H	H	H	H	H	H	H	M	H	H
Gambling	L	M	L	H	H	L	M	M	L	L	M	L	M	H	M	M
Tax cheating	M	H	M	H	H	M	M	M	M	H	L	M	M	M	M	M
Welfare cheating	M	H	H	H	H	M	H	M	H	H	M	H	M	M	M	M
Contributing to minor's delinquency	L	M	M	H	M	L	M	M	L	L	M	L	L	L	L	M
Child abuse	H	H	H	H	H	M	M	H	M	M	M	M	M	M	H	H
Drunken driving	H	H	H	H	H	H	M	M	H	H	H	M	M	M	M	H
Liquor law offenses	H	L	L	L	L	M	M	L	L	L	H	L	M	L	L	L
Disorderly conduct	M	L	L	L	M	H	M	M	M	H	M	M	M	M	M	H
False fire alarms	M	H	M	H	M	M	M	L	M	L	M	L	L	M	L	M
Perjury	M	M	H	M	M	M	M	M	H	M	M	M	M	H	M	M
Contempt of court	H	L	M	L	H	L	H	M	L	L	M	L	L	H	L	M

Note: L = low third; M = middle third; H = high third of possible scores for each factor. In the computation negative replies have been subtracted from positive replies. Qualified answers (for example, little, some, a lot) received stepwise point increases, starting at zero for "none."

[a]For computation detail, see Chapter 1.

[b]Based on self-estimated seven-point scale. Extreme conservatism = 1; extreme liberalism = 7.1

[c]Same as b, but based on protection of rights of accused.

[d]People classified economically, ethnically, and demographically.

Source: Original research.

97

is interested, yet lacks the time to avail herself of most of the information within her reach.

Ms. A. depends primarily on the media for crime information because she lives in a low-crime neighborhood where children and home activities, rather than crime, are the staple of discussion among young mothers. As crime news has low utility for her, she pays little attention to it, particularly as she is also dissatisfied with the manner in which the media cover crime. She considers it inaccurate, superficial, and sensational. However, general inattention to news did not keep her from being well informed about crime stories like the Hearst and Chowchilla cases. She believes that she knows much about these stories because the details were covered repeatedly, particularly on television. Because she misses the bulk of ordinary crime and justice coverage due to limited media use, stories that she does hear do not compete with much other information. Therefore they leave an exceptionally vivid impression on her mind.

Although Ms. A. is by nature optimistic and trustful, a constant barrage of news in the past two years about public and private breach of faith and crime has left its mark. This explains her turn toward a middle-of-the-road position, away from the liberalism of her college days (though this does not extend to civil rights positions) and her fairly low trust in government and in various population groups.

Her generally rosy view of life does show in her exceptionally low appraisal of the seriousness of various crimes. She is most concerned about crimes that involve the possibility of serious physical harm, such as child abuse, drunken driving and other liquor law offenses, and drug offenses and weapons violations. She also views parole violations as leading to physical harm because of frequent press reports that violent crimes have been committed by persons free on parole. Her high seriousness rating for fencing of stolen goods and contempt of court relates to her concern about proper functioning of the social system. She believes that this requires obedience to the courts that are enforcing the law and avoidance of activities that make it easier for criminals to profit from their crimes.

Mr. I. is retired from a blue-collar job, but remains active in gardening and home maintenance activities. He retains a strong interest in current affairs because of participation in precinct politics in his younger years, and because of his penchant for political discussions with his large family and with friends. He is an avid newspaper reader and conveys much of what he reads and sees on television to his wife, who does little reading and watching on her own. Mr. I. has only a grade school education, but his children are college graduates.

Mr. I. scores in the top group for news interest and access. But because of his advanced age (he is in his middle seventies), he has some difficulty occasionally in recalling specific facts quickly. This explains his midlevel scores for knowledge of crime control steps and knowledge about the Hearst and Chowchilla cases. In addition, crime stories are not a matter of primary concern for him, even though he lives in a high-crime neighborhood. Because of lack of interest, he does not pay as much attention to crime stories as he does to other types of media fare. A further damper on his learning about crime and justice news is the fact that most of his news comes from the media and is presented in a manner that he finds only moderately satisfactory. It does not come from interpersonal sources, which he trusts more than the media, and does not form an important part of his interpersonal discussions, which generally deepen his knowledge about current affairs.

Mr. I.'s estimate of increasing crime is based on his personal observations of deteriorating conditions in his own neighborhood. Because of this increase, which threatens him and his family personally, he considers most crimes as intrinsically very serious. However, he moderates this rating for crimes that he judges as occurring fairly rarely and for offenses that seem to him to carry an inappropriately heavy social stigma. He places gambling, tax and welfare cheating, and liquor law offenses other than drunken driving in the latter group.

While he is concerned about crime and many other problems, Mr. I. retains an essentially optimistic and liberal outlook toward life. This explains his high ratings on scales measuring support for civil rights and trust in government.

The experiences and lifestyles of the other panelists, like those of Ms. A. and Mr. I., are also useful in making sense out of cognitive patterns and shedding light on otherwise unexplainable idiosyncrasies, such as the frequent negative correlation between fear of victimization and taking protective measures. A few highlights for each person provide illustrations of salient lifestyle characteristics and give the reader a chance to examine the individual cognitive patterns in Table 5.4 with greater insight.

Throughout, three basic factors appear to be the strongest influences on individual cognitive maps. They are past background, current lifestyle, and attitudes toward the news. The most salient background factors generally are personality traits related to trust and distrust and optimism and pessimism, lifestyle patterns and orientations and concerns acquired during the formative years, educational status, and major historical experiences affecting the individual's life. Current lifestyle factors are important as they relate to time available for media use and need for information for social and occupational purposes. Current lifestyle also affects perceived vulnerability to crime for one's self and one's family, and the sharpening of interest in crime and justice matters brought about by vulnerability. Finally, the credibility of news in general affects learning from the mass media. Repetition helps because it retards forgetting and prevents much accidental skipping. However, exposure to large quantities of information often turns out to be more confusing than enlightening when people, particularly older folk, find the large bulk unmanageable.

Ms. B. is a young, unmarried black woman who works as an insurance clerk. She lives with her parents, who also work, in a high-crime neighborhood. The family obviously takes great pride in its material acquisitions and is very careful about home security. While generally liberal in outlook, Ms. B. favors strict treatment for lawbreakers who, she thinks are a threat to the possessions she and her family have acquired through hard work. Like other respondents who have been crime victims or live or work in high-crime areas, her judgments about the seriousness of various crimes fall into the upper ranges. Her low dependence on the media for crime and justice system information reflects general inattention to media, coupled with an abundance of interpersonal information about crime.

Ms. C. is a young matron who splits her time between care of an infant and a part-time professional job. Her husband, too, is a professional and both are much concerned about government issues. Despite high interest in the political world, Ms. C.'s busy schedule prevents her from paying much attention to mass media news in general. She does make time for news about the crime and justice system, as this is an area of professional concern for the family. As is true of most other panel members who are lawyers or work with them, her appraisal about the seriousness of various crimes falls into the lower ranges of the scale, with many "moderately serious" ratings. Although she and her husband have been previously mugged, albeit in a different part of town, they report no unusual protective measures. They consider victimization a matter of chance, unpredictable and unavoidable.

Ms. D., a nurse, has two middle-grade schoolchildren and a husband in a white-collar job. During the year of interviews, she was working a number of night shifts as well as attending classes to upgrade her nursing skills. Her home, job, and school tasks left little time to pay attention to the news and sapped whatever interest in the news she had in more leisurely phases of her life. However, she has stored up a good fund of knowledge and opinions from earlier years that she applies readily to whatever current situations come to her attention. Ms. D. was raised on a midwestern farm in a family with high respect for law, which is reflected in her strong feelings about the seriousness of law infractions.

Ms. E. runs her own business and combines very liberal family orientations with the down-to-earth caution that springs from brushes with crime in the business world. Crime is a personal threat to her in her store so that she opposes lenient treatment for criminals. While she does not take much time to read or watch the news in general, she does pay attention to topics of special interest to her, such as Middle East news, business news, and news about crime. Her business dealings with government agencies and with low-income, slow-paying customers have made her wary of trusting public officials and the general public. Her ratings of the seriousness of crime fall into the lower range, overall. In typical liberal fashion, she normally gives low seriousness ratings to offenses. But this changes to high ratings when experience supersedes ideology for those offenses that touch her life directly.

Ms. F., a middle-aged, well-to-do widow who lives in a low-crime residential neighborhood, was the only panelist victimized by a serious crime — armed robbery — during the course of the study. This may explain why she was one of only two women panelists who recalled a large number of details about specific

crime stories, like the Hearst and Chowchilla cases. She also reported more precautions against victimization than other panelists. She was tied with Ms. G. for
highest place in the seriousness ratings of various white-collar crimes. While her
recent victimization may explain the grave view she takes of crime, there is
another plausible explanation. Her husband was a local judge and she has maintained close contacts with other judges involved in local law enforcement.

Ms. G. is, in many respects, the most vulnerable panelist. She is a poorly
educated black woman of upper middle age, of somewhat precarious health,
living on the edge of a high-crime area. The household consists of an extended
family, including several young children. Ms. G. works as a maid in the daytime,
using public transportation to get to and from work. She is frequently out at
night, attending church functions. She is very concerned about the safety of her
grandchildren, although much less concerned about her own safety from crime.
As mentioned, she ties with Ms. F. in the seriousness ratings of various white-
collar crimes, and, like Ms. F., considers crime to be on the increase. But her low
interest and attention for mass media information keep her from scoring well on
knowing details about crimes committed outside her neighborhood, such as the
Hearst and Chowchilla cases. Her diary entries, however, abound with stories
about local crime learned through word-of-mouth channels.

Ms. H. is an elderly bookkeeper who lives alone in a small high-rise apartment. The building has good security. She claims to be relatively unconcerned
about possible victimization, but her cautious behavior in allowing people access
to her apartment and her use of various precautionary measures tell a different
story. In response to direct questions about the importance and seriousness of
crime, she expresses only moderate concern. However, in open-ended questions
about major problems in the nation, the local community, and in her own
personal life, crime themes are dominant. It is difficult to judge from the recorded
conversations what the precise mixture is in her case between personal fear, on
the one hand, and thrill-seeking that comes from vicarious participation in the
world of crime and corruption. Ms. H. seems to think that it is chic to be cynical
about life and not shocked by anything. An attempt to convey this impression,
rather than genuine beliefs, may explain her below-average appraisal of the
seriousness of white-collar crime. Of all the respondents in the core panel, Ms. H.
was the only one who frequently conveyed the impression of insincerity. Outright contradictions between her open-ended conversations and more directed
questions support this impression.

Ms. I., at age 78, was the oldest member of the core panel. Despite her
advanced years, she lives alone, spending much of her time in a well-kept high-rise
apartment. She maintains contact with life in the local community through
regular social service volunteer work and through her children and grandchildren.
While she does venture out by herself during the daytime to go to familiar
places, she usually calls on her family to take her to unfamiliar locations. This
family support gives her a sense of personal security and trust. Because she lives

alone, television and radio are steady, much-appreciated companions. As is true of other older respondents, she feels personally close to a number of media figures, including commentators as well as fictional characters and their actors.

Turning to the men, Mr. A., a hospital clerk, who lives in a high-crime neighborhood, pays relatively little attention to the mass media. However, because he talks with many people throughout the day, he picks up much current information through casual conversations. Like other low media users, he pays comparatively high attention to crime stories in his diary entries – the highest among the men. This is coupled with comparatively low recall of crime stories selected from the media by the interviewer. Among the men, he ranks in second place in the seriousness scales for white-collar crime. He is tied with Mr. C., who lives in a somewhat safer neighborhood but works in the inner city, and topped by Mr. D., who lives close to A., but also commutes to the inner city. These three young men demonstrate what appears to be a pattern: Those who perceive themselves as vulnerable to crime, take a more serious view of it. However, Mr. A., in his typical casual approach to life, reports no precautionary measures against the victimization that seems so probable to him.

Mr. B. is single and lives with his mother and siblings in a neighborhood bordering on a high-crime area. His job as a grocery clerk entails some night work. His free time, especially in the summer, is taken up by sports. In the winter, he attends night school classes to advance his skills in the professional area for which his college training prepared him, but in which he has been unable to obtain work. His attention to the media and knowledge of media information are quite variable, depending on available time after he has taken care of his other interests. Given his reserved personality, which occasionally borders on hostility, neither his job nor his home and social life provides much information through conversation. Hence the gaps remain unfilled whenever his mass media exposure is low.

Mr. C. is a young research engineer who shares an apartment with several professional peers in a middle-income area. Among young male panelists, he was by far the most avid consumer of mass media information, as well as an avid participant in conversations at work and in his home setting. He was dissatisfied with media crime coverage because he realized, thanks to an excellent memory for details, that many news stories were imprecisely reported. His distrust in government and people stemmed from numerous incidents in which his work had been hampered by bureaucratic bungling or institutional politics. While his sense of the seriousness of white-collar crime sprang in part from exposure to crime situations, it also was fueled by a strong sense of morality and intolerance for lawbreakers.

Mr. D.'s low interest in using the media is due to time pressures. Although he is single and has few family obligations, his job, social life, and numerous hobbies crowd his schedule. But, like other societally involved low-media-use males with moderately outgoing personalities, he picks up a good deal of information from his work and social contacts. This makes him and other males far better informed than most low-media-use women, who ordinarily lack the information-rich contacts available to employed males. Among the males, Mr. D., whose job exposes him to many instances of white-collar crime, ranks highest in considering such crimes very serious. His family background gives him a high degree of social consciousness and predisposes him to intolerance toward violations of law.

Mr. E. works in the inner city as a professional for a federal agency. He lives with his family, consisting of his wife and two young children, adjacent to a high-crime neighborhood. By keeping the exterior of his home in somewhat decrepit condition, by dressing inexpensively like a blue-collar worker, and by installing a number of security devices in his home, he feels he has markedly reduced his chances of victimization. His job involves a fair amount of travel and he also works part time in the evening. His tight schedule keeps his media exposure moderate. But, as with many of the men in this study, conversations at work fill in for information gaps whenever he neglects his own reading and listening.

Mr. F. is an administrator in an organization dealing with legal questions. He commutes on public transportation from his home in an upper-class residential neighborhood to his job in the city. He uses the long commuting time to read several newspapers. However, given the distractions during such a trip and the preoccupation of a full career, a busy home life, and heavy community involvement, he retains comparatively few details from his ample reading. He is the only panelist who does not rate a single white-collar crime as very serious. He also reports no anticrime measures for himself or his family. The fact that neither he nor his wife and children seem to be particularly vulnerable to crime at this point in their lives may account for his comparative unconcern.

Mr. G., a middle-aged bachelor, lives alone in a high-rise apartment building in a high-crime neighborhood. His work requires a lot of travel away from the city, but rarely keeps him out in the late evening hours. He is an almost compulsive consumer of mass media news, reading several papers besides a host of professional journals. When out-of-town trips keep him from reading all the papers to which he subscribes, he saves them and reads them later, often several months after publication. His sense of personal vulnerability to crime is low and he pays relatively little attention to crime news and takes no special precautions against victimization. However, thanks to the nature of his work and life and career experiences, he is very interested in public policy issues in general and the law and order issue in particular. This alerts him to stories about the courts and the correctional system. His evaluation of the seriousness of white-collar crime is moderate, compared to other panelists. It is based largely on societal considerations, rather than personal concerns.

At 74, Mr. H., a respected lawyer, continues to practice at an inner-city location. He commutes to his job by public transportation from his home in an upper-class residential neighborhood. He and his wife also travel a great deal to spend time with their children and to enjoy various leisure pursuits. Mr. H. reads widely, but very selectively. He rarely watches television. His diary, recall, and interview patterns reflect his sharply focused interests. He is exceptionally well informed about those matters to which he chooses to pay attention, but draws blanks or near-blanks for many others. His diary entries gave by far the lowest emphasis to individual crime stories. However, his recall of mass media crime stories was average, evidently on the basis of information from personal contacts. Because his law practice does not generally involve white-collar crime cases, his exposure to this type of law violation is comparatively low, as is his concern about its seriousness. He reported only slight worry about becoming a street crime victim and took no special precautions against victimization.

These sketches of various panelists are full of conjectures about the linkages among various facets of their cognitive maps. While there is a good deal of backup information in the data for these conjectures, proof positive of the linkages is, of course, impossible. More important than such proof is the fact that the study of individual cognitive maps indicates that the numerous individual variations that one encounters in perceptions and attitudes hinge to a large degree on current lifestyles, personality, past experiences, and the quantity and perceived quality of available media information. Without knowledge of the kinds of lifestyle, personality, and experience factors gathered for this study, perception and opinion profiles defy accurate interpretation.

COGNITIVE MAP COMPARISONS AMONG THE THREE CITIES

Do the images of crime made available to residents of a huge metropolitan area, a middle-sized town, and a small rural community vary substantially? How do the residents of such communities respond to media offerings, in light of differences in the local incidence of crime and the handling of local crime problems? The evidence of this study is limited to three locations, but appears to be common enough to permit some tentative generalizations.

Panelists at all three sites were exposed to the same national television fare. This involved roughly 60 crime and justice news stories per month and constituted 7.4 percent of all television news stories. Of these, roughly 25 stories per month involved violent crime. The substance of newspaper crime and justice stories was also quite similar in the three locations.[2] However, the quantity of newspaper crime stories and the balance between stories involving violent and nonviolent crimes varied considerably among the three sites. In Indianapolis, 14.5 percent of all newspaper stories in the papers used by respondents dealt with crime, with 10.1 percent covering violent crime, such as criminal homicide, rape, or robbery. For Evanston respondents, crime newspaper coverage was slightly less, at 12.1 percent of total story coverage; but coverage of violent crime was only 5.3 percent, just over half of the Indianapolis rate of violent crime stories. This left a far heavier emphasis on nonviolent crime than was true for Indianapolis. In the *Lebanon Valley News*, 6.7 percent of all stories dealt with crime, with 0.4 percent covering violent crimes. Table 5.5 gives the actual numbers and proportions, estimated on a monthly basis, with 25 violent and 35 nonviolent television crime and justice news stories added to each monthly newspaper score. Even though Indianapolis papers carried 15 percent fewer stories than Chicago papers (Lebanon papers carried 70 percent less), the total number of crime stories was higher in Indianapolis than in Chicago. Lebanon's monthly total for violent crime stories was a miniscule two.

Because images of crime conveyed by the mass media are tempered by personal experiences within one's community, a look at actual crime figures in the three locations is appropriate. It should be clear, however, that one cannot automatically assume that respondents are familiar with real-world data in their communities. As the victimization rates (noted below) for the three communities show, most people are neither victims of crime nor likely to encounter many people in any given year who have been victimized. Nor are people likely to see crime statistics except when these statistics are published in the media. Even then, statistical information generally does not receive a great deal of attention. The genuine real-world data for most people, against which media data compete for credibility, are more likely to be the impressions that people accumulate over a lifetime from their environment and combine with snatches of current information. These, then, become part of the public folklore. They are what "everybody around here knows."

What was the actual crime situation in the three communities in 1976? FBI crime statistics for 1976 for Evanston, Indianapolis, and Lebanon will be used as indicators. Evanston, rather than Chicago, figures were chosen because the bulk of Evanston panelists spent most of their home and work life there, rather than in Chicago. This made Evanston crime figures somewhat more salient to them. The *Evanston Review*, the Evanston weekly paper, reported an average of 48 crimes per month in the town, with 37.5 percent (18) of them violent crimes. Table 5.6 presents comparative data on the frequency of mention of all types of crime by ABC national news, the *Evanston Review*, and the *Chicago Tribune*.

For 1976, the FBI reported one crime for every 20 people in Indianapolis, for a total of 38,972 crimes for the 715,000 population. Of these, 4,145 were violent crimes, or one for every 167 people. Evanston recorded one crime for every 14 people, for a total of 5,074 crimes. Of these, 336 were violent crimes, or one for every 250 people in its 77,000 population. Lebanon, with a population of 11,300, recorded a total of 302 crimes, or one for every 33 inhabitants. Of these, five were violent, amounting to just one violent crime per 2,500 population. Victimization rates were undoubtedly substantially higher because one crime frequently has many victims. The incidence of repeated victimization of vulnerable individuals, however, reduces the membership of the victim corps.

TABLE 5.5
Newspaper and Television Crime Stories (Monthly Average Estimates) and Panelists' Concern about Crime[a]

	Total Crime	Violent Crime	Nonviolent Crime	At All Concerned[b] (All Media)	Very Concerned[b] (All Media)	Very Concerned (Paper Only)
Indianapolis	253	159 (63%)	94 (37%)	60%	43%	63%
Evanston	243	105 (43%)	138 (57%)	47%	27%	26%
Lebanon	89	27 (30%)	62 (70%)	36%	14%	14%
				(N = 133)	(N = 63)	(N = 48)

[a]The question was: "Are you personally concerned about becoming a victim of crime?" If the answer was yes, the follow-up was "Are you very concerned, moderately concerned, or slightly concerned?" The latter two categories have been combined in the table.
[b]Combined figures for people who claim to use television primarily and newspapers primarily.

Source: Walter B. Jaehnig, David H. Weaver, and Frederick Fico, "Reporting Crime and Fearing Crime in Three Communities," *Journal of Communication* 30 (Spring 1980): forthcoming.

On a per capita basis, Indianapolis ranked first in violent crime, while Evanston ranked first in nonviolent crime. Lebanon was in last place by far on both counts. However, a computation of the ratio of actual crime in each town to stories about violent crimes reported in the media used by the panelists, yields an inverse relationship. For every 100 violent crimes in Indianapolis, 46 crime stories are reported in the media. In Evanston the figure is 64, while for every 100 violent crimes in Lebanon, there are 162 media crime stories.

What does this medley of figures mean in terms of the respondents in the three locations? Assuming that they are aware of the FBI data, and that news of crime breeds fear — questionable generalizations, of course — Evanston respondents should be most fearful of crime in general. However, their fears might possibly be moderated by the knowledge that there is only one chance in 18 that the crime would be violent. Fears might also be dampened because they are exposed to fewer violent crimes in their mass media than is true in Indianapolis.

For Indianapolis residents, despite an overall lower crime rate, the figures are less reassuring. If victimized, the chances are one in eight that it will be through violence. This fact probably outbalances the security that springs from the overall lower crime rate. Moreover, Indianapolis papers report the highest number of crimes and the highest proportion of violent crimes. Hence, overall statistics to the contrary notwithstanding, one may well predict that Indianapolis residents will be most concerned about possible victimization.

Lebanon residents should be at the bottom rung of concern, particularly as the number of recorded violent crimes in the town is so small. This should be true even though available violent crime stories exceed the actual numbers of local crimes by far and even though local crime is likely to be more salient to residents because it occurs in well-known locations and often involves personal acquaintances.

Table 5.5 shows that actual data about concern about crime correspond to these conjectures. When respondents in the three locations were asked how concerned they were about victimization, Indianapolis respondents had the highest proportions of concerned and very concerned people. Evanston respondents were next and Lebanon respondents last. However, the gap in concern between Lebanon respondents and their counterparts in larger cities was not nearly as large as one might expect from the differences in crime rates and crime reporting. Ceiling and bottom effects may be at work. There appears to be a ceiling for concern within a community so that concern no longer rises, or rises at only a very moderate pace after a ceiling has been reached. Similarly, news of even a few crimes seems to stimulate fear levels in the most fear-prone segments of the population so that a base plateau is reached just as soon as a community reports crime incidents.

In light of the heavy violent crime coverage in Indianapolis newspapers, it is interesting to note in Table 5.5 that Indianapolis newspaper readers show vastly exaggerated concerns over victimization, compared to readers in Evanston

TABLE 5.6
Frequency of Mention of Street and White-Collar Crime: ABC National News, Evanston Review, and Chicago Tribune
(N = 342 for ABC, based on six months coding, 573 for the *Review*, and 2,619 for the *Tribune*, both based on 12 months coding)

Crime	Tribune	ABC	Evanston Review	Crime	Tribune	ABC	Evanston Review
Murder/manslaughter	26.2	16.9	1.6	Contempt of court	1.1	0.0	0.0
Robbery	10.8	5.8	27.4	Lesser assault	0.8	2.3	0.9
Consumer fraud	5.9	3.5	0.5	Vandalism	0.8	0.0	19.2
Assault	5.8	4.3	2.3	Sex offenses	0.7	5.8	0.2
Kidnapping	5.1	8.5	0.0	Vehicle theft	0.7	0.0	0.5
Bribery/kickback	4.6	5.6	0.0	Prostitution	0.7	0.2	0.5
Arson/bombings	4.5	5.6	3.1	Fencing stolen property	0.6	0.2	0.0
Rape	3.4	0.2	2.1	Disorderly conduct	0.6	1.5	0.7
Larceny/theft	3.4	4.1	13.6	Gambling	0.5	0.0	0.5
Drug offenses	2.8	1.8	2.1	Illegal wiretap	0.4	0.4	0.4
Tax cheating	2.3	1.8	0.0	Piracy	0.4	0.0	0.0
Burglary	2.1	1.1	23.2	Embezzlement	0.4	0.9	0.0
Extortion	2.1	1.8	0.3	Obstruct justice	0.3	0.0	0.0
Weapons violations	1.6	0.2	0.3	Welfare cheating	0.3	0.0	0.0
Official misconduct	1.5	17.5	0.3	Child abuse	0.3	0.2	0.0

Corruption	1.3	7.3	0.0
Perjury	1.2	0.9	0.0
Forgery	1.2	0.0	0.5
Custody escape	1.1	0.2	0.0
Contributing to minor's delinquency	0.2	0.0	0.0
Drunken driving/traffic offenses	0.2	0.2	0.0
Liquor law violations	0.1	0.1	0.2
Parole violations	0.1	0.1	0.0
Miscellaneous	3.6		

Source: Original research.

and Lebanon. This phenomenon becomes considerably directed when data from the television audiences, which share common fare at all three locations, are added to the newspaper data. Overall data thus support the conclusion that the extent of crime coverage is reflected in the extent of fear about victimization.

Fear of victimization appears to spur attention to news about crime. Thus more Indianapolis residents reported that they paid "a great deal of attention" to crime news (56 percent) than did Evanston residents (38 percent) or Lebanon residents (42 percent).* When figures for "a great deal of attention" and "a little attention" were combined, the Evanston score of attention to crime stories (92 percent) exceeded the Lebanon score (86 percent). Lebanon had the largest percentage of respondents who paid no attention at all to crime stories (14 percent).

When asked about the crimes about which they read or hear most, panelists most often mentioned murder, robbery, rape, and violent crime in general. But Indianapolis panelists mentioned murder, robbery, and rape more than three times as often as did Lebanon panelists, a difference that was significant at the .01 level. The Indianapolis figures also exceeded those recorded in Evanston, although statistical significance was not attained. Comparisons among all three panels showed differences that were statistically significant at the .01 level for murder and rape reports. Given the differences in media fare and actual crime conditions, the perceptual differences are not surprising.

Compared to panelists from other areas, fewer Indianapolis residents complained about excessive attention to crime by the media (22 percent), despite the heavier crime emphasis in the Indianapolis papers. More of them approved the amount of crime information offered by the media (62 percent) and requested increased crime coverage (17 percent) than did respondents at the other locations. Greater perceived need for crime information, differences in personal vulnerability, and preferences linked to educational levels are plausible explanations. Evanston residents, who were most nightly educated, were at the opposite end of the scale from their Indianapolis counterparts, with 74 percent complaining about excessive crime coverage by the media, 23 percent approving of the available fare, and only 2 percent demanding more. Lebanon figures were 44 percent complaining about excessive coverage, 51 percent approving existing coverage, and 5 percent demanding more. These responses differed significantly (.05 or .01 level) for 8 out of 12 possible combinations.

Turning to stereotypes concerning criminals' race, age, sex, and, to a lesser degree, occupation, Table 5.7 shows great similarity among the three locations. By contrast, the victim characterization diverged. Demographic differences among the three communities partly explain the disparities. These real-world factors are apt to be more powerful for victim than criminal images because most people personally know many more victims than criminals.

---

*The difference between Lebanon and Evanston residents was not statistically significant.

TABLE 5.7
Criminals' and Victims' Race, Age, Sex, and Occupation as Depicted by Illinois, Indiana, and New Hampshire Panels
(in percentages; N = 52 responses for race, 241 for age, 230 for sex, 154 for occupation[a]; FBI, *Tribune*, and television crime fiction data added for comparison[b])

	Criminals						Victims					
	Illinois	*Indiana*	*New Hampshire*	*Tribune*	*FBI*	*TV*	*Illinois*	*Indiana*	*New Hampshire*	*Tribune*	*FBI*	*TV*
Race												
White	0	0	5	70	70	93	37	61	100	67	44	73
Nonwhite	100	100	95	30	30	7	63	39	0	33	56	27
Age												
Under 35	88	83	83	61	69	39	40	60	60	61	54	66
Over 35	12	17	17	39	31	61	60	40	40	39	46	34
Sex												
Male	95	96	90	86	85	84	47	35	28	63	78	80
Female	5	4	10	14	15	16	53	65	72	37	22	20
Occupation[c]												
Business/professional	0	0	0	62	13	13	9	6	43			
Clerical/sales	8	0	0	3	13	17	11	15	6			
Skilled labor	0	4	7	8	0	0	0	4	11			
Unskilled labor	13	0	5	7	0	0	0	0	9			
Student	4	2	5	8	0	0	0	0	17			

continued

111

TABLE 5.7, continued

	Criminals						Victims					
	Illinois	Indiana	New Hampshire	Tribune	FBI	TV	Illinois	Indiana	New Hampshire	Tribune	FBI	TV
Homemaker	0	0	0	1	0	8	0	2	5	3		
Retiree	0	0	0	0	0	8	0	19	23	0		
Unemployed	67	76	65	11	31	25	31	4	2	11		
Drifter/criminal	0	7	2	0	31	0	31	11	0	0		
Miscellaneous	8	11	16	0	12	33	12	38	50	0		

[a] Indefinite answers, such as "any age," were allocated to match the distribution of definite answers in the corresponding category.

[b] FBI and television crime fiction data are based on figures reported by Joseph R. Dominick for 1972 in "Crime and Law Enforcement on Prime-Time Television," *Public Opinion Quarterly* 37 (Summer 1973): 241-50. Ninety-six criminals were in the television sample. All 26 victims in the television sample were murder victims.

[c] FBI and television data unavailable except for TV criminals' occupation.

Source: Original research.

When audience responses at all three locations are compared to print media data, data from fictionalized television crime, and to real-life data supplied by the FBI, there are substantial discrepancies. The respondents had indicated that they accepted and internalized information according to a hierarchy of source credibility. Information about conditions in their own community, which had been acquired and substantiated through direct and indirect personal as well as media contacts, had been ranked first in credibility. Information attributed by the media to respected sources, such as the FBI or local police chiefs, had been ranked second. Media appraisals and appraisals that the respondents derived from media stories through their own reasoning came third. Impressions gained from television fiction were in last place. Respondents claimed that the more credible sources, if available, would supersede the less credible ones, with information rarely averaged to a midpoint. However, some respondents said that they never used fictional crime and justice stories for image creation, even if other information sources were lacking. Accordingly, it was expected that real-life FBI and panel data would show closer resemblances than FBI and media data. As Table 5.7 shows, this did not happen.

Newspaper and FBI statistics on the characteristics of criminals showed the closest correspondence. Even television fictional criminals bore a closer resemblance to FBI data than did the images depicted by the respondents. The picture was a bit more mixed for victims, where Illinois and Indiana respondents were more realistic about fact than the *Tribune* or crime fiction. On age, Illinois and New Hampshire respondents were more accurate than the mass media, but the latter did better in depicting the sex distribution realistically. FBI occupational data were unavailable for both criminals and victims so that one cannot tell whether the widely diverging images of media or panelists are correct.

Other comparisons among the three panels likewise show major similarities along with major differences. For instance, answers were essentially similar to the question "In what places is the average city resident most likely to become a victim of crime?" The sole exception was mention of the inner city, which was rare in Lebanon and most common in Indianapolis. The differences between Evanston and Lebanon responses and Indianapolis and Lebanon responses were statistically significant at the .05 level, using chi square.

When asked "What causes more and more people to commit crimes?" responses mentioning the home environment, need for money, drugs, unemployment, and the judicial system were common. Frequencies were similar, except for mention of home environment, for which differences significant at the .05 level occurred among all panels. Home environment was mentioned least frequently in Evanston as a cause of crime and most often in Lebanon, with Indianapolis in between.* These differences probably reflect sociocultural and religious

---

*The difference between Evanston and Lebanon responses was significant at the .01 level.

differences among residents of a comparatively sophisticated midwestern university community on the outskirts of a large metropolis, inhabitants of a small, heavily Catholic working-class New England town, and residents of a lower-middle-class midwestern middle-sized city.

Diversity was even greater in response to a question about "What could be done to reduce the number of crimes that are committed in this country?" Among the four main remedies cited – creation of jobs, better education, better home life, and improvement in the quality of the judicial system – there was agreement only on the importance of creation of jobs. For the other answers, emphasis differences were statistically significant at either the .05 or .01 level in 8 of the 12 possible combinations. Better education and a better home life were stressed most strongly in Lebanon, while improvement of the quality of the judicial system was paramount in Indianapolis. Responses from Evanston fell into the middle ranges. Again, sociocultural and political differences furnish plausible explanations.

There was also substantial diversity when panelists were asked to appraise the seriousness of 15 white-collar crimes (see Table 3.17). In each case, the crime was considered most serious in New Hampshire and least serious in Illinois, with Indiana in the middle. Differences were generally significant at the .05 level, except for offenses against public morals, such as gambling, prostitution, and tax cheating, where differences reached .01 significance levels. The difference between appraisals of the seriousness of extortion also was at the .01 level in comparisons between Illinois and New Hampshire. All three panels agreed on the degree of seriousness of weapons violations, wiretaps, and drunken driving.

It is difficult to summarize the findings about cognitive map differences and similarities among the three sites because the trends are blurred. Obviously, there are major contextual differences among the three sites. Indianapolis had most violent crimes per capita, Evanston had most nonviolent crimes and Lebanon ranked low on both. The substance of crime stories was similar in the three locations, but this did little to create uniformity because the images held by media audiences in all three locales did not conform to media images.

The three sites differed in quantity of media stories, in the proportion of stories of violent and nonviolent crime, and in the relation of actual to reported crime. Overall, data from the three sites suggest that concern about crime rises and falls, within a threshold and ceiling range, depending on the levels of violent crime and crime coverage. As concern rises, attention to and desire for crime news mount as well and become focused on the types of crimes that abound in the particular community. Because crime occurrence and media crime coverage do bear a rough resemblance in the three sites, it is impossible to assess their respective impact on audience perceptions.

While concern about crime and attention to crime stories vary, images of the crime and justice process are shared in the three locations except in matters where personal experiences are fairly common. For instance, stereotypes of criminals are shared while stereotypes of victims differ. Most, but not all, perceptions about location of high-crime areas and causes of crime are shared; differences that do occur can be explained quite readily by local conditions. However, differences become marked when one looks at matters of evaluation and policy choices that are linked to moral and political preferences. Accordingly, evaluations of the seriousness of crime vary among the three locations, as do suggestions about reducing crime.

SUMMARY AND CONCLUSIONS

The cognitive maps supply ample evidence that images and image combinations at the individual level are rich, amazingly similar in general configuration and some specific details, while diverging substantially in other details. These divergencies at the individual and group levels make it clear that a full picture of the impact of crime and justice news requires examination of impact in specific contexts as well as generally. The meaningfulness of cognitive maps increases sharply when one understands the social and cultural setting of the community from which the data are drawn, including prevailing beliefs and opinions about crime and justice. Close study of personal settings, along with psychological typing, are needed for accurate interpretations of cognitive maps at the individual level.

For most purposes, crime and justice news can be adequately assessed by studying news supply and general community perceptions. Such perceptions usually are widely shared, akin to the sharing of "public opinion" on other public issues. This does not mean that the existence of significant individual variations can be safely ignored. Minority cognitions and configurations of cognitions have often spread to majorities.

In the final analysis, the most important actors in determining the impact of crime and justice news are the millions of individual news recipients. While they depend on the media for the bulk of their informational raw material about current happenings, they are free to pick and choose among news offerings. They can, and often do, ignore them in whole or in part. They can also transform the contents to complement their preconceived notions or to assuage their existing hopes or fear. When it comes to image formation, they are not puppets whose strings are pulled by the media or by the pronouncements of public officials. Rather, they are the puppeteers who work with available resources in ways suited to their own experiences, needs, and expectations.

NOTES

1. Wesley Skogan has reported data that indicate that "measures of direct victimization cannot explain much of the variation in measures of fear of crime." See his "Public Policy and the Fear of Crime in Large American Cities," in *Public Law and Public Policy*, ed. John A. Gardiner (New York: Praeger, 1977), p. 9.

2. Table 2.2 provides comparative data on press and television coverage. For data indicating that media coverage differences produce minimal perceptual differences, see Lutz Erbring, Edie Goldenberg, and Arthur Miller, "Front Page News and Real-World Clues: Another Look at Agenda-Setting by the Media," *American Journal of Political Science* 24 (1980): 16-49. The authors claim that actual differences in crime rates explain perceptual differences. Similar conclusions have been drawn by Skogan, "Public Policy and the Fear of Crime in Large American Cities." These authors do not explain in what ways, other than through media coverage, people become aware of the actual incidence of crime in their often large communities.

Six

RESEARCH AND POLICY IMPLICATIONS

At the outset of this book, five major questions were posed: (1) Do mass media supply adequate and accurate news about the crime and justice process? (2) What sorts of images of the crime and justice process does the public hold, and what attitudes and evaluations does it develop from them? (3) What kinds of politically significant behaviors spring from these images? (4) What are their implications for political life and public policy? Finally, (5) What contributions does this study make to communication research in general, in substance as well as methodology?

The first three questions have been answered in great detail. Therefore, the bulk of this final chapter will be devoted to the remaining two. The last question will be considered first and some major general findings and conclusions will be outlined. This will be followed by a discussion of public policy implications in general and their possible impact on media policies and the policies pursued by governmental bodies.

GENERAL PROBLEMS AND FINDINGS

Representativeness

As is true of most work in the social sciences, resource constraints limited subject matter and sources used for this study. Nonetheless, evaluation of the data in the light of communication theories, and comparison with findings from related studies give confidence that the findings have general application. This confidence is strengthened by an analysis of data outside the crime and justice realm that was carried out in tandem with the study reported here. The combined findings support a tentative conclusion that the types of considerations that go into crime and justice news reporting and crime and justice news image formation by the public are applicable to other types of news.

Separating Media Effects

The problem of isolating media effects from each other and from other effects has long plagued communication research. It could be solved if investigators could take identical audiences and expose them to well-defined media treatments, while leaving an untreated control group. But such ideal experiments are not possible in real-life field research situations. Investigators must deal with people who have been simultaneously exposed to real-life events, to media reports about these events, and to third-person reports. Additionally, people bring stored information to bear on much of the new information that comes to their attention. Wherever media and audience images coincide, this mixture of stimuli makes it difficult to ascertain what portions of audience images and evaluations are attributable to media stories and what portions spring from other influences.

We attempted to cope with these problems through asking our respondents to list story sources in their diaries, and through asking for sources while testing story recall. These efforts to use individual memories as clues to the mystery were largely unsuccessful. In most instances, people failed to recall sources or recalled a combination of them. We therefore concluded that it is well-nigh impossible to assign effects to particular sources when people have been exposed to a variety of sources which carried similar information. We were able to establish that people mention media more often than interpersonal contacts as their best sources of crime and justice news, except for local crime where neighbors are generally ranked first. Among media, television gets first place.[1] Given the general vulnerability of global self-judgments, when compared to actual behavior, this finding remains tentative. At best, media influence was moderate, judging from limited conformance of audience images to media images.

Audience Factors

Assessing the impact of media information proved equally complicated. A host of mediating factors intervene, such as lifestyle, personality, social environment at the time of message reception, and even moods and whims of audience members. The findings parallel the work of other researchers and indicate that mass media impact involves transactional processes, rather than straightforward stimulus-response situations. In-depth interviewing over a prolonged time span helped to shed light on these processes generally and learn what impacts are likely under various circumstances. It is a promising approach to solve some of the major problems faced by less intensive methods of impact measurement.

Refining Concepts

The need to specify questions precisely enough so that the answers are sharp rather than blurred presented the usual difficulties for this study. For instance, one cannot ask generally about "media exposure" and equate exposure with transmission of particular information reported by a given news channel. If one wants to know whether Jane Doe was exposed to a specific kidnapping story through the *Middletown News,* one cannot assume so merely from knowing that she reads that paper regularly. One must combine content analysis of the *Middletown News* with specific questions about the story, and rule out the possibility that sources other than the *Middletown News* were used.

For full understanding of what is meant by "knowing" a story, one needs to ask a series of questions about it. It is not enough to present the respondent with a statement of story content and ask for agreement or acknowledgment of recall or some other overall judgment. The answers must be verified through examining the contents of the media and other messages that reach the respondent. To assess how meaningful findings are, one needs standards for comparison. Whether recall of one third of the facts of a crime story is high or low depends on knowing rates of recall for other subject matter, the ranges of recall among comparable groups of people, and the expectations against which the rates are measured. To deal with such problems, the interview questions were defined more sharply than usual. Accordingly, issues were probed in a variety of contexts and from different vantage points and the answers were appraised in light of the contexts that impinged on their meanings. The results have been encouraging and point to the need for further refinements along these lines.

Statements referring to media content, too, require much finer specifications than ordinarily used. One should not, for instance, talk broadly about "crime news" without specifying the type of story content and the manner and context of presentation. Findings about the impact of a murder story may not hold true for a tale of child abuse or vandalism. To make them comparable requires scales of variable impact that are difficult to produce. Is one murder the equivalent of two rapes in shock value? How many robberies equal one rape? It is a tricky calculus.

Assessment of story impact requires more than knowing story topic and frequency. It also matters a great deal whether the story involves distant locations or the audience's immediate neighborhood. The facts should be provided. The play given to a story in terms of language, position, and graphics is also tremendously important. The context of other stories appearing with a crime story is crucial, as is the social context existing at the time the story is reported. Criminal activities are far more frightening, for instance, if they are attributed to a terrorist gang and are part of a series of similar crimes than if they are linked to an individual acting on impulse.

The media tend to call attention to selected serious crimes by giving them more space, time, graphics, and bigger headlines than they give to more numerous lesser crimes. Sensational coverage of just one mass murder may send shock waves through a wide area and profoundly affect the behavior of millions of people, while other murders may be all but ignored. Content analysis should take note of such prominence factors in studies concerned with mass media impact.

The Frequency-Impact Relationship

Story recall patterns provide evidence that the relation between frequency of coverage and audience attention and recall is far from perfect. Judging from their diaries and recall of story details, the respondents gave proportionally more attention to street crime stories than did the media, but with different emphases on particular crimes. For instance, murder played a smaller part, relatively, in the audience's diaries and recall tests than in the *Tribune*. Investigators for the Reactions to Crime project found that more people remembered murders in Chicago than in Philadelphia, despite similar newspaper coverage. In high-crime areas, people were apt to recall crimes involving people of similar life-styles, regardless of prominence and frequency of media coverage. In low-crime areas, the match between frequency of coverage and prominence in memory was closer.[2]

People also paid substantially less attention to police, court, and correctional system stories than was true of the media. These choice patterns appear to be related to people's feelings of need and interest in certain information, or lack of interest, as the case may be. This suggests that an increase in the usual stories about a given subject, such as the police, the courts, or prisons, is unlikely to enhance consumption of such news proportionately. Enhancing the attention-arousing features of stories, such as placement, language, or graphics, appears to be a somewhat more promising approach, if it serves to increase the story's salience to the audience.

The Attitude-Behavior Connection

This study demonstrates anew the tenuous connection between various attitudes and behaviors. For instance, expressed interest in news does not necessarily mean that people will pay attention to it. Most respondents were seriously concerned about crime and crime fighting and had repeatedly mentioned it spontaneously as a serious problem in the United States. Yet less than half (48 percent) professed to pay a lot of attention to crime and justice news. Most said that they paid only limited attention.

Likewise, expressions of high concern and belief in the effectiveness of protective measures did not necessarily mean use of such measures. Nonetheless, crime avoidance and protective behavior are generally greatest among people who perceive a high crime risk to themselves and believe that avoidance and protective measures are effective. The explanation for frequent divergences between attitudes and behaviors seems to be that their determinants are influenced by different mediating factors. This does not mean that attitudes do not influence behaviors, and vice versa, only that additional factors may modify the direction of this influence.

The study demonstrated the fragility of news attention behaviors, even for audiences expressing high interest and enjoying easy access to news. Attention to news is readily displaced by most serious as well as most casual pursuits. For instance, when people are on vacation and have ample time and resources available to keep up with the news, few make the effort. When illness strikes a family or excess work pressures mount, news consumption may stop almost entirely.

This low priority for news in the hierarchy of interests is coupled, nonetheless, for many people with a very high rate of exposure. For many news consumers, the mass media provide a pleasant, fairly effortless way to fill idle hours. They give people "someting to do," akin to gazing casually out of a train window at the passing scenery. For much of the time, inertia, rather than strong attraction to the flow of news offerings, maintains the superficial contact.

Information-Processing Traits

A number of general conclusions about information processing emerge from this study. Most, though by no means all of them, provide fresh support for the findings of other researchers. The relevant data have been presented, albeit in other contexts, throughout the book and therefore need not be repeated here.

The finding that people do not fully adopt the images and priorities of the media indicates some of the limitations of general agenda-setting theories that investigators have been trying to specify. The relationship between crime news and media images fits more closely into the modulator model of audience effects than in the basic agenda-setting model.[3] Proponents of the modulator model argue that effects of the media on the audience are modulated by the sensitivity of the audience to a particular issue and by the background and demographic characteristics and experiences of individual audience members. Modulation enhances or decreases media impact, depending on the salience of a specific issue to an individual. Personal experiences are an especially strong influence on social judgments and almost invariably override media images and evaluations.[4]

For many topics, crime among them, people have a backlog of stored knowledge because these problems recur over the years. Stories about these topics therefore are not genuinely "news" in the sense of something that has not happened before. They are episodes in a continuing story that simply reinforce whatever has been previously perceived as the main story theme. This main theme is modified only occasionally when new episodes clash markedly with established stereotypes and the clash becomes apparent to the audience. This study therefore indicates that audiences select mass media crime and justice information to reinforce existing attitudes. They ignore those aspects of the information that clash with existing perceptions and the implications drawn from them. This explains why sensational crime coverage does not automatically lead to panic reactions among most people.[5] However, jolting evidence that disconfirms the audience's mental status quo may lead to rapid reshaping of perceptions.[6] The study also provides evidence of more gradual incremental reshaping that occurs through the combined impact of media and other stimuli over extended time periods. In this process, existing attributes are first weakened and then gradually modified to conform to the new images and attitudes conveyed by credible information sources.

The study sheds some light on primacy and recency effects: the question of whether, in the case of clashing information, that which is presented first or that which is presented last tends to make the strongest impact and leave the firmest memories. In crime news coverage, primacy apparently holds sway, when the information is presumed to be fairly stable and when there are only small discrepancies between successive bits of information. For instance, once the impression has been conveyed that an area suffers from a heavy incidence of crime, that impression persists, despite occasional stories that the crime situation has improved. Recency effects obtain when the phenomena are presumed to be unstable and when conditions believed to cause change occur. For example, if crime is attributed to corrupt police officials, a well-publicized change to honest personnel is apt to change the impressions.

The study supports the common finding that negative information has a stronger impact than positive information, assuming that everything else is equal, especially the salience of the story to the personal lives of audience members. Stories about rising crime rates make a greater impact on memories, attitudes, and behaviors than stories about declining rates. Crimes that involve more violence receive more attention than those that involve lesser infringements of personal and property rights. However, there are ceiling and threshold phenomena. This study provides evidence that initial stories, if noticed, may quickly raise perceptual and behavioral responses to a minimum level. From this threshold, responses such as fear of crime and avoidance behavior may change more gradually until a ceiling is reached. Then additional information brings no further changes in responses. In fact, it is often ignored because a saturation level of information has been reached. A similar process occurs in learning story details. Once saturation has been reached – the point varies with memory capabilities – no further details are absorbed.

A major confounding factor in predicting how stories will be processed is personal salience. If a particular story is highly salient to the personal lives of audience members, normal responses may be either enhanced or diminished. For instance, news that indicates that a respondent's neighborhood is a highly dangerous place is frequently rejected by the people who live in the neighborhood even though it bears all the marks of authenticity. People are willing to accept danger elsewhere, but not next door. On the other hand, people who may be very casual about protective behaviors when crime hits other parts of town may become highly protective when it appears in their own communities. Credibility of the sources from which a crime story originates may also determine its salience. Stories from personal experience have the greatest impact on perceptions and behaviors. Interpersonally conveyed stories are generally next, followed by media reports attributed to credible government and private sources. The run of the mill media story comes last.

Once information has been processed into images of reality, the "pictures in our heads," as Walter Lippmann called them, are vastly more important in shaping behaviors than the conditions that actually exist in "the world outside." People act on the basis of their own perceptions of crime, regardless of what the circumstances appear to be to a dispassionate observer. Explanations for behavior and attempts to change it therefore require first of all an understanding of the perceptual reality that exists in people's minds.

Research Strategies

The study has provided many useful lessons about research strategies. Most importantly, it has demonstrated the feasibility of working intensively with small panels over a lengthy period of time. This is significant because many of the wide knowledge gaps left by large-scale survey research projects can only be filled through intensive work with small panels. The study demonstrates that membership in small panels can be maintained for a year and possibly much longer, given good contact procedures based on personal rapport. It helps to keep panel members fully informed about the general thrust — though not the specific goals — of the study and to recognize their contributions through material or immaterial rewards.

Working repeatedly with the same group of people always raises questions about sensitization effects that may destroy the validity of the findings because the reactions of previously questioned subjects are contaminated by prior interviews. As indicated, this study shows that major sensitization effects are not inevitable. They can be minimized through dispersion tactics by asking respondents a large number of questions about a wide array of issues so that no single major issue focus emerges. It then becomes too troublesome for panel members to keep track of their answers or to concentrate on the multitude of issues raised in the interview. Urging respondents to behave as normally as possible and explaining to them why this is important also help. Likewise, the sheer length of a project serves to diminish sensitization. In this case, ten repetitions spaced out over a year made it too burdensome to increase attention to mass media stories beyond normal time budgets. While attention to the media increased slightly after the first interview, the respondents told us in individual and group interviews essentially normal patterns resumed thereafter.

The experiment of supplementing personal interviews with group interviews turned out to be worthwhile. The group sessions became a form of aided recall where participants reminded each other about shared experiences. But just as an aided question by an interviewer may lead a respondent into answers that do not accurately reflect what that person thought, so a group session may lead respondents into a "me-too" syndrome, lacking a factual basis. It is not known at this point how frequently this happens, or even how to judge when it happens.

Similarly, comparisons among groups showed that some sessions produced greater frankness than individual interviews in the expression of views on socially sensitive issues because people felt reinforced by the knowledge that their views were shared. On the other hand, in other sessions, the tenor of discussion shied away from sensitive, possibly hurtful comments. This seemed to constrain some respondents from discussing sensitive issues as openly as they had done during individual interviews. It takes a perceptive analyst to sense such group dynamics in group interviews and to apply correctives to the interpretation of group interview results.

THE STATUS QUO AND POLICY IMPLICATIONS

This study has shown that the mass media produce a steady flow of crime and justice news. By its steadiness, it constantly reinforces whatever reactions it arouses. The flow is largely immune to variations in actual crime statistics. It is not merely a mirror or random sampling of known events. Rather, it is shaped by journalists' choices. It therefore seems appropriate to question how well crime news policy serves the public, and what, if anything, can be done to improve it. Our evaluation criteria for media performance are drawn from the professional standards proclaimed by journalism educators since "setting criteria for the definition of public objectives and the appraisal of public programs" is "the essential function of the expert."[7] Journalism texts generally stress that crime news, besides making interesting reading or viewing, should alert the public to the dimensions of the crime and justice problem. It should also provide sufficient information so that citizens can cope with the problem personally or through the political process. How well are these purposes fulfilled?

Alerting the Public

Judging from the attention paid to it, crime and justice news seems to fascinate the public and seems to provide a psychologically satisfying way to pass idle hours. Attention to crime news may even be a form of catharsis. The audience observes and weeps and rejoices that it has escaped the misfortunes that have befallen others. This fulfills one major journalistic purpose: providing interesting news, and often excitement and relaxation as well.

But does crime and justice news inform the public adequately? Is the community kept aware of all major dimensions of the crime and justice problem? Is it alerted to the need for measures to prevent crime and reduce victimization? Is it assisted in implementing these measures through public and private action? Based on the 1976 data, the answer is "no" for the most part.

Obviously, the media alert the public and politicians to the fact that crime and organized social responses to it constitute major political problems. The polls and political rhetoric bear ample testimony to this awareness. But, although individual stories are reasonably accurate, the media do not inform the public well. Stories are written as isolated events, which the audience finds hard to weave into meaningful patterns. The media do little to put crime news into perspective, to help the audience to correct the distortions that inevitably spring from the need to select and condense. The fact that people are aware that selection leads to imbalanced presentation does not mean that they know how to devise corrective lenses.

Stimulating Defensive Behavior

Do the media provide adequate information to assist citizens to protect themselves against crime? The answer is both "yes" and "no." The media do generate fear of crime, which stimulates people to practice previously known protective behaviors. People use media facts about crime to draw conclusions about dangerous areas or to support preestablished conclusions. People also scan the media for news about the safety of locations important to their personal lives. A single nearby crime may produce strong reactions in terms of protective behavior, at least temporarily.

On the negative side, most stories lack the kind of detail that would help people to know how to protect themselves and their property. They also lack information about ways to cope with various crime and justice problems through public actions by government officials or groups of citizens. This finding supports the observation by other investigators that implementing information is generally missing from media stories.[8]

Providing Evaluation Criteria

Does crime and justice news produce sufficient criteria for appropriate evaluations of the public institutions that deal with crime and justice problems? Is it designed to generate support for them? Once again, the answer to both questions is "no." The media provide little information by which to judge whether the job done by public institutions involved with crime and justice problems is as good as the public has a right to expect. Comparative performance data, cost-effectiveness data, and differential data for handling of various types of crimes are rare or totally absent. The 1976 sample of newspaper stories, for instance, told nothing about police turnover rates and morale and success of various crime prevention efforts. Most evaluation stories that, despite their lack of evaluation criteria, might have been valuable, were buried in the back pages and back sections of newspapers. Only severely negative criticism was featured in more prominent places.

Judging from the content analyses, crime and justice news supports a generally negative view of the courts, the correctional system, and, to a lesser degree, the police. However, as explained earlier, the public uses somewhat different evaluation criteria to arrive at a more sympathetic view of the problems of the crime and justice system. Blame for the inadequacies of the system is tempered by recognition that the magnitude of the problem makes adequate coping well-nigh impossible.

The public images of institutions like the courts, correctional facilities, and the police are matters of public concern, of course, because they become translated into support and compliance or its opposites. Lack of support, in turn, makes the work of these institutions far more difficult and success less likely. It may also lead to reduced appropriations, particularly in periods of tight money when public officials become more conscious of linking budgets to demonstrations of satisfactory performance and public approval. The evidence does not indicate that any of these consequences currently flow from media publicity, but the potential exists. It is quite likely that adverse media stories have been used by parties to political discourse to erode support for these institutions, as currently constituted.

Deleterious Consequences

The Hippocratic Oath taken by physicians commands them, above all, to avoid doing harm. Can one judge the media by the same standard and praise their policies on the ground that they avoid news that seriously damages the public trust? A weak "yes" is the answer. Despite widespread popular belief that media crime coverage, especially coverage in fiction stories, stimulates people to commit crimes, the evidence is not clear-cut. Intensive research has failed to denote the precise connection between crime news and crime and the magnitude of the ensuing problems. Very few of the panelists admitted to ever having been tempted to criminal activity by media stories. Of those who did, all denied that they had succumbed.

It also is questionable that crime news leads to disdain for minorities who are considered crime prone. Though the panelists saw blacks as the most likely contributors to rising crime rates and whites as the most likely victims, their level of trust in blacks remained comparatively high and stable. What is more, they saw social conditions, particularly poverty and poor home life, as the primary causes of crime, thus absolving individual criminals and their ethnic groups, at least in part. However, those views did not make them any less wary whenever they considered themselves in danger by proximity to crime-prone ethnic groups.

We have already discussed how media-stimulated fear of crime may produce protective behaviors. Some of these, while personally beneficial, may be socially harmful. For instance, the common practice of avoiding high-crime neighborhoods at night may leave streets comparatively empty and more hazardous than before. Abandoning inner-city businesses may leave the heart of the town a boarded-up, unproductive, and costly wasteland. Similarly, unfavorable images of public institutions may harm the institutions involved. Such images may also reflect on the political system generally. Negative news appears to lower general feelings of political trust and efficacy.[9]

The Pros and Cons of Media Reform

Suggestions for changes in media policies run into many serious objections. First of all, there is the basic question of the priorities to be assigned to various media goals. It can be argued that the media should place primary emphasis on presenting lively stories that attract large audiences. Providing information for coping with social problems should be a distinctly secondary goal. The present crime and justice format allows reporters assigned to the police beat to take police blotter news and, with minimal effort, shape it into a steady stream of "newsworthy" stories. The public wants to be entertained, primarily, and not educated and prodded into social action. It would probably ignore much of the action and evaluation information if it were presented. Given such reader and viewer trends, and the fact that the current police beat system is well established, it can be argued that major changes would be foolish.

These arguments can be countered by pointing out that the media, whether they like it or not, play an important role in U.S. political life that entails public service obligations. They serve as public agenda setters for political authorities and pressure groups and their publics. If media stories do not stimulate the kinds of social changes that may be required to cope with crime, undesirable status quo policies are apt to persist.[10] The news profession should therefore feel compelled to take its public responsibilities seriously.

An even more fundamental bar to change is the fact that media presentations apparently make very little difference in audience images, audience evaluations, and audience knowledge about crime protection programs. Established stereotypes persist. Attention rates to various types of stories hinge more on interest in them than on their frequency and the amount and kind of display, except when the latter are truly extraordinary. Learning from the media is imprecise, often full of errors, and memory is short. Whenever possible, people use their own views to make performance judgments, rather than adopting media evaluations.

These contentions have merit, of course, but do not tell the full story. Despite the fact that crime images are heavily influenced by personal experiences, interpersonal information transmission, and stored knowledge, media information continues to make an important contribution of new facts that can either reinforce or subtly change existing stereotypes. The media are most important when a new problem first emerges for which preconceived ideas are scarce. Coping with airline hijacking is an example. The media may also make problems seem more or less urgent by their reporting. They can, for instance, create perceptions of general crime waves or rape epidemics or bank robbery sprees, even when there has been no change in the actual crime rates. Occasionally, a single story can even bring about major changes in public attitudes, as happened with the Watergate story of crime and corruption in the highest government echelons.

Besides, today's news becomes part of tomorrow's history and joins the fund of stored information. Learning about new developments may be slow, but it does occur. Knowledge patterns about new crime protection programs demonstrate this quite well. People become familiar with new programs of peripheral salience to them personally after they have been mentioned repeatedly over a period of several years. The importance of media content cannot be belittled, therefore. In fact it can be likened to the impact of stories in presidential elections. Although people are strongly predisposed to use election news to reinforce existing views and to behave according to existing patterns, some stories do stimulate rethinking. This may lead to significant new conclusions and attitudes, immediately or eventually.

For policymakers in the media and elsewhere, this means that it is by no means impossible to overcome stereotypes. However, the current approach of presenting stories about ongoing events appears to be ill-suited for this purpose because it relies on the audience to draw its own generalizations from a mass of data. And people largely fail to do this. Making these generalizations explicit for the public might help. It would also aid public understanding if crime were examined in more depth than is apparent from police records. Stories should explore the origins of crime in greater depth. Reporters might look at the home life, economic status, and work history of criminals and victims in an attempt to produce information that could provide leads to the causes and cures of crime, rather than merely chronicling the problem. They might also explain the operations of the courts and correctional system more fully.

Currently, stories about individual crimes far outrank emphasis on stories dealing with criminal justice issues and crime prevention. "Robbers and Cops" rather than "Cops and Robbers" is the name of the news-reporting game. That a different emphasis is possible and makes for interesting stories is well illustrated by most fictional crime stories on radio and television. It might be tried as a news story format as well.

SOCIAL POLICY REFORMS

Several general public policy areas are affected by the types of perceptions of the crime and justice process that the public harbors. The first of these concerns general social policies to aid the disadvantaged. Given public beliefs that poverty and crime are linked, programs to reduce poverty among population groups with high crime incidence should be able to win wide public support. In an era when there is general reluctance to maintain or even increase welfare obligations, making the crime-poverty link explicit may aid in passage of programs that might otherwise fail.

The fact that the public recognizes the difficulties faced by the police, correctional institutions, and the courts ought to augur well for policies designed to improve the operations of these institutions. This could mean support for new personnel, new equipment, and for new procedures to make the process of justice swifter and punishment more certain. The public's view that penalties are far too lenient and the net of justice much too coarse provides support for hardening penal laws and making it more difficult to escape the system through the use of legal technicalities. Politicians can tap this potential or use it as a warning of public pressures that may lead to policy consequences they ought to fight.

Efforts to stimulate more public involvement in the crime and justice process may also be useful because there is general recognition that public involvement is lagging and might be beneficial. Knowing the difficulties of using the media to generate such support provides a real challenge to newspeople and public authorities alike. Because information transmission is a transactional process, both must make better use of available information on public perceptions and reactions. Armed with such knowledge, newspeople and public authorities ought to be able to devise more effective messages to stimulate desired responses. If this becomes possible, without degenerating into propaganda efforts, the long underused potential of the media to become a major force in the solution of public policy problems may come closer to realization. All of us will benefit.

NOTES

1. The findings from Northwestern University's Reactions to Crime project parallel those obtained from this study. Center for Urban Affairs, Northwestern University, *Crime in the Newspapers and Fear in the Neighborhoods: Some Unintended Consequences* (Evanston, Ill.: Center for Urban Affairs, Northwestern University, 1979), chap. 7, p. 23.

2. Ibid., chap. 8, pp. 9-10.

3. Lutz Erbring, Edie Goldenberg, and Arthur Miller, "Front Page News and Real-World Clues: Another Look at Agenda-Setting by the Media," *American Journal of Political Science* 24 (1980): 16-49.

4. The respective influence of personally versus vicariously experienced events is discussed by Tom R. Tyler, "Drawing Inferences from Experiences: The Effect of Crime Victimization Experiences Upon Crime-Related Attitudes and Behaviors" (Ph.D. diss., University of California, Los Angeles, 1978), and sources cited there.

5. Jeffrey C. Hubbard, Melvin L. DeFleur, and Lois B. DeFleur, "Mass Media Influences on Public Conceptions of Social Problems," *Social Problems* 23 (October 1975): 22-35.

6. Leslie T. Wilkins, *Social Deviance: Social Policy, Action and Research* (London: Tavistock, 1964), p. 163.

7. Charles W. Anderson, "The Place of Principles in Policy Analysis," *American Political Science Review* 73 (September 1979): 711-23.

8. James B. Lemert et al., "Journalists and Mobilizing Information," *Journalism Quarterly* 54 (Winter 1977): 721-26.

9. Arthur H. Miller, Edie N. Goldenberg, and Lutz Erbring, "Type-Set Politics: Impact of Newspapers on Public Confidence," *American Political Science Review* 73 (March 1979): 67-84.

10. Roger Cobb and Charles Elder, *Participation in American Politics: The Dynamics of Agenda-Building* (Boston: Allyn and Bacon, 1972).

Appendix A

PRINT MEDIA CODEBOOK

CODING UNIT

1. Newspaper and news magazine content will be differentiated into stories and nonstories. Only stories will be analyzed.
2. The coding unit is the individual story. This is defined as an entire item presented under one or more headlines. A story may have more than one theme in it.
3. The following items are considered nonstories:

Short stories no longer than three column inches (columns time inches) inclusive of heading and/or picture (see pages 140-48 for instructions on measuring headlines and stories).
News in brief with or without headlines and pictures if the main stories appear elsewhere
Tables of contents, including headlines or pictures
Lottery announcements
Announcements of all sorts
Sports score tables
Stock market lists
Obituaries
Meeting notices
Radio-TV listings
Puzzles, bridge columns
Brief weather forecasts
Advertisements
Other miscellaneous items of similar nature (for example, "Quote of the Day")

Note: Drawings and comics will be considered stories.

COMBINING STORIES
(rules based on test panel perceptions)

1. When the same story is continued on separate pages, or when only the headline appears on the front page and the main body is elsewhere, the sum of all parts is considered as one story.

131

2. When two or more related or similar stories are side by side with a common title, they will be coded as one story. Such stories are frequently found in columnist sections (for example, "Newsmaker" in *Daily News*, "Action Line" in *Tribune*).

3. Neighboring stories not belonging to any particular columnist section but closely related to each other in subject matter will be considered one story.

4. Substories (for example, inset stories, background analysis, supplementary explanations, maps or illustrations) are considered part of the main story.

5. Two closely related stories appearing in different sections will be coded separately.

SPECIAL SECTIONS

1. All special sections (for example, People, Leisure, Food, Entertainment) except the business section will be grouped together as one story. The business section will be considered one story independent from the other special sections.

2. Occasionally a few regular political/social stories may be found in special sections. These stories should be coded separately as if they appeared in regular sections.

3. For the grouped stories from special sections and the business section, do not code page number, section number, type of story, picture size, or size of headline. Incorporate picture size and headline size into story length.

4. Omit such special sections as "Suburban Week" in the *Daily News* and "Metronorth" in the *Tribune* from coding, as these sections do not appear in all issues of the paper.

CODING DIRECTORY

Variable	Name	Column	Code	Explanation
1	Newspaper name	1	1	*Chicago Tribune*
			2	*Sun-Times*
			3	*Daily News*
			4	*Time*
			5	*Newsweek*
			6	*Evanston Review*
			7	*Indianapolis News*
			8	*Indianapolis Star*
			9	*Valley News*
2	Date	2-3	01-31	Day of month
3	Month	4-5	01-12	January-December
4	Year	6		Code last numeral only
			6	1976
			7	1977
5	Story number	8-9	01-99	Each story is numbered consecutively per paper per day.
6	Page number	10-11	01-99	When a story appears on more than one page, or when the headline appears on the front page and the main body is elsewhere, code the page number on which the main body appears.
7	Section number	12-13	01-99	Code by section numbers provided by the paper. If no section numbers are given (as in *Sun-Times, Time, Newsweek*), assign section numbers consecutively.
8	Story type	14		Use the following categories to code each story according to the format of presentation:
			1	News report: General news reports and special news (indicated as such by the papers) on current daily events or issues.
			2	Featured news, news analysis: Distinguished from general news reporting by an in-depth investigation, analysis, interpretation, or opinion commentary. Most

Variable	Name	Column	Code	Explanation
				stories in news magazines are featured news. News commentaries and analyses written by columnists whose columns appear daily in the same paper will be included elsewhere (see code 5).
				Note: A simple rule to follow in distinguishing general news from featured news in *Time* and *Newsweek* is to code as featured news (code 2) stories that are approximately one page or longer. Code as general news reports (code 1) stories that appear side by side with other stories on a single page.
			3	Featured human interest story: More or less detailed coverage of various human interest stories with emotional, personal, or humorous slant. Most of the stories in special sections fit into this category (for example, "A complete guide to roasting your holiday turkey"; "Do the wealthy pay their bills like the rest of us?").
			4	Editorials: Stories that represent views and opinions of the publisher or editor with or without names. The stories generally appear on the editorial page.
			5	Columnist section: Distinguished from other types by regular (daily or weekly) appearance, a distinct outline that physically separates the column from other stories on the same page, and/or a unique column name (frequently columnist's own name).

Variable	Name	Column	Code	Explanation
			6	Letters and public opinion polls: Letters from readers, reports on the results of public opinion polls, or opinions directly quoted or written by individual citizens (for example, "Letters" in *Tribune* and *Newsweek*; "Forum" in *Time.*
			7	Drawings, cartoons, political comics: Drawings, cartoons, or political comics are coded as independent stories unless they appear as part of another main story.
9	Picture size	15		Picture size will be measured by multiplying width in inches by length in inches. Code according to one of the following categories:
			0	No picture
			1	3 square inches or smaller
			2	3.1 through 12.0 square inches
			3	12.1 through 24.0 square inches
			4	24.1 through 40.0 square inches
			5	40.1 through 60.0 square inches
			6	60.1 square inches or larger
				When a story is accompanied by one or more pictures or drawings, indicate the picture size by combining the sizes of the individual pictures.
				Exclude words that explain a picture in measuring picture size. In some columns the picture of the columnist is attached to the column's name or included in a box together with the column's name (see Figure A1 for examples). In these cases code the picture as part of the headline, not as a picture. However, if the

FIGURE A.1
Examples: Headline with Picture

Vernon Jarrett

What if Brown never happened?

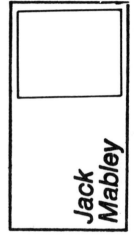

Jack Mabley

Variable	Name	Column	Code	Explanation
				columnist's picture appears distinctly apart from the column name, code it as a picture, not as part of the headline.
10	Headline size	16-17	01-99	Headline size and story length are coded by multiplying the column width by length in inches.
11	Story length	18-21	0001-9999	See 140-48 for detailed instructions on column width and measuring headlines and stories.
12	blank			
13		24-26	Codes	Instructions for selecting categories:
14	Subject	27-28	appear	gories:
15		30-32	on	1. Up to three subjects may be
			pages	coded for each story. The num-
			149-56	ber of categories per story will depend on the complexity of the story.

2. When a story concerns more than one subject category, code the most salient and important theme first, and the remaining themes in descending order of importance. When themes are of equal importance, code them in random order.

3. Code foreign/international stories that are political by region (see subject categories 112-118). Nonpolitical foreign/international stories will be coded as if they were ordinary domestic stories. By combining the subject categories with the impact level (5 or 6), a story can be identified as domestic, international, or foreign.

4. Code combined stories as follows:

Combined story for special section − 500

Variable	Name	Column	Code	Explanation
				Combined story for business section — 400
				Combined story for special columns — depends on the dominant theme, for example, "Action Line" in *Tribune*, 500; "Newsmakers" in *Daily News*, 401, 402, or both; "People" in *Time*, 401, 402, or both.
				5. New subject categories may be created after careful appraisal and consultation with the project director. Use the space on the far right of the coding sheet to jot down any uncertainty or ambiguity regarding coding.
16	Impact level	33		Refers to the geographic area to which a story is relevant, meaningful, or important.
				The geographic origin of the story does not necessarily determine its impact level. For example, stories on New York City's financial trouble should be coded as having national impact.
			1	Local: Stories largely limited to one particular city, county, or intraurban area (for example, local election campaign in Chicago).
			2	State: Stories with potential impact on entire state (for example, Illinois governor versus Chicago mayor on education fund issue).
			3	Regional: Stories relevant to people in several adjacent states, but not nationally significant (for example, East Coast storms, West Coast fires).

Variable	Name	Column	Code	Explanation
			4	National: Stories important to entire U.S. population.
			5	International: Stories involving two or more countries including United States (for example, Ford visits China).
			6	Foreign: Stories involving foreign countries and not directly related to United States (for example, India-China trade).
			7	All: Stories of general human interest (for example, people, food, sports, and other stories, with no geographic implications). Include in this category combined stories in special columnists' sections (for example, "Newsmakers," "Action Line"). These stories cannot be categorized into any one impact level because of the different impact levels of individual items within the story.
17	Local relevance	34	0 (X)	Stories that are not directly concerned with people in the local area (Chicago, Indianapolis, Lebanon).
			1	Stories that are directly concerned with or relevant to people in the local area. Note: National, international, foreign, and all impact level stories should not be coded in this column.
18		35-36	Codes	Instructions for recording topics:
19	Topic	37-38	appear	1. Up to three topics may be
20		39-40	on pp.	coded for each story. Topic
		41-80	149-57	codes are identical to topic categories used to code individual interviews. They represent a refinement of the subject

Variable	Name	Column	Code	Explanation
				categories, which was added to permit better coordination between topics mentioned by interviewees and media presentations.

2. To retain information on the content of each story, record the headline or a brief written summary in columns 41-80.

3. For 1976 election stories, specify the names of the candidates involved (for example, Walker's tax plan, Reagan's conservatism). ·

4. For items related to international/foreign policy, specify the names of countries (for example, United States-Japanese trade).

5. If an item contains several topics, some of them with code numbers and some without (because interviewees did not mention them), code only the items that have numbers. Record the remainder in writing.

MEASURING COLUMN WIDTH, HEADLINE SIZE, AND STORY LENGTH

Column Width

1. Size of headline and stories are measured by multiplying the width in columns by length in inches.

2. Columns may vary in width. Column width is found by determining how many columns of the same width would fit on one page. Use the following rules to simplify measurement:

Paper/Magazine	Number of Identical Columns per Page	Width of Single Column
Tribune, Daily News	6 or 8	1
	4 or 5	2
Sun-Times	5 or 6	1
	3 or 4	2
Time, Newsweek	3 or 4	1
	2	2

Adapt this format for other publications.

Length: General Instructions

1. To find the length of a headline or story, round off to the nearest whole inch (for example, 3.5 becomes 4; 5.2 becomes 5).

2. If a headline or story is less than 0.5 inch long, count as 0.1.

Note: As mentioned previously, stories shorter than 3 column inches (columns x inches), inclusive of headline and picture, will not be coded.

Headline Size

1. When there is more than one headline per story, count only the largest headline.

2. If, however, the subheadline(s), including the names of reporter, writer, or column, appear next to the main headline without any intervening text, count them as part of the main headline (see Figure A2 for examples).

3. Measure only the letters and blank space to the right or left of the headline within the appropriate column width. Do not measure blank space above or below headline.

4. If a columnist's picture is attached to the headline, measure the picture as part of the headline. (See the Coding Directory, Variable 9, for instructions.)

5. Headlines that run across an entire page are counted as width 8.

Story Size

1. If a story is extremely long, as in combined stories of special sections, estimate the percentage of each page that is devoted to the story, add the percentages for all pages of the story (or combined stories), and multiply the total by the size of the page (in column inches). The size of each page for the *Tribune* and *Daily News* is 168 column inches, 84 for the *Sun-Times*, and 44 for *Time* and *Newsweek*.

FIGURE A.2
Examples: Measurement of Headline Size

Column 1

Graduation—
but first, a
word from...

Speakers seek 'issue'
on commencement trail

1(COLUMN) × 2(INCHES) = 2

Kissinger stumbles
on diplomatic no-no

2(COLUMN) × 1(INCH) = 2

For example, if the total number of pages for stories in special sections of the *Tribune* (calculated by summing the percentages per page devoted to stories) is 17, the story length will be: 168 column inches times 17 (pages) = 2,586 column inches.

2. Include names of reporters in measuring story length.

Special instructions for *Time* and *Newsweek:*

1. Measure headlines for *Time* and *Newsweek* by the method used for newspapers, that is, multiply column width by length in inches.

2. Since headlines in *Time* and *Newsweek* do not vary much in size, do not code the size if under 2 column inches. Consider them part of the story length.

3. Measure story length for *Time* and *Newsweek* by the method specified above for measuring special sections in newspapers. The percentage of each page devoted to the story, excluding nonstories, will be multiplied by the total size of each page (44). If a story is longer than one page, multiply the sum of the percentages per page devoted to the story by the size of each page.

Use the table in Figure A3 to simplify measurement of headlines and stories.

CODING EXAMPLES

The following examples (Figures A4 to A7) were selected to show different types of stories and the coding of picture size, story length, topic, subject categories, impact level, and relevance to Chicago. Name of paper, date, month, year, story number, page, and section are omitted.

FIGURE A.3
Headline Story Length Measured by Column x Inch

LENGTH (INCH)	WIDTH (COLUMN)										
	1	2	3	4	5	6	7	8	9	10	11
.1	.1	.2	.3	.4	.5	.6	.7	.8	.9	1	1.1
1	1	2	3	4	5	6	7	8	9 .	10	11
2	2	4	6	8	10	12	14	16	18	20	22
3	3	6	9	12	15	18	21	24	27	30	33
4	4	8	12	16	20	24	28	32	36	40	44
5	5	10	15	20	25	30	35	40	45	50	55
6	6	12	18	24	30	36	42	48	54	60	66
7	7	14	21	28	35	42	49	56	63	70	77

FIGURE A.4

Provident settles for 340-bed unit

By James Pearre

PROVIDENT HOSPITAL'S board has dropped a two-year-old plan for a 500-bed replacement hospital, approving an alternate proposal for a 340-bed facility with provision for future expansion to 500 beds.

John Sengstacke, Provident board chairman, said the first stage of the project will cost an estimated $63 million, $30 million less than the former 500-bed proposal.

The savings includes elimination of an underground parking garage, use of the existing, 200-bed hospital for outpatient clinics and offices, and lower interest on construction loans, Sengstacke said.

Sengstacke confirmed Wednesday that the two-stage project was approved July 7. He said he had hoped to delay announcing it until approval is obtained from the federal Department of Health, Education and Welfare [HEW] for a federally guaranteed construction loan.

HEW EARLIER REFUSED a Provident application for a $63.5-million loan to to build the 500-bed hospital, offering instead to approve $40 million in loans and grants for a 300-bed facility.

"HEW now is talking about a loan in the area of $35 million, but negotiations' are not complete and we still have to obtain state approval of the new plan," Sengstacke said.

The new hospital is to be built on a site immediately east of Provident's present building at 426 E. 51st St. Efforts to replace the obsolete facility began in 1971, when the state Department of Public Health warned that it did not meet fire and safety codes. The state could close the old hospital if construc-

John Sengstacke

tion of a new facility is not begin by Dec. 31.

Provident officials originally laid plans for a 300-bed replacement but increased the size to 500 beds at the urging of Dr. James G. Haughton, executive director of the county Health and Hospitals Governing Commission. Haughton agreed last year to provide staff and financial support to Provident and to phase out 200 beds at Cook County Hospital if the 500-bed Provident replacement was built.

Friction between the Provident and Cook County Hospital staffs and lack of funds in the County Hospital budget has stalled implementation of the agreement.

- **TOPIC = "NEW HOSPITAL UNIT"**
- **TYPE = 1**
- **SUBJECT CATEGORY = 212**
- **PICTURE SIZE = 2**
- **IMPACT LEVEL = 1**
- **HEADLINE SIZE = 2**
- **RELEVANCE TO CHICAGO = 1**
- **STORY LENGTH = 8(1×8)**

FIGURE A.5

India and Pakistan resume ties despite Delhi-Dacca crisis

From Tribune Wire Services

INDIA AND Pakistan agreed to exchange ambassadors after four years of rivalry Friday, but a crisis developed along India's northeast frontier as 300,000 Bengalis were reported gathering for a march on the India-Bangladesh border to protest diversion of the Ganges River.

Statements released in both Islamabad and New Delhi announced the reestablishment of diplomatic relations at the ambassadorial level following a week of negotiations.

India and Pakistan broke relations during the war of December, 1971, which Pakistan lost, and which saw the creation of Bangladesh from the former East Pakistan.

THE NEW DELHI government warned Bangladesh Friday for the second time in two days not to allow a leftist-led mass march into Indian territory in the dispute over the River Ganges.

Reports from across the border said followers of 97-year-old Bangladesh leftist Maulana Bhashani were grouping for the march on the Farakka Dam 10 miles inside India on the Ganges.

The leftists reportedly have vowed to "demolish" the dam.

Indian Foreign office spokesman Sheel Haksar told newsmen:

"All necessary measures are being taken to meet the situation arising from the threatened march on Farakka by Maulana Bhashani and his followers . . . In any event, it is the responsibility of the Bangladesh government to see that there is no violation of international border by its nationals."

THE INDIAN government Thursday ordered its border security forces to throw back the Bangladesh marchers if they crossed into India.

The Farakka Dam has become a bone of contention between the two nations since the assassination of the pro-Indian Bangladesh President Sheik Mujibur Rahman last August.

Tribune Map
Cross marks site of Farakka Dam

India put the dam into operation two months ago to divert river water to the Calcutta port in the lean summer months.

BANGLADESH PROTESTED the Indian move and said it was done without its consent. The Dacca government alleged that the diversion of water caused the drying up its irrigation canals and crops and also resulted in a serious drinking water shortage for its people living along the river.

In the Bangladesh capital, Rear Adm. Mosharraf Hossain Khan, naval chief in charge of flood control and water resources, expressed surprise over what he called India's "baseless charges and allegations."

He said the march would be a peaceful expression of "the people's sentiment."

* * * * *

- TYPE = 1
- PICTURE SIZE = 2
- HEADLINE SIZE = 4
- STORY LENGTH = 10 (1×10)
- TOPIC = "INDIA AND PAKISTAN RESUME TIES"
- SUBJECT CATEGORY = 115
- IMPACT LEVEL = 6
- RELEVANCE TO CHICAGO = X

FIGURE A.6

Claes Oldenburg

Oldenburg sculpture on baseball set

By Alan G. Artner

CLAES OLDENBURG is bringing a baseball bat to Chicago.

The locally trained artist whose work is noted for its whimsy has created a 100-foot high red steel sculpture called "Batcolumn" for the new Social Security Administration Program Center, 600 W. Madison St.

Scheduled for "unveiling" late in the fall, "Batcolumn" is an open latticework structure whose crisscrossing steel makes a diamond pattern, at once suggesting the baseball diamond and batter's cage.

Oldenburg said his work "could be called a monument, both to baseball and to the construction industry," as well as "to the ambition and vigor Chicago likes to see in itself."

THE PIECE IS being constructed at Lippincott, Inc., a steel foundry in New Haven, Conn. At its widest point, it will be 12 feet in diameter and will rest on a four-foot high steel base in front of the center's Madison Street side.

In addition, the main lobby will have a 50 by 14-foot abstract mural by Ilya Bolotowsky, the famed Russian-American painter.

"Batcolumn" was commissioned for $100,000 under the General Services Administration's art-in-architecture program to place contemporary American art in new federal buildings. Chicago's first GSA artwork was Alexander Calder's "Flamingo," erected on Dearborn Street in 1974.

- TYPE = 1

- PICTURE SIZE = 2

- HEADLINE SIZE = 1

  STORY LENGTH = 6(1×6)

- TOPIC = "OLDENBURG BASEBALL SCULPTURE"

- SUBJECT CATEGORY = 403

- IMPACT LEVEL = 1

- RELEVANCE TO CHICAGO = 1

FIGURE A.7

Action line

Q—I bought a car cover from Warshawsky & Co., a year ago last January. The cover was guaranteed against cold, rain, drying out, and fading. A large rainfall a month later proved this wasn't so, as the cover leaked. I called the company and was told the cover would be replaced but that it would take a few months because it was a factory item. It wasn't until December that I received the second cover. This one didn't leak but stuck to the car. I had to wait until the snow melted before I could remove it. When I did, I discovered it had ruined the paint job. I began calling the company about filing a claim with their insurance company. The customer relations department was very helpful but was unable to get an answer. In the meantime, my car began to rust. Is there a way Action Line can help get this settled?
George Street, Bensenville

A—We have been told that your insurance company will pay for the new paint job. Marge Brychel, special contact manager at Warshawsky & Co., is presently trying to reorder a new cover for you. There is going to be another wait, however, because the item has to be ordered from the manufacturer in California.

Q—Our 14-year-old son recently purchased a glass-blown item from the Glass Blowing Shoppe in the Woodfield Shopping Center. He had purchased the item as a gift but it was unacceptable. When he tried to return it for a refund, he was told that there wouldn't be one. After several calls and visits to the shop, we were told to contact the owner who lives in Indiana. We've written and called but have received no acknowledgment whatsoever from him. Shouldn't store owners be obligated to inform minors of any restrictive policies when purchasing anything? He was not told there would be no refunds and now he has to pay the $10.71 item. Can you help us? Richard W., Palatine

A—The Glass Blowing Shoppe has a sign near the cash register which says "no refunds". Since your son did not take notice of it, the shop cannot make any exceptions. The store, however, is willing to accept the item and issue a different one of the same value.

Q—I wonder why the Water Tower and pumping station on either side of Michigan Avenue have been allowed to fall into such disrepair. As landmarks of our city, all one sees is a fine example of architecture that has paint peeling from the window sashes and doors. The windows are no longer glazed but now have plywood coverings. The sidewalks are cracked and broken. I hope those responsible for maintaining these landmarks will hasten to correct the situation soon.
Gilbert Marcus, Chicago

A—The maintenance of the Water Tower and pumping station falls under the jurisdiction of the city's Department of Water and Sewers. Commissioner Richard Pavia tells us he will inspect the structures and do

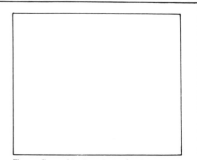

The peeling paint of a city landmark.

all necessary minor repairs. We were also told new windows are being installed, which is the reason for the plywood coverings. "We also have plans to replace the shrubbery, which is an annual event," Pavia said. A new copper roof was installed last year. A revision of the sidewalk layout is being considered. Even routine upkeep of the sandstone structures is difficult because it is very porous and subject to weather conditions. Pavia says experiments with preservatives have not been successful. Sandstone blocks are replaced from a supply the city has from structures torn down in the past.

Q—You answered a question about the music in "Peanuts;" how about answering a question about music for me? Could you please tell me the name of the symphony music that's played in the old "Flash Gordon" series? Janice T., Palatine

A—The music most often used in the Flash Gordon serials was Franz Liszt's "Les Preludes" and Richard Wagner's "Ride of the Valkyries," The Record Center, 1614 S. Pulaski Rd., informed us. Both items are on hand at The Record Center if you wish to order them. The Liszt composition is in an album titled "Liszt's Greatest Hits," and sells for $6.98. The Wagner tune is in the album "The Sound of Wagner," and sells for $3.98.

Sound off

This is in regards to the ruling that people who work for a city must live in the city. There may be some merit for this but it creates a lot of hardship for some who are close to retirement. This is a Supreme Court ruling. Mayor Daley, who is a strong supporter of this issue, forgets that he is closely guarded by men who are constantly at his side. Also, his kids are no longer in school. He should remember that those he forces to move back into the city will then have a vote. These votes can be used against "his honor."
R. K., Valparaiso, Ind.

- TYPE = 5
- PICTURE SIZE = 2
- HEADLINE SIZE = 2
- STORY LENGTH = 26(2×13)

- TOPIC="ACTION LINE"
- SUBJECT CATEGORY = 500
- IMPACT LEVEL = 7
- RELEVANCE TO CHICAGO = X

SUBJECT CODES (Variables 13, 14, 15)

Code Number	Explanation	Example
Political/Government Stories: Stories related to broad public concern, actually or potentially involved with governmental action of the United States related to domestic affairs (101-111), foreign affairs (112-118), election (119, 123), and other political stories (199, 200)		
100	General discussion of foreign affairs, no area focus mentioned	
101	The president and his public, official activities	"Ford to tell NY aid" (101, 304)
102	Former U.S. presidents and their public, official activities	"Kennedy assassination" (102, 204, 206)
103	Cabinet members and their performances (vice-president, secretaries, attorney general)	"Rumsfeld confirmed as Defense Chief" (103, 108)
104	Congress, Senate, and their activities	"Senate cuts missile system" (104, 108)
105	Other federal government officials and their activities (ambassadors and the like)	"US Ambassador to UN meets with Ford" (105, 118)
106	State government, legislatures, and their performances	"Governor Walker vetoes education bill" (106)
107	Local city government, mayor, city council, and their activities	"Mayor's proposal for 1976 budget" (107)
108	National defense, military-army, and other defense-related stories	"New missile system in California" (108)
109	Security-related stories such as stories on police departments, FBI, CIA, military security, and so forth	"Senate report on CIA" (109, 104)
110	Judicial systems of all levels, their performances, legal issues involved with court, law and justice	"Illinois Supreme Court tryout" (110)
111	Other domestic-national politics	"HEW agricultural policy" (111)

149

Code Number	Explanation	Example
112	U.S. foreign policy, international politics, international war, domestic issues of foreign nations, with or without direct involvement of United States, concerned with nations in Western Europe and Commonwealth, including Canada, Australia, and New Zealand	"Western Summit meeting" (112) "Ford-Wilson Talk in London" (112) "London bombing" (112)
113	Same as 112, concerned with nation(s) in Eastern Europe, including Soviet Union and other Communist bloc countries	"Detente and Kissinger's foreign policy" (113, 103)
114	Same as above, chiefly concerned with one or more nations in the Middle East, including Arab countries, Israel, and Turkey	"Saudi Arab aid plan halted" (114) "Arab-Israel dispute" (114) "US bars PLO in Geneva" (114)
115	Same as above, concerned with nation(s) in Asia, including People's Republic of China, Taiwan, India, South and North Korea, Japan, Vietnam, Thailand, Laos, and so on	"Inflation in Japan" (115) "Ford visits China" (115, 101)
116	Same as above, concerned with nation(s) in Africa	"South African force at Angola" (116)
117	Same as above, but concerned with nation(s) in Latin America	"Peron ousts cabinet" (117)
118	Same as above, concerned with nation(s) in more than one region as categorized above, including activities of such international organizations as UN, OPEC, NATO, and so on	"UN votes against Zionism" (118, 114)
119	Stories directly related to 1976 election (general and local levels), campaign activities, and other related stories	"Reagan's conservatism" (119) "Ford's visit to the South" (119) "Hartigan to seek Secretary of State nomination" (119)

120	Actual or alleged crime/other illegal activities of political institutions or of politicians	"Tax fraud by Nixon" (120, 102) "CIA assassination attempt revealed" (120, 109) "Watergate trial" (120)
121	Discussion of political ideologies	"Ford calls Reagan too conservative to win" (121)
122	General discussion of bureaucracy when no specific governmental level is mentioned	"The government is riddled with red tape" (122)
123	Stories related to elections other than 1976 election	"Analysis of election patterns in 1972" (123)
124	Military politics	"Influence of military on foreign policy" (124)
125	Leadership	"This country is in a crisis of leadership. We need more strong leaders" (125)
126	President-elect stories	Carter activities between election and inauguration (126)
199	Other political stories that do not belong to any of the above categories	"Essay: America – Past, Present, Future" (199)
200	Discussion of domestic politics in general	"Politics in the US has become very confusing" (200)

Societal Stories: Stories concerned with matters of social issues, problems, activities; stories related to minority groups (201-203); social problems involved with unlawful activities (204-206); and other social phenomena (207-217, 299)

201	Racial issues and related stories directly involved with the black population	"FBI's effort to smear Dr. King revealed" (201, 109)
202	Issues involved with women's rights	"ERA activities" (202) "Abortion law" (202)
203	Stories related to other minority groups	"Mexican-Americans" (203) "Illegal immigrants from South America" (203)
204	Crime, terrorism, and violence directly related to small or large groups of individuals that are politically antiestablishment	"SLA terrorism" (204) "London bombing" (204, 112) "Kidnapping of Patricia Hearst by SLA" (204)

Code Number	Explanation	Example
205	Individual crime, violence (murder, burglary, robbery, rape, arson, bombing, and so forth), and organized crime syndicates (Mafia)	"Mafia today" (205) "Crime in Indianapolis reduced last year" (205)
206	Gun control issues and related stories	"Should handguns be banned by law?" (206) "Gun manufacturers lobbying" (206)
207	Hard-drug-related stories	"3 arrested for drug-abuse" (207) "Legalization of Marijuana" (207)
208	Strikes, demonstrations concerned with labor problems, labor unions	"Suburban doctors on strike" (208, 212) "Northwest Airline on strike" (208, 210)
209	Issues related to environmental protection (for example, air pollution, animal protection)	"Pollution of Lake Michigan" (209)
210	Stories related to transportation and traffic	"CTA on strike" (210, 208) "Holiday traffic jam" (210)
211	Accidents and natural disasters (for example, traffic accidents, fire, flood, earthquake, storm)	"Woodfire at Los Angeles" (211) "2 cars collide on Lebanon highway" (211)
212	Medicine, medical activities, and organizations, other health-related social issues	"Quinlan Case: Let Live or Die?" (212) "Doctor's malpractice" (212)
213	Religious groups, their activities, and other religion-related stories	"World Council of Religion" (213) "First woman priest" (213, 202)
214	Schools, education, and other stories related to education	"Chicago public schools" (214) "Teachers on strike" (214, 208)
215	Press, journalism activities, including radio-TV news and other journalistic programs, related stories	"Latin staff needed for better coverage of minority group" (215, 203) "Press-Government relationship" (215, 199)
216	Stories related to family life, for example, effects of divorce on children, interracial adoption, permissiveness	"Series on runaway wives" (216)

152

217	Social injustice	"Ability of rich to get good lawyers — get off from stiff sentences" (217)
218	Bicentennial stories	"NBC Bicentennial series" (218)
219	Postal/telephone service	"Stories on communications services" (219)
220	Agriculture and agricultural activities	Problems of farmers, crops, and so forth (220) "Farm exports decline" (220, 305)
225	Space exploration	Satellites, Mars exploration, and so forth (225)
299	Other stories on social problems and issues	"American Civil Liberties Union helps open US files" (299, 199)
300	General discussion of social issues	"Social issues ignored in 1976 election" (300, 119)

Economy/Business Stories: Stories concerned with money, economic activities, economic state of individuals, groups, corporations, problems in the business world, business crime, international business transactions, other money-related stories

301	General economic state of individual citizens or the country — such as stories concerning inflation, living costs, salary, unemployment, taxes	"Meat prices rise" (301) "US economy 1977" (301) "Unemployment rate down" (301)
302	Energy policy, energy research, other energy-related stories, including gasoline-fuel price	"Sea power energy plan" (302) "New energy legislation criticized as unrealistic" (302) "Oil companies meet" (302)
303	Housing problems, housing policy, other housing-related stories, hotels	"Redlining in Indianapolis" (303) "Housing construction becomes active" (303)
304	Financial issues directly related to public, governmental, or other organizations	"NY City's financial crisis" (304) "Dam project over cost" (304)
305	Business transactions, issues in the business world, other business-related stories, including international trades	"General Motors' financial trouble" (305) "US-Japan trade more active" (305)

153

Code Number	Explanation	Example
306	Business crime, illegal business transactions, and so on	"Illegal contribution of Gulf Oil to politicians" (306, 119, 120)
307	Consumer protection stories, for example, checks on taxis	"Mislabeling, poor service, etc." (307, 120)
308	Stock market news	(Only where this is a regular story) (308)
399	Other money-related stories	"Illinois lottery" (399)
400	Combined business/money-related stories	"Business gains increase" (400)

Human Interest Stories: Stories concerned with people and their lifestyle, various cultural activities, including sports and entertainment, hobbies and games, and other leisure activities; other human interest stories; combined stories concerning human interests.

Code Number	Explanation	Example
401	Touching, interest arousing, or shocking stories, rumors, and gossip about current or past politicians' and their families' private lives; political gossip	"Ford family adopts 2 Vietnamese orphans" (401) "John Dean's wife publishes a book on Watergate" (401) "Kissinger on golf course" (401)
402	Same as above, concerned with people other than politicians	"Liz and Burton remarried" (402) "Ali and his wife fight in Manila" (402)
403	Cultural activities and entertainment; people engaged in such performances as art, music, theater, ballet, books, science, humanities, academics, religion, architecture, poetry, TV-radio entertainment and cultural programs, sports, movies, and so on	"TV networks' fall season programs" (403) "Ali's victory" (403) "Architectural innovation in Chicago" (403)
404	Hobbies, leisure activities such as travel, gourmet foods, games, drinks, and so forth	"Winter tourists in Hawaii" (404) "Games for holidays" (404)

Note: Categories 401-404 should be used only when the human interest items appear in regular sections. For coding of special sections, see instructions on p. 132.

154

406	Regular discussion of weather other than disaster conditions	"Trend toward colder winters" (406)
407	Discussion of sports events	Olympics, tennis matches, and so on (407)
499	Other human interest stories	"Baby Panda born in Zoo" (499)
500	Combined human interest stories	Combined special sections (500), special columns, for example, "Action line"

155

TOPIC CODES (Variables 18, 19, 20)

Code	Explanation
	Government Stories — General
06	Government credibility
08	Size of government
· 20	National defense
23	Communism
26	Urban problems
41	Corruption
43	Philosophical issues
47	Domestic problems
	Government Stories — Elections
16	Gerald Ford
33	Ronald Reagan
35	Elections
45	Campaign finances
51	Jimmy Carter
52	Walter Mondale
53	Robert Dole
54	Hubert Humphrey
55	Sargent Shriver
56	Fred Harris
57	Birch Bayh
58	Morris Udall
59	Henry Jackson
60	George Wallace
61	Edward Kennedy
62	Eugene McCarthy
63	Frank Church
64	Jerry Brown
65	Richard Schweiker
	Government Stories — Foreign Affairs
13	Foreign affairs/world affairs
14	Foreign aid
42	U.S. prestige
48	Panama Canal

Code	Explanation
	Social Issues
01	Welfare
02	Pollution
04	Elderly/social security
05	Crime
11	Education
17	Unions/labor
19	Environment
22	Health care
24	Busing
25	Individual rights
27	Poverty
29	Racial problems/immigrants
30	Population
34	Women's liberation
38	Malpractice
39	Alcohol, drugs
40	Abortion, Right to Life
44	General social services
46	Minority problems
	Economy and Business
03	Taxes
07	Government spending
09	Energy
10	Unemployment
12	Inflation/recession (stagflation)
15	Personal income
18	Fuel shortage
21	Big business
28	General economy
32	Housing/rent
36	Food crisis
49	Socialism
	Human Interest, Miscellaneous
31	Other
37	Personal defense
50	There are none
98	Don't know
99	Have not discussed

Appendix B

TELEVISION CODEBOOK

CODING UNIT

1. The basic coding units are the story and the episode within a story.

2. A story is an item with a common theme, for example, 1976 election or airport bombing, told without intervening stories on different themes.

3. A story may discuss several subthemes. For example, a story on the main theme "1976 election" may run as follows: after the subtheme, "Ford's press interviews," the newscast may turn to the second subtheme, "Reagan's campaign in the South," and to the third subtheme, "Recent public opinion polls." Similarly, the same speaker, for example, President Ford, may be shown at separate campaign affairs, for example, first at a press conference, then at a meeting of farmers, then at a college rally. In both cases, each of the distinct subthemes will be defined as an episode and will be coded individually. In network abstracts supplied by the Vanderbilt Television Archives, stories are identified by underlined headings; episodes are separate paragraphs under these headings.

4. When the introductory or concluding comment by the television reporter is merely a lead-in into the story or a summation of the story told by others, the introduction and windup are counted as part of the subtheme that they complement.

When the television reporter's story has substantial additional data, it counts as a separate episode. When the reporter's story is interrupted by two or more subthemes, but then concludes the initial discussion, it is counted as one episode.

5. Subthemes (episodes) in weather reports and sports stories will not be coded individually, but will be collapsed into one story.

6. Sometimes, at the beginning of a news program, reporters introduce a limited number of major headlines before starting their reports. These announcements will not be considered as part of the stories, but as attention drawing factors. (See Variable 8, "Presence of Headline," for coding instructions.)

7. The following portions of news programs will be excluded from the analysis:

    a. Commercials

    b. Beginning and closing statements (for example, "Good evening . . ." or "That's the way it was . . ."

c. Jokes, gags, or other conversations of reporters that are not related to any particular news story or episode

8. National network news will be coded from abstracts, rather than from live telecasts. Special directions for this "Abstract Coding" are provided throughout the coding directory.

CODING DIRECTORY

Variable	Name	Coumn	Code	Explanation
1	Network	1-2	02	CBS local news
			05	NBC local news
			07	ABC local news
			12	CBS network news
			15	NBC network news
			17	ABC network news
2	Date	3-4	01-31	Day of month
3	Month	5-6	01-12	January-December
4	Year	7		Code last numeral only
			6	1976
			7	1977
5	Story number	10-11	01-99	Each story is given an identification number corresponding to the sequential order of presentation. Each program is coded separately.
6	Episode number	12-13	01-99	Number each episode within each story according to its sequential position.
7	Story/episode length	14-16	001-999	Actual number of seconds of broadcast time for a story (which has only one episode in it), or for an episode (if the story has more than one episode). Episode length is unavailable in abstracts; as an approximation, divide total story time by number of episodes and code episode time accordingly.

160

8	Headline presence	17	As limited numbers of major items are introduced in the headline, it will be assumed that those items receive more emphasis than other items.
			Blank
		0	No headline announced in program.
		1	Headline announced, but particular story not mentioned.
			Headline announced, particular story mentioned.
9	Mode of	18	Up to three modes may be coded for each story or episode.
10	visual	19	
11	presentation	20	
		1	Newsroom/studio
		2	Graphics/photos
		3	Film
		9	Other
			For abstracts, code "3" unless abstract is marked (S) to indicate studio. Code "2" only if it is specifically noted.
12	Mode of	21	Up to three modes may be coded for each story or episode.
13	verbal	22	
14	presentation	23	
		1	Narration by reporter
		2	Question/answer or interview
		3	Formal speech/conference
		4	Chatter
		5	Filmed conversation
		9	Other
			Material in brackets in abstracts should be coded "2" except when different coding is explicitly indicated.

161

Variable	Name	Column	Code	Explanation
15	Type of story	24	1	News reporting
			2	Commentaries/editorials
16	Reporter	25		Up to three categories of reporters may be coded for each story
17		26		or episode.
18		27	1	Anchor
			2	Field reporter
			3	Reporter in studio
19	Subject	28-30	Codes appear	Instructions for selecting categories: See Appendix A,
20		31-33	on pp. 149-55	Variables 13-15.
21		34-35	in Appendix A.	
22	Impact level	37	1-7	Instructions for selecting categories: See Appendix A, Variable 16.
23	Local relevance	40	0-1	Instructions for selecting categories: See Appendix A,
			x	Variable 17
24	Topic	41-42	Codes appear	Instructions for selecting categories: See Appendix A,
25		43-44	on pp. 156-57	Variables 18, 19, 20.
26		45-46	in Appendix A.	
		47-80		

Appendix C

CRIME STORY CODEBOOK

GENERAL CODING INFORMATION

Crime news to be coded includes all U.S. news about infractions of criminal law involving injury to persons and property. It also includes stories about crime prevention, general discussions of the crime problem, stories about the police that relate to its crime-fighting mission, and stories about the criminal justice system. General discussions of policies to deal with crime, such as gun control, reform of the parole system, the status of the death penalty, and the like, are also considered crime news. Traffic offenses are excluded.

Coding is designed to gain information about the images of crime depicted in the mass media through selective attention to various types of crime and various aspects of crime. It is most detailed in those areas that are most likely to be noticed by the average reader. Where stories discuss several crimes, coding follows the main thrust of the story. No distinctions are made between alleged or suspected criminal activity and proven criminal activity. Coding is based on story content rather than the coder's knowledge of facts that might have been incorporated into the story but were omitted. However, in stories involving the criminal justice process, the alleged crime should be coded; details about the crime, criminal, and victims should be omitted.

CODING DIRECTORY

Variable	Name	Column	Code	Explanation
1	Name of newspaper/ magazine	1	1	*Tribune*
			2	*Sun-Times*
			3	*Daily News*
			4	*Time*
			5	*Newsweek*
			6	*Evanston Review*
2	Date	2-3	01-31	Day of month
3	Month	4-5	01-12	January-December
4	Year	6		Code last numeral only
			6	1976
			7	1977
5	Story number	7-8	01-99	Stories are numbered to correspond to numbers used for *Chicago Tribune* general coding.
6	Page number	9-10	01-99	When a story appears on more than one page, or when the headline appears on the front page and the main body is elsewhere, code the page number on which the main body appears.
7	Section number	11-12	01-99	Code by section numbers provided by the paper. If no section numbers are given (as in *Sun-Times*), assign section numbers consecutively.
8	Nature of story	15-16		Each story will be categorized according to its major emphasis. Use narrowest applicable category.
			1	General discussion of crime
			2	Specific crime(s)

3	Combination of general discussion and specific discussion
4	Crime fighting in general (includes crime statistics stories)
5	Crime prevention
6	Mafia
7	Crime syndicate
8	Gang violence
9	Juvenile delinquency
10	Confidence games
11	Biography of criminals – predominantly successful (do not code crime incidents separately)
12	Biography of criminals – predominantly unsuccessful
13	Biography of criminals – mixed success
14	Free press – fair trial – general discussion (or both pro and con)
15	Free press – fair trial – pro
16	Free press – fair trial – con
17	Police activities – general (or both favorable and unfavorable) (exclude personnel activities such as pay, hiring, union activities except when specifically related to crime-fighting activities)
18	Police activities – favorable appraisal
19	Police activities – unfavorable appraisal
20	Prison reform – pro
21	Prison reform – con
22	Prison reform – mixed
23	Criminal justice process, other than police activities
24	Prison escape or attempted escape
25	Prison riot
26	Terrorism

Variable	Name	Column	Code	Explanation	
			27	Court reform	
			28	Criminal law changes, proposed and actual	
			29	Nonspecific, general discussion of pretrial or trial procedures	
			30	Police violation of civil rights of citizens	
			31	Support for victims of crime	
			32	Prison conditions	
			33	Victims of crime – specific incidents	
9	Nature of	17-18		Three crimes may be coded. Select in order of emphasis. When more	
10	alleged crime	19-20		than two crimes are mentioned to some extent, use columns 21-22	
11		21-22		for combination codes:	
			01	Murder, nonnegligent manslaughter	(A)
			02	Negligent manslaughter	(A)
			03	Rape	(A)
			04	Assassination attempt	(A)
			05	Robbery	(A)
			06	Aggravated assault/battery	(A)
			07	Burglary, breaking or entering	(B)
			08	Larceny-theft	(B)
			09	Motor vehicle theft	(B)
			10	Kidnapping	(A)
			11	Piracy/hijacking	(B)
			12	Extortion	(C)
			13	Other assault	(C)
			14	Arson	(C)
			15	Forgery and counterfeiting	(C)
			16	Fraud/consumer deceit/disservice	(C)
			17	Embezzlement	(C)

166

18	Bribery/kickbacks/payoffs	(C)
19	Corrupt practices ("deals")	(C)
20	Dealing in stolen property	(C)
21	Vandalism	(C)
22	Weapons violations	(C)
23	Escape from custody	(C)
24	Parole violation	(C)
25	Illegal wiretapping	(C)
26	Prostitution, commercial vice	(D)
27	Other sex offenses	(D)
28	Illegal drug offenses	(D)
29	Gambling	(D)
30	Tax cheating	(D)
31	Welfare cheating	(D)
32	Contributing to minor's delinquency	(E)
33	Child abuse	(E)
34	Drunken driving	(E)
35	Drunkenness, liquor law violations	(E)
36	Disorderly conduct, vagrancy	(E)
37	False fire alarms	(E)
38	Contempt of court (criminal or civil)	(E)
39	Perjury	(E)
40	Obstruction of justice	(E)
41	Inciting to riot	(E)
42	Homosexuality	(D)
43	Official misconduct	(E)
47	Witchcraft	(E)

167

Variable	Name	Column	Code	Explanation
			51	Traffic offenses/scofflaw (E)
			52	Resisting arrest (E)
			54	Criminal pollution (E)
			44	Group A + B
			45	Group A + C
			48	Group B + C
			49	Group B + D + E
			50	Group A + D + E
			46	Specific nature of crime not clear (E)
			53	Other.
12	Causes of	23-24		Up to three causes may be coded. Select in order of emphasis
13	crime	25-26		delineated explicitly in the story.
14		27-28		
			01	Heredity, genetic factors (includes race)
			02	Methods of child rearing, includes permissiveness
			03	Poor home life, includes parental absence, illness, poverty, marital strife, alcoholism, rejection
			04	Adolescent stresses
			05	Religious deficiencies
			06	Materialism
			07	Economic stress, unemployment
			08	Slum/ghetto conditions
			09	Inefficient police-criminal justice system
			10	Judicial leniency
			11	Prison conditions/recidivism
			12	Alcohol/drugs
			13	Abuse of political power

14   Welfare state mentality (somebody owes me a living)
15   Influence of mass media: movies, TV/radio
16   Moral bankruptcy
17   Racism
18   Faulty coordination between judicial and legislative branches
19   Other
20   Availability of guns

16   Motives,   29-30
17   triggering   31-32
18   incidents   33-34

Up to three may be coded. Select in order of emphasis delineated explicitly in the story.

01   Fight among strangers — argument
02   Fight among acquaintances — argument
03   Family fight/argument
04   Racial/ethnic incident
05   Gang violence
06   Sex (rivalry, infidelity, promiscuity, and the like)
07   Labor/union problems
08   Political differences (partisan strife, radicalism, left-right clashes, and the like)
09   Mental derangement/going berserk
10   Prison inmate strife
11   Prison inmate — authority strife
12   Opportunity
13   Intimidating potential witness
14   Robbery
15   Rape
16   Protecting national security

Variable	Name	Column	Code	Explanation
			17	Drugs/alcohol
			18	Influence of mass media: movies/TV/radio
			19	Money
			20	Occult worship
			21	Kicks
			22	Other
19	Criminal(s)' sex/identity	35	1	Male
			2	Female
			3	Both
			4	Institution acting through agent
			5	Unknown
			6	Not applicable
			7	Institution + individual
				Note: When story involves individual participant in collective crime, code only for individuals to which story pertains.
20	Victim's sex/identity	36	1-7	See Variable 19.
21	Criminal(s)' age group at time of crime	37-38		(May be inferred from clear picture if not in story.)
			01	Young child – (0-7)
			02	Preteen – (8-12)
			03	Young teen – (13-16)
			04	Juvenile – (17-21)
			05	Young adult – (22-25)
			06	Premiddle age – (26-35)
			07	Middle age – (36-65)
			08	Seniors – (66 & over)
			09	Members of 13-25 group (3 + 4 + 5)

170

		10	Members of 13-25 group + 26-65 group (3, 4, 5 + 6, 7)
		11	Members of 26-65 group + over 65 group (6, 7 + 8)
		12	Other combinations
		13	Private institutions, companies, corporations
		14	Public institutions
		15	Combination private + public institutions (13 + 14)
		16	Named individuals + institutions
		17	Unidentified/not given
22	Victim(s)' age group at time of crime	39-40	1-17 See Variable 21.
23	Number of criminals	41-42	01-90 Use actual number or estimate. When ranges are given, use midpoint.
		91	More than 90
		99	Indeterminate number (use this category when criminal is an institution)
24	Number of victims	43-44	01-90 See Variable 23.
25	Criminal(s)' ethnic/racial/religious tag	45-46	Use narrowest identification. If name, address, or organizational identification is an obvious clue, identify accordingly.
		1	White
		2	Black
		3	Oriental
		4	American Indian
		5	Latino
		6	Jewish
		7	Southern European (Italian, Greek)

171

Variable	Name	Column	Code	Explanation
			8	Hillbilly, Appalachian
			9	Other
			10	Mixed
			11	No identity tags
26	Victim(s)' ethnic/racial/ religious tag	47-48	1-11	See Variable 25.
27	Criminal(s)' occupation	49, 50, 51		Three occupations may be coded. Retired people should be coded for most prominent past occupation. Code only one occupation per person.
28				
29			1	Professional/technical (college degree required, generally)
			2	Business-managers/union officials
			3	Politician/bureaucrat/police, clergy, career army
			4	Clerical/sales
			5	Skilled workers/trades/farmers/military personnel
			6	Nonskilled workers/ex-taxi drivers
			7	Students
			8	Homemaker
			9	Not identified
			0	Unemployed
30	Victim(s)' occupation	52, 53, 54	0-9	See Variables 27, 28, 29.
31				
32				
33	Previous crime record	55		Code only fact of mention. Do not code details of previous alleged offenses.
			1	None
			2	Some mention (1-3 sentences)

172

		3	A lot (4 or more sentences)
		4	Mention as recidivist – some
		5	Mention as recidivist – a lot
		6	Mention as on parole – some
		7	Mention as on parole – a lot

Note: Use discretion on sentence measures. One very long, packed-with-detail sentence may be counted as two normal sentences. Two very brief, sparsely descriptive sentences may be counted as one.

34	Crime neighborhood	56		
				Code smallest identifiable area.
			1	City
			2	Suburb
			3	Nonurban
			4	Downtown (for example, the Loop)
			5	Rim of city core – roughly to midpoint between core and boundary
			6	Outer rim of city – midpoint to boundary (from 40,000 outward in Chicago)
			7	Mixed
			8	Not identified
			9	Evanston

35	Site of crime	57-58		
			1	School and schoolyard
			2	Church
			3	Home
			4	Street or alley
			5	Outdoors, parks, fields
			6	Factory
			7	Store/restaurant
			8	Government building

Variable	Name	Column	Code	Explanation
			9	Transportation facility, car, truck
			10	Mixed
			11	Not identified
			12	Prison/other correctional facility
			13	Tavern
			14	Shopping center (if labeled)
			15	Public housing
			16	High-rise — flats to 6 stories
			17	Office building
			18	Warehouse and storage
			19	Sports facility
			20	Bank/currency exchange/Brinks
			21	Hotel/motel/transient facility
			22	Retirement home
			23	Gas station
			24	Museum/theater
			25	Hospital
			26	Parking lot
			27	Lake/ocean
			28	Apartment building, 7 + stories
			29	Vacant building
36	Details of injuries	59	1	None
			2	Some mention (1-3 sentences)
			3	A lot (more than 3 sentences)
				(See note for Variable 33)

174

37	Details of crime execution	60	Refers to who did what, where, with what tools
			1 None
			2 Some mention (1-3 sentences)
			3 A lot (more than 3 sentences)
			(see note for Variable 33)
38	Details of apprehension measures/arrest	61	Code only if there is description of specific actions taken to bring about arrest, regardless of success or failure.
			1 None
			2 Some mention (1-3 sentences)
			3 A lot (more than 3 sentences)
			(see note for Variable 33)
39	Apprehension success rate	62	1 No arrests, bookings, preliminary charges
			2 Arrests, bookings, preliminary charges for some suspects
			3 Arrests, bookings, preliminary charges for all suspects
			4 Arrests, and so forth and release pending trial – some suspects
			5 Arrests, and so forth and release pending trial – all suspects
			6 Mixture – no suspects released
			7 Mixture – some suspects released
			8 Suspect detained but not charged
			9 Suspect deceased or in hospital
40	Details of pretrial action	63	Code for discussion of such matters as indictments, grand jury action, pretrial detention, jury selection, bail questions, trial delays, lawyers' motions, and so on
			1 None
			2 Some mention (1-3 sentences)
			3 A lot (more than 3 sentences)
			(see note for Variable 33)

Variable	Name	Column	Code	Explanation
41	Civil rights of accused	64-65		Code only if specifically mentioned (for example, double jeopardy, effective council, speedy trial, and so on).
			1	Police violation charged
			2	Police protection claimed
			3	Police – mixed action
			4	Court violation charged
			5	Court protection claimed
			6	Court – mixed action
			7	Prison violation charged
			8	Prison protection claimed
			9	Prison – mixed action
			10	Combination – violation charged
			11	Combination – protection claimed
			12	Combination – mixed action
			13	Mass media violation charged
			14	Mass media protection claimed
			15	Mass media – mixed action
			16	Prosecution violation charged
			17	Prosectuion – mixed action
42	Discussion of courtroom procedures	66	1	None
			2	Some mention (1-3 sentences)
				A lot (more than 3 sentences)
				(see note for Variable 33)
43	Sentence/ disposition	67-68	1	Dismissal – innocent
			2	Dismissal – insufficient evidence
			3	Dismissal – technical details
			4	Guilty – no penalties (or penalties already served)/instant parole

5	Prison – less than one year	(L)
6	Prison – 1-10 years	(M)
7	Prison – 11 or more years	(H)
8	Prison – indeterminate	
9	Hospital commitment/criminally insane	
10	Fine – less than $100	(L)
11	Fine – $100-$10,000	(M)
12	Fine – more than $10,000	(H)
13	Combinations for individual – Low prison, low fine	
14	Combinations for individual – Low prison, medium fine	
15	Combinations for individual – Low prison, high fine	
16	Combinations for individual – Medium prison, low fine	
17	Combinations for individual – Medium prison, medium fine	
18	Combinations for individual – Medium prison, high fine	
19	Combinations for individual – High prison, low fine	
20	Combinations for individual – High prison, medium fine	
21	Combinations for individual – High prison, high fine	
22	Group combinations – Low and medium prison	
23	Group combinations – Medium and high prison	
24	Group combinations – Low and high prison	
25	Group combinations – Low and medium prison + any fine	
26	Group combinations – Medium and high prison + any fine	
27	Group combinations – Low and high prison + any fine	
28		
29	Parole after serving part of sentence	
30	Other penalties	
31	Mistrial declared	

177

Variable	Name	Column	Code	Explanation
			32	Death penalty
			33	Not identified
			34	Not given, but on appeal
			35	Retrial ordered
			36	Appeal denied
			37	Freed after serving sentence
			38	Pardon requested
			39	Pardon granted
			40	Appeal denied for some, granted for others
			41	Parole denied
			42	Retrial under consideration
			43	Innocent on appeal
			44	Guilty on appeal
			45	Sentence commutation considered
			46	Death penalty considered
44	Overall evaluation of police system	69-70	1	Code only if specific evaluations are made. Good job – stable
			2	Bad job – stable
			3	Mixed – stable
			4	Good job – declining
			5	Good job – improving
			6	Mixed – declining
			7	Mixed – improving
			8	Mixed-mixed
			9	Bad job – declining
			10	Bad job – improving
			11	Bad job – mixed

178

45 Overall evaluation of court system   71-72   Code only if specific evaluations are made.

1 Good job – stable
2 Bad job – stable
3 Mixed – stable
4 Good job – declining
5 Good job – improving
6 Mixed – declining
7 Mixed – improving
8 Mixed – mixed
9 Bad job – declining
10 Bad job – improving
11 Bad job – mixed

46 Overall evaluation of correctional system   73-74   Code only if specific evaluations are made.

1 Good job – stable
2 Bad job – stable
3 Mixed – stable
4 Good job – declining
5 Good job – improving
6 Mixed – declining
7 Mixed – improving
8 Mixed – mixed
9 Bad job – declining
10 Bad job – improving
11 Bad job – mixed

When juvenile correctional system is involved (without mention of general court system), use the following subcategories:

31 Good job – stable

Variable	Name	Column	Code	Explanation
			32	Bad job – stable
			33	Mixed – stable
			34	Good job – declining
			35	Good job – improving
			36	Mixed – declining
			37	Mixed – improving
			38	Mixed – mixed
			39	Bad job – declining
			40	Bad job – improving
			41	Bad job – mixed
47	Overall evaluation of crime danger	75-76		Code only if specifically mentioned or if statistics are given, indicating trends.
			1	Serious crime (A, B, C) on increase
			2	Serious crime (A, B, C) on decrease
			3	Serious crime (A, B, C) stable
			4	Serious crime (A, B, C) mixed change
			5	All crime on increase
			6	All crime on decrease
			7	All crime stable
			8	All crime, mixed change
			9	Lesser crime (D, E) on increase
			10	Lesser crime (D, E) on decrease
			11	Lesser crime (D, E) stable
			12	Lesser crime (D, E) stable
			13	Serious crime on rise, lesser crime on decline
			14	Serious crime decreasing, lesser crime rising

180

48	Discussion of crime prevention devices	77	1	General discussion
			2	Specific how-to advice for citizens
			3	Societal programs – to remedy economic causes of crime
			4	Societal programs involving high-crime potential population (for example, summer jobs, recreational facilities, job training)
			5	Stress on penalties/dangers of crime commission
			6	Witness protection
			7	Citizen watch groups
			8	Blank
			9	Other
49	Discussion of criminal justice policies	78-79		Code "mixed" if no evaluation is provided, or if both positive and negative evaluations are given.
			1	Gun control – pro
			2	Gun control – con
			3	Gun control – mixed
			4	Death penalty – pro
			5	Death penalty – con
			6	Death penalty – mixed
			7	Fixed sentences – pro
			8	Fixed sentences – con
			9	Fixed sentences – mixed
			10	Parole reform – pro
			11	Parole reform – con
			12	Parole reform – mixed
			13	Plea bargaining – pro
			14	Plea bargaining – con
			15	Plea bargaining – mixed

181

Variable	Name	Column	Code	Explanation
			16	Marijuana decriminalization – pro
			17	Marijuana decriminalization – con
			18	Marijuana decriminalization – mixed
			19	Prostitution decriminalization – pro
			20	Prostitution decriminalization – con
			21	Prostitution decriminalization – mixed
			22	Granting repeat continuances – pro
			23	Granting repeat continuances – con
			24	Granting repeat continuances – mixed
			25	Granting immunity from prosecution – pro
			26	Granting immunity from prosecution – con
			27	Granting immunity from prosecution – mixed
			28	Free press/fair trial – pro
			29	Free press/fair trial – con
			30	Free press/fair trial – mixed
			31	Prison reform – pro
			32	Prison reform – con
			33	Prison reform – mixed
			34	Use of lie detector tests – pro
			35	Use of lie detector tests – con
			36	Use of lie detector tests – mixed
			37	Change in criminal law – greater
			38	Change in criminal law – less
			39	Change in criminal law – mixed
			40	Compensation for crime victims – pro
			41	Compensation for crime victims – con
			42	Compensation for crime victims – mixed

182

	43	Right of wife to prosecute husband for "attack" – pro
	44	Right of wife to prosecute husband for "attack" – con
	45	Right of wife to prosecute husband for "attack" – mixed
	46	Rape laws/prosecution reform – pro
	47	Rape laws/prosecution reform – mixed
	48	Rape laws/prosecution reform – con
		Use this category to indicate an unfolding story of specific crimes and court cases. Do not use it to indicate repeat discussions of policy issues such as free press-fair trial, death penalty merits, and so on, unless they are discussed in connection with a specific case.
50 Novelty of story	80	
	1	New story (to coder's best knowledge)
	2	Update of existing story – no major new developments
	3	Update of existing story – major new developments

183

_____Appendix D

CRIME QUESTION CODEBOOK

Crime questions in interviews were coded to facilitate cross-referencing to crime story coding for mass media (see Appendix C). Questions have been divided into seven groups. There were ten interviews altogether. The number(s) in parentheses after each of the following questions indicate the interview in which the question was asked. (The first interview contained no crime questions. Therefore, no questions from that interview appear below.) For some interview codes, there were no questions. This happened (a) if people answered things that were not asked but we chose to code them, or (b) when the answer permitted certain inferences, for example, we concluded that answer A differed from answer B.

GROUP 1. USE AND APPRAISAL OF MASS MEDIA

1.1   During the past month, how much attention did you pay to newspaper and television stories about crime? (3, 10)
         1 = None
         2 = A little
         3 = Some
         4 = A lot

1.2   What kinds of crime did you read or hear about most? Any others? (3, 10)
         01 = Murder
         02 = Robbery/burglary
         03 = Kidnapping/hostages
         04 = Rapes
         05 = Vandalism
         06 = Arson
         07 = Murder – women and children
         08 = Juvenile crime
         09 = Assault
         99 = Don't recall/don't remember specifics

1.3　In general, do you feel that the newspapers report crime accurately? How about television, radio, news magazines, fiction stories? (3, 10)

      1 = Accurate in general
      2 = Inaccurate in general
      3 = Depends on the stories
      4 = Don't know
      5 = Don't care

Why or why not?

Positive aspects of newspaper reporting on crime stories:

      01 = No bias
      02 = In-depth

Negative aspects of newspaper reporting on crime stories:

      01 = Sensationalism
      02 = Brevity/incomplete
      03 = Unfair treatment (minority group, and so forth)
      04 = Protection of privacy not related to the crime itself
      05 = Imbalance between crime and other stories (which produces distorted view of the world in readers)
      06 = Imbalance between blue-collar crime vs. white-collar crime reports
      07 = Accuracy

1.4　In general, do you feel that newspapers give too much or too little coverage to crime stories, or is coverage about right? How about television, radio, news magazines? (3)

      1 = Too much
      2 = Too little
      3 = About right
      4 = Don't know
      5 = Don't care
      6 = Too much, but not media's fault

1.5　What about stories about white-collar crime? Are they adequately covered? (The meaning of "white-collar crime" was explained.) (3, 10)

      1 = Too much
      2 = Too little
      3 = About right
      4 = Don't know
      5 = Don't care
      6 = Too much, but not media's fault

1.6　Do you learn about crime mostly from mass media, personal knowledge, or from conversation with others? (3, 10)

      1 = Mass media
      2 = Personal knowledge

         3 = Conversation

         4 = Job-related special sources (reported documents, and so on)

         5 = All three (1, 2, 3)

1.7   Do you recall whether newspapers generally describe the kinds of injuries that victims suffer?

         1 = Yes

         2 = No

         3 = Don't know

         4 = Depends

What do you remember about injury description? (5)

         1 = Nature of injury — general

         2 = Nature of injury — specifics

         3 = General nature of injury + gun mention

         4 = Specific nature of injury + gun mention

         5 = General nature of injury + knife mention

         6 = Specific nature of injury + knife mention

         7 = General nature of injury + rape

         8 = Specific nature of injury + rape

         9 = More than two crime methods

1.8   Some people say that the media teach people how to commit crimes by describing crimes in detail. Do you think that people learn how to commit crimes by watching television shows/reading newspaper accounts of crime/reading crime fiction in books or magazines? Is it a serious problem? Why or why not? What, if anything, can/should be done about it? (6)

a. Do people learn how to commit crimes by watching television shows?

         1 = Yes

         2 = No

         3 = Indirectly

         4 = A little (only a small number of people)

         9 = Don't know

b. Is this a serious problem?

         1 = Serious

         2 = Not serious

         3 = In between

         4 = Potentially serious

         9 = Don't know

c. If serious, why?

         1 = Television shows help form public climate of tolerance toward crime

         blank = Not mentioned

d. Remedies for the problem (up to 3)

    0, blank = None
    1 = Censorship by government
    2 = Self-censorship by networks
    3 = Consumer boycott/public pressure
    4 = No censorship
    5 = Regulation to reduce crime stories
    6 = Consumer discretion
    7 = Self-discretion by media to give less details
    8 = Other
    9 = Don't know

Do people learn how to commit crimes by reading about them in newspapers?

    Same as a above.

Is this a serious problem?

    Same as b above.

If serious, why?

    Same as c above.

Remedies for the problem (up to 3)

    Same as d above.

Do people learn how to commit crimes by reading crime fiction in books or magazines?

    Same as a above.

Is this a serious problem?

    Same as b above.

If serious, why?

    Same as c above.

If not serious, why?

    1 = Not too many people read books
    2 = Criminals don't read books in general
    blank = Not mentioned

Remedies for the problem

    Same as d above.

GROUP 2. PERSONAL EXPERIENCE AND CONCERN WITH CRIME

2.1   Have you or your friends or your family ever been a victim of crime? What happened? (3)

    1 = Yes
    2 = No
    3 = Don't know

What happened?

    Use "Nature of Alleged Crime" categories, Appendix C, Variables 9 to 11.

2.2   Have you ever personally known a person accused of crime or convicted of crime? Tell me some of the details. (3)

    1 = Yes

    2 = No

    3 = Don't know

Nature of crime

    Use codes in Appendix C, Variables 9 to 11.

2.3   Are you personally concerned about becoming a victim of crime? If yes, how much? (4)

    1 = Yes

    2 = No

    3 = Don't know

How much?

    1 = Very concerned

    2 = Somewhat concerned

    3 = Slightly concerned

2.4   Recently, there have been many stories about crime and illegal activities involving people in all walks of life. As a result of these, do you trust any of the following less than you did five years ago? Or are things pretty much the same − doctors/ lawyers/ big business/ repairmen/ merchants/ politicians/ Congress/ courts/ police/ Greeks/ Italians/ Latinos/ Swedes/ blacks/ teenagers/ neighbors? (9)

    1 = Less

    2 = Same

    3 = Don't know

2.5   Do you do anything special to protect yourself against becoming a victim of crime? What is that? (4)

    1 = Yes

    2 = No

    3 = Don't know

What is that?

    01 = Curtail night activities

    02 = Travel in group − any sex (no sex mentioned)

    03 = Travel in group including males

    04 = Inconspicuous dress, car, house, and so on

    05 = Carry no ID, valuables, money

    06 = Locks, burglar devices

    07 = Stay away from danger areas

    08 = Stay visible/avoiding people

    09 = Do not stay out late at night

10 = Tough look on the face

11 = Avoid eye contacts with strangers (suspicious)

12 = Move constantly, do not stay at one spot

13 = Safe place to live/neighborhood

14 = Watch for police reports to be aware of the areas of danger

15 = Carry no guns to protect myself

16 = Carry enough money to make criminals happy

2.6   Do you avoid going to certain neighborhoods or places because you think they are dangerous? Which ones do you consider dangerous? Which ones do you avoid? (4)

1 = Yes

2 = No

3 = Don't know

In Chicago:

Which places are perceived to be dangerous or avoided?

01 = None

02 = Elevated train/night

03 = Addison/night/White Sox Park

04 = Westside of Chicago

05 = Southside of Chicago

06 = Howard Street

07 = Loop area

09 = Most of Chicago

10 = Cicero

11 = Old town – new town area (including Rush Street)

12 = Black neighborhoods

13 = Halstead

14 = Parks

15 = Parking lots

In Evanston:

Which places are perceived to be dangerous?

01 = None

02 = Unfamiliar places

03 = North West area

04 = Chicago Avenue/Dempster/(especially at night)

05 = South Evanston

06 = Black neighborhoods

07 = Howard Street

08 = Northwestern University campus

09 = Main Street

10 = Church Street and Dodge

11 = Home

2.7 What makes you think that place X, Y, Z, and so on, is dangerous? Who told you that? (4)

    01 = Mass media

    02 = Personal experience (of being assaulted, and so on) or personal observations of crime being committed

    03 = Word of mouth

    04 = Fear of slum areas — personal feelings and general observations

    05 = Fear of black areas — personal feelings and general observations

    06 = Experiences of friends/family members

    07 = Other sources of facts of crime

2.8 Do you think that most crimes occur outdoors or inside buildings? What kinds of outdoor locations are most dangerous? What kinds of indoor locations are most dangerous? Why? (5)

    1 = Outdoors

    2 = Inside

    3 = Half/half

    4 = Don't know

Most dangerous places

    01 = School and schoolyard

    02 = Church

    03 = Home

    04 = Street or alley (of ghetto area)

    05 = Parks, fields

    06 = Factory

    07 = Store

    08 = Government building

    09 = Transportation facility

    10 = Not identified

    12 = Prison/other correctional facility

    13 = Tavern, pub, bar

    14 = Shopping center

    15 = Public housing

    16 = High-rise apartments (with many entries)

    17 = Office building

    18 = Warehouse and storage

    19 = Sports facility

    20 = Bank

    21 = Hotel/motel/transient facility

    22 = Small apartment buildings

    23 = Any streets

    24 = Movie houses

25 = Dark places (dark and quiet)
26 = Public transportation
27 = Beaches
28 = Public washrooms
29 = Deserted buildings
30 = Forests
31 = Business places
32 = Open basements
33 = Inside of auditorium
34 = Parking lot
35 = Stairways

2.9 Do you try to avoid these places? How? At what times? (5)

1 = Yes
2 = No
3 = Depends on the areas
4 = Depends on day
9 = Don't know

GROUP 3. IMAGES OF CRIME, CRIMINALS, AND CAUSES OF CRIME

3.1 Do you have any ideas about what causes people to commit crimes? Which of these causes is most important? What, if anything, can be done about it? (3)

Causes of Crime (Code up to 3)

01 Heredity, genetic factors (including race)
02 Methods of child rearing, includes permissiveness
03 Poor home life, includes parental absence, illness, poverty, marital strife, alcoholism, rejection, and so on — relevant to juvenile crime mainly
04 Adolescent stresses
05 Religious deficiencies
06 Materialism/greed — individual characteristics
07 Economic stress, poverty, unemployment, out of necessity
08 Slum/ghetto conditions — more emphasis on total environment inclusive of crime
09 Inefficient police-criminal justice system
10 Judicial leniency
11 Prison conditions/recidivism
12 Peer group pressure
13 Social pressure to succeed

14 Biological human nature — passion (crime of passion)
15 Circumstances — opportunity
16 Alcoholism/drug influence
17 Insanity/psycopathic causes
18 Educational cause/school
19 Whole combination of all factors possible
20 Thrill/impulse/out of boredom, and so on
21 Social isolation/lack of hope/desperateness
22 Laziness/don't want to work
23 Lack of conscience/morality/ethics
24 Difficulty to get in the mainstream of society
25 Success of crime provides the criminals gratifications
98 Can't categorize
99 Don't know

Crime Prevention Devices

01 General discussion
02 Specific how-to advice for citizen
03 Societal programs — to remedy economic/educational causes of crime
04 Societal programs involving high-crime potential population (for example, summer jobs, recreational facilities, job training)
05 Stress on penalties/dangers of crime commission
06 Witness protection
07 Citizen watch groups
08 Gun control
09 Reform of court system
10 TV and mass media (other) to reduce crime coverages
11 Enforcement of police/security
12 Death penalty
13 Family unity (better family ties)/ better child-rearing practices/more discipline
14 Certitude of penalty
15 Drug control
16 Alcohol control
17 Fair tax structure
18 Mental institution to be enforced
99 Don't know

3.2 If you had to describe the person most likely to commit a crime, how would you describe that person? (Probe for age, sex, occupation, national background, and so on, if not supplied spontaneously.) (4)

Use codes in Appendix C, Variable 19 (sex), 21 (age group), 25 (ethnic/racial/religious group), and other codes below.

Criminal(s) occupation (up to 3):

01 = Professional/technical/college degree required in general
02 = Business manager
03 = Politician/bureaucrats
04 = Clerical/sales
05 = Skilled workers/trades/farmers
06 = Nonskilled workers
07 = Students
08 = Homemaker
09 = Unemployed
10 = Employed – general
11 = Public guards, police
19 = Don't know

Criminal(s) economic status (up to 3):

1 = Extremely rich (upper-high)
2 = High-rich
3 = 1 + 2
4 = Middle class
5 = Poor (lower-middle)
6 = Extremely poor (low class)
7 = 5 + 6
9 = Don't know

Criminal(s) residence (neighborhood) (up to 3):

1 = City
2 = Suburb
3 = Nonurban
4 = Downtown (for example, Loop)
5 = Rim of city core (roughly to midpoint between core and boundary)
6 = Outer rim of city midpoint to boundary
7 = Mixed
8 = Evanston
9 = Poor section of the city (ghetto)

Criminal(s) other characteristics (up to 3):

1 = Drug users (addiction)
2 = Alcoholism
3 = Education – low

       4 = Emotionally unstable/mental problem

       5 = Related to victims

       6 = Family disharmony, lack of love from the family, unhappy family life

       7 = People on the street

3.3   If you had to describe the person most likely to become a victim of crime, how would you describe that person? (Probe for age, sex, occupation, national background, and so on, if not supplied spontaneously.) (4)

       Use codes in question 3.2 and below.

       Victim(s) other characteristics:

       1 = Those who carry money/who appear to have money

       2 = Alcoholism

       3 = Isolated/loners

       4 = Widowed

       5 = Trusting soul

       6 = Unpreparedness, lack of caution, carelessness

       7 = Out of school (kids)

       8 = Wandering around the streets

3.4   Do you think that most crimes are committed by people acting alone, or are there usually several people involved? How many? (4)

       01-90 Use actual number of estimate (use midpoint of ranges)

       91 More than 90

       96 Several (specific numbers not mentioned)

       97 Group of varying sizes

       98 Depends (sometimes alone and sometimes in groups)

       99 Indeterminate number, don't know

       In case of one point difference (for example, three or four), use *lower* figure

3.5   Do you think that in most crimes just one person gets hurt, or are there usually several victims? How many? (4)

       Use codes in question 3.4.

3.6   Do you think that most people who commit crimes already have a record of crime? Why is that? (4)

       1 = Yes

       2 = No

       3 = Don't know

       Why is that?

       Use "Causes of Crime" categories, question 3.1.

3.7   I am going to mention a list of nonviolent and white-collar crimes. In each case, tell me how often it occurs, whether it happens more or less frequently than violent crimes, and who the most likely criminals and victims are: extortion/forgery/counterfeiting/fraud/consumer deceit/embezzlement/bribery/kickbacks/corrupt deals/dealing in stolen property/weapons violations/escape from custody/parole violations/illegal wiretaps/prostitution/other sex offenses/drug offenses/gambling/tax cheating/welfare cheating/contributing to minor's delinquency/child abuse/drunken driving/vagrancy/disorderly conduct/perjury/false fire alarm/civil or criminal contempt of court. (8)

Frequency of Crime

  1 = Rare
  2 = Common
  3 = Moderately common (in between)
  9 = Don't know

Frequency of crime — comparison with violent crimes

  1 = Rare
  2 = Same
  3 = More
  8 = Can't compare
  9 = Don't know

Overall, is it a serious social problem?

  1 = Very serious
  2 = Moderately serious
  3 = Not serious
  4 = Depends
  8 = Can't answer
  9 = Don't know

What kinds of people are most likely to commit white-collar crimes/ to become victims?

White-Collar Crime Actor Characteristics

  01 = Anybody
  02 = Person who has access to money
  03 = Poor, low SES, underprivileged
  04 = People who don't have proper way of making living
  05 = Less educated
  06 = People who had unfortunate childhood
  07 = Higher/middle SES
  08 = Organized crime group
  09 = Educated/intelligent/skillful
  10 = Felons/prisoners/convicted and in custody/accused/ and so on
  11 = Couples in the process of divorce
  12 = Emotionally/mentally ill/unstable

13 = Murderers
14 = Thieves
15 = Unhappily married couples
16 = Dope addicts
17 = Alcoholics
18 = Bankers
19 = Single persons (unmarried)
20 = Sportsmen
21 = Criminals in general
22 = High SES
23 = Young, married couples
24 = Dope pushers
99 = Don't know

White-Collar Crime Victim Characteristics

1 = Persons known to have property
2 = All of us/any of us/general public
3 = Middle-class/upper-middle-class
4 = Less educated
5 = Less privileged
6 = Banks
7 = Criminals/suspects/accused/and so on
8 = Married couples (husband-wife)
9 = Don't know

GROUP 4. COPING WITH CRIME: THE CRIMINAL JUSTICE SYSTEM

4.1 Do you feel crime is on the increase, decrease, or about the same in Evanston/Chicago compared to last year? Compared to five years ago? Why is that? (5)
1 = Increase
2 = Decrease
3 = About the same
9 = Don't know
Why increase? (up to 4) Evanston/Chicago area/in general.
Use "Causes of Crime" categories, question 3.1 and additional categories below.
26 = Population increase
27 = Population change (general, without specifications)
28 = Tolerance of crime/lack of community concern or action
29 = Increase of low-income housing
30 = Decrease of middle-class families

31 = Media violence/desensitization to crime
32 = Media reporting more crimes than before
33 = Unemployment
34 = Increase of black people in the city
35 = Increase of other ethnic groups
36 = Inability for police to catch criminals
37 = National mood, climate/loosening of authority

4.2 Do you think that the police are very successful or very unsuccessful in catching criminals? Why is that? What proportion of criminals are caught? (6)

Are police very successful in catching criminals?
1 = Yes
2 = No
3 = In between
4 = Depends on crime
9 = Don't know

Reasons for success rate (up to 3):
1 = Difficulty of problem
2 = Lack of skill
3 = No public cooperation
4 = Depends on the nature of crimes
5 = Insufficient manpower
6 = Murder crime − success rate high, others − vary
blank = Not mentioned

What proportions of criminals are caught?
1 = Most of them
2 = Three fourths
3 = One half
4 = One fourth
5 = Less than one fourth
6 = 10 percent or less
7 = One third
8 = 60 percent
9 = Don't know
blank = Not mentioned

4.3 People accused of crime often complain that the police violate their civil rights. Do you feel, in general, that these claims are justified? Why or why not? In what ways are civil rights most often claimed to be impaired? (6)

Is the complaint of the accused that the police violate their civil rights justified?
1 = Justified
2 = Not justified

3 = In between

9 = Don't know

blank = Not mentioned

If not justified, why? (up to 3)

    1 = Criminals' false justification

    2 = Police mistreat criminals only when necessary

    3 = Criminals have no right to complain

    blank = Not mentioned

In what ways are people's civil rights most often impaired? (up to 3)

    1 = Physical brutality

    2 = Not told of rights

    3 = No access to counsel

    4 = Lack of care for victims

    5 = Illegal searches

    6 = Unfair treatment of minority

    7 = No opportunity to defend themselves

4.4   In general, would you say that the police are doing a good job, fair job, or poor job in protecting the community? Explain. (6)

    1 = Good

    2 = Fair

    3 = Poor

    4 = Evanston — good, Chicago — poor

    5 = Evanston — good, Chicago — fair

    9 = Don't know

Reasons for rating of the police (up to 3):

    1 = Difficulty of problems

    2 = Lack of skills

    3 = (No) public cooperation

    4 = Not enough crime prevention

    5 = Caliber of police

    6 = Unsuccessful experimental programs (for example, public relations)

    7 = Insufficient manpower/increase of crime

    8 = Unwillingness/lack of dedication

    9 = Media report

    0 = Good knowledge of society, crime, and law

    blank = Not mentioned

4.5   Compared to five years ago, are they doing a better, worse, or stable job? Why or why not? (6)

    1 = Better

    2 = Worse

    3 = Same

    9 = Don't know

Reasons for the above rating:

    1 = Increase in police training and education

    2 = Increase in police force

    3 = Better technology/skill

    4 = Increase in crimes

    5 = Unemployment has increase 1 crimes

    6 = Reduced crime rate

    blank = Not mentioned

4.6   How about the correctional system — prisons, parole boards, and so on? Are they doing a fair, good, or poor job? Why or why not? (6)

    1 = Good

    2 = Fair

    3 = Poor

    9 = Don't know

Reasons for the above rating (up to 3):

    1 = Poor prison staffs

    2 = Poor prison facilities

    3 = Failure to rehabilitate

    4 = High crime repeat rate

    5 = Homosexual problems

    6 = High escape rate

    7 = Mixed-up purposes of the institution

    8 = Insufficient jail facility (se urity)

    9 = Poor management (politic.1 deals)

    0 = Improvement in prison condition

    blank = Not mentioned

4.7   Compared to five years ago, are they doing a stable, worse, or better job? Why or why not? (6)

    1 = Better

    2 = Worse

    3 = Same

    9 = Don't know

Reasons for the above rating:

    1 = Today's situation is more mixed up

    2 = More minimum security facilities

    3 = More people need to get into jail

    4 = More efforts to improve

    5 = More criminals to handle

    6 = Don't know enough to compare with five years ago

    blank = Not mentioned

4.8   What about the courts? Are they doing a poor job, fair job, or good job? Why or why not? (6)

        1 = Good
        2 = Fair
        3 = Poor
        9 = Don't know

Reasons for the above rating (up to 3):

        1 = Inadequate sentencing
        2 = Long delays
        3 = Cases judged on technicalities (good lawyers can win the case)
        4 = Lazy judges
        5 = Mean treatment of the accused by the judges
        6 = Parole system
        7 = Judges leaning back to give doubt to criminals
        8 = Briberies, corruptions
        9 = Insufficient number of judges – overloaded, overcrowded
        0 = Don't know
        blank = Not mentioned

4.9   Compared to five years ago, are they doing a better, worse, or stable job? Explain. (6)

        1 = Better
        2 = Worse
        3 = Same
        9 = Don't know

Reasons for the above rating (up to 3):

        Use codes in question 4.8.

4.10   Some people feel that the courts are far too lenient in imposing penalties. Others feel that penalties are too severe. Others think they are just about right. What do you think? How would you determine the kind of penalty that is right for a particular offense? (6)

        1 = Too severe
        2 = Too light
        3 = Just about right
        4 = Depends on cases
        9 = Don't know
        blank = Not mentioned

Reasons for the above evaluation of penalties:

        1 = Not given maximum sentences
        2 = Depends on case/judge must decide
        3 = Heavy penalties for repeaters
        4 = Overcrowded condition of prisons
        5 = Past records of penalties

6 = Social consequences/severity of crime

7 = (Lack of) standard sentences for standard crime – consistency in penalties

8 = Other suggestions (for example, death penalty)

9 = Don't know/respondent does not understand question

0 = Depends on socioeconomic class of the criminals

blank = Not mentioned

4.11 Do you think the federal/state/local/subdivisional government is doing all it can to reduce crime in the United States/state/city/subdivision? Do you think that citizens are doing all they can? What else could be done? What is your source of information? (9)

1 = Yes

2 = No

3 = In between

9 = Don't know

What else could be done? (up to 4)

Use "Crime Prevention" categories in question 3.1 and additional categories below.

19 = Better rehabilitation system

20 = Reduce unemployment rate

21 = Racial integration

22 = Better fund management (from federal government to local law enforcement agencies)

23 = Decriminalization of drugs

24 = Dispensing programs for opium/and so on

25 = Recreational facilities for youngsters (to provide creative outlets)

26 = Basic research on crime to be encouraged/funded

27 = Witness protection from financial loss

28 = Better funding for law enforcement agencies

blank/98 = None

99 = Don't know

Source of information?

1 = Newspapers

2 = Radio

3 = Television

4 = Conversation

5 = Personal experience/thinking

6 = Professional source (publications, and so on)

7 = News magazine

8 = Combination of above/general

9 = Don't know

Do you think citizens are doing all they can to reduce crime?
Same as above.
What else could be done?
01 = More careful burglary protection system at home
02 = Other precautions of crime (stay away from dangerous areas, avoid bad neighborhood, and so on)
03 = Report of crime to police
04 = Fight unemployment
05 = Stop illegal activities
06 = Citizen watch group
07 = Attitude change/more cohesive community involvement (informal)/more common concern
08 = Raise conscience/morality
09 = Formally organized citizen pressure group
Source of information:
Same as above.

4.12 Corruption in government is considered to be a serious problem. Tell me briefly what the problem is. Is it serious or not? Why do we have it? What can be done about it? What are your sources of information about the problem? (6)
Seriousness
1 = Serious
2 = Not serious
3 = In between
4 = Potentially serious
9 = Don't know
Conceptualization of problem (5) (up to 3):
01 = Stealing
02 = Self-enrichment
03 = Morals infringements
04 = Dishonesty in general
05 = Sex scandals
06 = Bribery
07 = Vulgar verbal behaviors
08 = Using government agencies (or power) for personal interests
09 = Mismanagement of public money
10 = Lack of commitment to important areas of problems
11 = Favoritism
12 = Lobbies
13 = Politicians conspiring with businesses
14 = CIA illegal activities
98 = None
99 = Don't know
blank = Not mentioned

Comparisons of government corruption with private sector:
    1 = Better
    2 = Worse
    3 = Same
    4 = Same but more publicity
    5 = Same but higher standard required
    9 = Don't know

Reasons for corruption (up to 3):
    01 = Human nature
    02 = Opportunity
    03 = Lust for power
    04 = Lax standards
    05 = Change in public (social) attitudes on sex, morals, honesty, education, and so forth
    06 = Access to money
    07 = Less danger to be caught
    08 = Low salary of elected officials
    09 = Social pressure for immediate results
    10 = Lack of ethics
    11 = Spirit of competition in U.S. culture
    99 = Don't know
    blank = Not mentioned

Remedies for corruption (up to 3):
    01 = More media disclosures
    02 = More internal checking procedures
    03 = Personal reforms
    04 = Electoral sanction
    05 = New laws
    06 = Public pressures
    07 = Government's self-conscience
    08 = Legislation to let government inform public of the facts (through publication)
    09 = Prosecution of accused/stricter punishment for corruption
    98 = Nothing
    99 = Don't know
    blank = Not mentioned

Sources of information
    Use codes in question 4.11.

GROUP 5. PUBLIC PROTECTIVE POLICIES

5.1   Do you think that guns are used frequently to help criminals commit crimes? (5)

        1 = Yes
        2 = No
        3 = Don't know

5.2   Are you in favor of gun control legislation? What kinds? Do you know any political leaders who favor gun control? What kind of control? (5)

        1 = Yes
        2 = No
        3 = Don't know
        4 = No, because not feasible

Kinds of gun control you favor:

        1 = Complete outlaw
        2 = Outlaw Saturday night special
        3 = Tighter registration
        4 = Age limits on ownership
        5 = Licensing handguns (police, hunters)
        6 = Renewal of license with tests
        7 = Somebody else's recommendation in getting license or registration
        9 = Don't know/don't have specific ideas

Do you know any politicians who favor gun control? Who are they?

        0 = None
        1 = One name
        2 = Two names
        3 = Three names
        4 = Four names
        5 = Five names
        6 = Some
        9 = Don't know

Kinds of gun control they favor:
See above.

5.3   Do you have any idea why attempts to pass gun control legislation have been largely unsuccessful? (5)

        1 = Gun lobby (NRA)
        2 = Specifics can't be worked out (difficulty in working out specifics)
        3 = Government lacks power to enforce
        4 = Pervasiveness of guns
        5 = Constitutional right to possess guns

6 = People's fear/necessary to have gun to protect themselves
7 = Legislators are affiliated with gun pressure groups
8 = Some success
9 = Don't know

5.4 Some people are primarily concerned with doing everything possible to protect the legal rights of those *accused* of committing crimes. Others feel that it is more important to stop criminal activity, even at the risk of reducing the rights of the accused. Where would you place yourself on a seven-point scale when point 1 puts the rights of the accused first and point 7 puts the need to stop crime first? Where would you place Gerald Ford/Jimmy Carter/the Democratic party/the Republican party/most blacks/most whites? Why? (7)

Protect Rights
of Accused

Stop Crime Regardless
of Rights of Accused

|_____|_____|_____|_____|_____|_____|_____|
1   2   3   4   5   6   7

Respondent's position on the scale of protection of accused criminals' civil rights:
  0 = Haven't thought about it much
  1 = Highest protection of civil rights
  2-6 = In between
  7 = Lowest protection of civil rights
  8 = Don't know
Reasons (up to 3):
  1 = Importance of fundamental human rights
  2 = Importance of crime protection
  3 = The accused are accused because they have done something against law
  4 = Importance of balancing the two positions
  5 = Too many get off by legal technicalities
  6 = Respondent's knowledge of a few cases of crime accusation
  9 = General impression
Ford's position:
  Same as above.
Reasons (up to 3):
  1 = Public pressure keeps him in the middle-of-the-road position
  2 = He hasn't spoken out for rights of accused
  3 = His middle-of-the-road attitude

4 = His statement
5 = Importance of balancing the two positions
9 = General impression

Carter's position:
Same as above.
Reasons (up to 3):
1 = To get votes from both groups
2 = To get votes from majority who are victims of crime
3 = Stop-crime attitude from his statements
4 = Importance of both ends
9 = General impression

Democratic party's position:
Same as above.
Reasons (up to 3):
1 = General party philosophy
2 = To get votes from majority who are victims of crime
3 = Anticrime position due to the illegal activities (scandal) within the party

Republican party position:
Same as above.
Reasons (up to 3):
1 = Emphasis on stop crime in previous election (1968 election)
2 = General party disposition
3 = Nixon campaign emphasis on law and order
4 = Reagan's influence
5 = Illegal activities within the party
6 = Party history
9 = General impression

Most blacks' position:
Same as above.
Reasons (up to 3):
1 = Blacks are majority of both accused and of victims
2 = Blacks are most of the accused
3 = Feeling of rejection from the society
4 = Blacks' antipolice attitude
5 = They are most of the victims
9 = General impression

Most whites' position:
Same as above.
Reasons (up to 3):
1 = Whites are most of the victims
2 = Whites are disgusted with malfunction of legal technicalities

3 = Whites always emphasize individual rights
4 = Whites, like blacks, are potential criminals
5 = Averaging variety of attitudes
9 = General impression

5.5 Have you read or heard anything about programs that provide for public compensation for crime victims? What is that? What do you think about it? What else could be done? (10)

1 = Yes
2 = No
3 = Not sure

What program(s)?

1 = Public payment
2 = Criminal pays
3 = Insurance pays
9 = Don't know
blank = None/not mentioned

Evaluation of the program(s) mentioned above (if more than one, code in the order of the programs mentioned):

1 = Approval
2 = Disapproval
3 = Neutral
4 = Indifference
5 = Mixed
9 = Don't know

Other alternative program ideas?

1 = Public payment/public aids
2 = Criminal pays
3 = Insurance pays
4 = To make testifying easier (by money compensation)
5 = Psychological therapy program for victims
6 = Stricter restriction in getting bonds
7 = Crime control
8 = Public payment to only the poor who are not covered by insurance
9 = None, don't know
blank = Not mentioned

5.6 Have you heard or read anything about programs to protect wives who are beaten by their husbands? What is that? What do you think about it? What else could be done? (10)

Awareness

Same as question 5.5.

What program(s)?
    1 = Women's group providing housing (temporary)
    2 = Charity organization providing housing (temporary)
    3 = County welfare department
    4 = Hot-line
    5 = Marriage counseling
    9 = None, don't know
    blank = None, not mentioned
Evaluation of the program(s):
    Same as question 5.5.
Other alternative program ideas?
    1 = Training programs for psychological solution
    2 = Religious group to provide counseling
    3 = Stronger women's group activities for protest actions
    4 = Program to encourage wives to call police
    5 = Better police protection against violent husbands
    6 = More news coverage and publicizing (to heighten public awareness)
    8 = Nothing should be done (or can be done)
    9 = Don't know/no specific idea
    blank = Not mentioned/don't know

5.7   Have you heard or read anything about protection of children from beatings by their parents? What is that? What do you think about it? Could anything else be done? (10)

Awareness
    Same as question 5.5.
What program(s)?
    1 = (Evanston) volunteer education program for parents
    2 = Counseling for parents
    3 = Hospital to be required to report to police about suspicious bruises on children
    blank = Don't know, not sure, not mentioned
Evaluation of the program(s) mentioned:
    Same as question 5.5.
Other alternative program ideas?
    1 = Educational program (counseling)
    2 = Schools to teach (from childhood) how to manage good family life
    3 = Stricter punishment of parents
    4 = Encourage neighbors to report to police
    5 = Special agency to handle the problems
    6 = Wider publicity through media — raise public awareness
    7 = Foster homes

8 = No program necessary (or possible)

9 = Don't know, none

blank = Not mentioned

5.8 Have you heard or read anything about help for people who believe that businesspeople have cheated them? What is that? What do you think about it? Could anything else be done? (10)

Awareness

Same as question 5.5.

What program(s)?

1 = District attorney general

2 = Better business bureau

3 = Media (action line or similar programs)

4 = Small claims court

5 = Police

6 = Ralph Nader organization

7 = City's consumer advocate

8 = Federal consumer department

9 = None

blank = Not mentioned

Evaluation of the program(s) mentioned:

Same as question 5.5.

Other alternative program ideas?

1 = Government agencies

2 = Better price-marking system in the market

3 = Write to president of company

8 = Not necessary

9 = Don't know/not any specific idea

5.9 Have you heard or read anything about places that will help a person annoyed or injured by environmental pollution (noise, air, garbage, and so on)? What is that? What do you think about it? Could anything else be done about it? (10)

Awareness

Same as question 5.5.

What are they?

1 = City agency (city hall, police)

2 = State agency (attorney general, and so on)

3 = Environmental Protection Agency

4 = Media (action line and other similar programs)

8 = Not necessary

9 = Don't know, no specific idea

blank = Not mentioned/don't know

Evaluation of the programs:

Same as question 5.5.

Other alternative program ideas?

    1 = Prosecution of violators (by police, by government)
    2 = Writing to representative/congressman
    3 = More power to Environmental Protection Agency
    4 = Public education program
    8 = Not necessary
    9 = Don't know, no specific idea
    blank = Not mentioned/don't know

GROUP 6. IMAGES OF SPECIFIC CRIMES

Periodically, detailed questions were asked about specific crimes that had received major attention in the news. The chief examples are the Hearst kidnapping/bank robbery case and the Chowchilla bus hijacking case.*

6.1   Are you watching the stories about the Patty Hearst/Chowchilla bus hijacking case? How closely? On what medium? (2, 7)

    1 = Yes, a lot (most available stories)
    2 = Yes, some
    3 = Yes, a little (off-and-on attention)
    4 = Hardly at all/none

Medium
    See "Sources of Information," question 4.11.

6.2   If you had to tell a friend very quickly what it was all about, what would you say? Why did you pick these facts? (2, 7)
Description of the stories regarding crime events/victims' escape/ suspect's apprehension/children's life and background/suspect's life and background/speculations about motivation (code each aspect separately).

    1 = No detail
    2 = Some detail (up to 3 facts)
    3 = A lot of detail

6.3   What outcome do you predict in the case? Do you think that is a good or a bad outcome, or partly good and partly bad? Why? (2, 7)
Respondent's prediction of outcome:

    1 = No penalty
    2 = Light penalty (fines, 2 years or less jail)
    3 = Heavy penalty (more than 3 years jail)

---

*The Hearst case involved criminal activity by kidnapped heiress Patricia Hearst as a member of a terrorist organization, the Symbionese Liberation Army. The Chowchilla case involved hijacking a school bus full of children and holding them captive for ransom.

> 4 = Family payoff for release
> 5 = Family payoff for lighter-than-normal penalty
> 9 = Don't know

6.4 Do you think that the media are doing a good job in reporting this kind of story? Why or why not? (2, 7)
Media coverage in reporting this (kind of) story:
> 1 = Good job
> 2 = Poor job
> 3 = In between
> 9 = Don't know

Reasons (up to 3):
> 1 = Completeness of coverage
> 2 = Unbiased presentation
> 3 = Accuracy
> 4 = Straightforwardness – no sensationalism
> 5 = Gave audience strong impact on recalling stories
> 8 = Respondent's general trust of media coverage (credibility)
> 9 = Don't know

6.5 Are there any other crime stories that stand out in your mind for the last month? What are they? Why do you remember them? (2, 7)
Number of other crime stories mentioned
> 00-99

Nature of crime stories remembered
> Use "Nature of Alleged Crime" categories, Appendix C, Variables 9 to 11.

GROUP 7. STORY RECALL QUESTIONS

Recall questions were asked to test short- and long-term recall of news stories. Some diary stories were included. The interval between first appearance of the story and the recall test ranged from one week to nine months. Coding for these questions includes both the respondent's answers and the interviewer's evaluation of respondent's recall.

7.1 Identification question (for interviewer only)
Story recall:
> 1 = Diary stories
> 2 = Regular interview story recall check (stories one to six weeks old)
> 3 = Long-term memory test stories (stories seven to forty weeks old)

Aided or unaided recall:
> blank = Aided stories
> 1 = Unaided stories

7.2   Do you recall the story about the bombs that went off downtown last week? (sample question)

Extent of memory:
> 1 = None
> 2 = A little
> 3 = Some
> 4 = A lot
> 5 = Recall, but extent of memory not mentioned
> 6 = Successful guesswork

7.3   Tell me what you remember about that story. What else?

Type of memory:
> 1 = Specific
> 2 = General

Emphasis of memory:
> 1 = Story substance
> 2 = Story style (of presentation)
> 3 = Story reaction
> 4 = Spinoffs
> 5 = Why interested
> 6 = Story source

7.4   Please tell me how you heard about the story. (Probe for television, radio, newspaper, friend, neighbor, and so on, if not supplied.)

Recall of source:
> 1 = Yes
> 2 = No

Sources of the story (medium) (up to 3)
> blank (or 0) = Not mentioned
> 1 = Tribune
> 2 = All other daily newspapers
> 3 = Weekly papers, including Evanston Review
> 4 = News magazine
> 5 = Book
> 6 = Television
> 7 = Radio
> 8 = Conversation
> 9 = Other sources

7.5   How do you feel about that story? Have you always felt this way about this kind of story?

Recall of previous reaction:
> 1 = Yes
> 2 = No
> blank = Not mentioned

Previous reaction (up to 2):

1st column for reaction type:

    1 = Story substance

    2 = Mass media reaction

    3 = Spinoffs

2nd and 3rd columns for reaction categories:

    Same as Appendix E, Variable 26.

7.6   What is your reaction to the story? Will it change what you think or do in any way?

Present reaction (up to 2):

    Same as above.

Change of reaction:

    1 = Same

    2 = Change a little

    3 = Change a lot

7.7   Identification question (for interviewer only):

Time lapse (from media date or diary entry to interview date)

    - 001 — number of days

Subject categories (code up to 3)

    See Appendix A, Variables 13 to 15.

Impact level of story

    See Appendix A, Variable 16.

Local relevance

    See Appendix A, Variable 17.

7.8   Why do you think you remember/fail to remember this story?

"Why Interested?"

    See Appendix E, Variable 23.

    01 = General interest

    02 = General entertainment

    03 = Human interest

    04 = Special interest

    05 = General importance

    06 = Personal importance

    07 = Job-related importance

    08 = Social life importance

    09 = Circumstantial reasons

    10 = Appealing presentation

    11 = Recommended by others

    12 = Following previous stories on the same line/was curious what happened

    13 = Content/subject matter shocking or unusual/very interesting

    14 = Multiple exposure to the same (kind of) story

15 = Don't know

16 = Personal relevance (or personally known to the people/ place)

17 = Personally known to similar case/situation

Why *not* recall?

1 = Too busy to remember/too long ago

2 = Getting old/memory getting poor

3 = Lack of interest — skeptical about the subject matter

4 = Lack of interest — same old story, predictable, bored, repetitive, insignificant

5 = Lack of interest — does not like media report

6 = Missed the story

7 = Lack of interest — not important (or relevant) to my personal life, too far away

8 = Lack of interest — simply no interest in the subject matter; no reason provided by respondent

9 = Story too complex to follow

7.9 How adequately did the media cover this story?

1 = Adequate/good job

2 = Inadequate — personal reason

3 = Inadequate — quantity lacking

4 = Inadequate — quality lacking

5 = Inadequate — both quantity and quality lacking

6 = Inadequate but that's media

7 = Don't know

8 = Depends on media

9 = Quantity — excessive coverage

7.10 Did you discuss this story with others?

1 = Yes

2 = No

3 = Don't recall

4 = Just briefly mentioned

7.11 Who were they?

1 = Friend

2 = Family

3 = Coworker

4 = Others

7.12 What were their reactions?

Use code for question 7.4.

7.13 Congruency of reactions between respondent and discussion partner(s):

1 = Congruent

2 = Incongruent

3 = Half-and-half
4 = Depends
5 = Discussion not serious enough to agree or disagree
9 = Don't recall

7.14 Who usually takes the lead in conversations with this person, you or the other person, or does it vary?

1 = Respondent
2 = Other
3 = Half-and-half

Appendix E

DIARY AND STORY RECALL INSTRUCTIONS AND CODEBOOKS

General Instructions

This diary should be filled out every day by you or by your interviewer. Put your name, day of the week, and date of diary entries on the top line. Start a fresh sheet for each day.

Record only those items of information to which you pay more than passing attention. You will forget most stories you hear each day almost immediately. Don't try to record them. In fact, after hearing a story, wait at least one-half hour before recording it in your diary. Do not try to pay more attention to news and fiction story sources than you normally do. Act naturally!

On days when you receive no information that requires recording, note the day and date and put "None" in the space set aside for the first information item. Information about your personal affairs, such as discussions about your personal life and your family, or about technical details of your job, should *not* be recorded.

1. *Source* Record personal and media sources that gave you information about the story. Newspapers, magazines, books, pamphlets, television, radio, friends, coworkers, or personal experiences are common sources. List these sources if they have provided you with stories about current happenings such as political events, the economy, the environment, sports, entertainment, crime, and so forth. Plays and variety shows should be included.

   Examples: 1. Source Chicago Tribune editorial

   1. Source Priest, sermon and after-church talk

   1. Source Playing cards with friends at my house

   1. Source Channel 5, 6 o'clock news

2. *Total Time* You learn about most stories during a conversation, or while reading the paper, or watching a television program. Record the total time spent for the conversation, or for reading the whole paper, or watching the whole television program in this space.

3. *Story Time* Record, in minutes or hours, how much time you spent learning about a particular story. For instance, if 5 minutes out of a 30-minute radio broadcast was spent on the story you remember, put down 5 minutes.

4. *Time Delay* Wait at least 30 minutes after hearing a story before you record it in your diary. In this space, note the length of the actual delay in hours.

5. *Attn: Full Part* Circle "Full" if you paid undivided attention to the information. Circle "Part" if your attention was divided. Examples of part-time attention are doing housework while listening to the radio, playing cards with the TV going, or taking part in conversation while skimming through the newspaper.

6. *Recall: Short Med. Long* Indicate here how long you believe you will remember the story. Circle "Short" if you think you will remember it for several hours or days; circle "Med." if you will remember it for more than one week; circle "Long" if you believe you will remember it for a year or longer.

7. *Theme* Record the main points of the story from memory. Do not review the paper or magazine or ask others about details you may have forgotten.

    Examples: 7. <u>Dem. Congressman from Wisconsin attacks Pres. Ford's economic program. Says unemployment benefits are bad.</u>
              7. <u>See also examples on sample sheet.</u>

8. *Info: New Old* Circle "New" if this is the first time you have heard this story. Circle "Old" if the story merely gives additional details about a story you had heard before. Circle both if part of the story is old, but there are *important new elements* you had not heard before.

9. *Coverage: Clear Confused* Circle "Clear" if the story makes sense to you. Circle "Confused" if the facts seem jumbled or there is not enough information to know what is going on. Circle both if part of the story is very clear and part is very unclear.

10. *Bias: None Some A Lot* Circle "None" if it seems to you that the story is told factually, without any attempt to persuade you to adopt a certain opinion. Circle "Some" if the story seems to favor a certain opinion. Circle "A Lot" if the story tells you outright which point of view you should adopt.

11. *Why Interested?* Write down your reasons for paying attention to the story. Or write down the numbers corresponding to the numbered reasons below. You may use several numbers.

    (1) *General interest:* Useful knowledge; interesting; I like to keep up with things; I feel I should keep up.

    (2) *General entertainment:* Fun to watch; amusing; enjoy listening; good way to relax; novelty; odd occurrence.

    (3) *Human interest:* Touching story about people; story about crime, sex, disaster. Story about exciting lifestyles.

    (4) *Special interest:* Story concerns a special interest or hobby of mine. I know or always like to hear about this person, or thing, or place.

(5) *General importance:* This story is important for people in general. The story is important for this country, this city, the world.

(6) *Personal importance:* This story is important for me as a person. It is important for my family, my race, my religion, my close friends.

(7) *Job-related importance:* This story helps me on my job; the story tells me things I need to know for my work.

(8) *Social life importance:* This information helps me in my social life; I can tell this story to my friends. This story helps me to know what others are talking about. I can discuss this story with others.

(9) *Circumstantial reasons:* I pay attention to this story because there is nothing else to do. I listen to be polite. I listen because somebody wants to tell me this story. Somebody else turned on the program. I happened to be there when the story took place.

(10) *Appealing presentation:* Interesting picture or headline caught my attention. Pretty to watch. I like to watch dancers and skaters. Pretty girls; beautiful scenery; lovely photography; rich sound; good graphics; magnificent color.

12. Reaction   Put down any ideas, feelings, or moods that you experience after receiving the information recorded in the story. They may be about the subject of the story, the source and its way of presenting the story, or about unrelated matters the story brings to mind.

Examples: 12. Reaction   Depressing to read about all these murders; makes me feel scared.

12. Reaction   The papers are always attacking the government. Makes people lose confidence. Is it worth it? Probably.

12. Reaction   Best story about teenage alcoholics I've ever seen. Really gripping. Well-acted.

SAMPLE INFORMATION DIARY

Name: Peter Mugow   Day: Friday   Date: Jan. 13

1. Source: Chan. 9 Saturday night movie   2. Total Time: 2 hours
3. Story Time: 40 min.   4. Time Delay: 8 hrs.
5. Attn:(Full) Part   6. Recall: Short (Med) Long
7. Theme: Story about English spy who gets mixed up with counterspies. He
         and girl friend are killed at Berlin Wall.
8. Info:(New) Old   9. Coverage: Clear (Confused)
10. Bias: None (Some) A lot   11. Why Interested: 1, 2, 8
12. Reaction: Spying is dirty, dangerous. I don't like black & white movies
         anymore. Like color.

---

1. Source: Daily News editorial   2. Total Time: 30 min.
3. Story Time: 2 min.   4. Time Delay: 1 hour
5. Attn:(Full) Part   6. Recall:(Short) Med. Long
7. Theme: Postal service getting worse. Steady rise in rates. This has got to stop.
8. Info: New (Old)   9. Coverage:(Clear) Confused
10. Bias:(None) Some A lot   11. Why Interested: 4, 6, 7
12. Reaction: Everything is getting worse. Depressing.

---

1. Source: Dinner talk with friend   2. Total Time: 1 hour
3. Story Time: 10 min.   4. Time Delay: 3 hours
5. Attn: Full (Part)   6. Recall: Short Med. (Long)
7. Theme: Should young singles buy life insurance when inflation is bad?
         Where should they put their savings?
8. Info: New (Old)   9. Coverage: Clear (Confused)
10. Bias: None Some (A lot)   11. Why Interested: 1, 6, 8
12. Reaction: Don't really care.

INFORMATION DIARY CODEBOOK

Variable	Column	Code	Explanation
1	1,2,3	1-25	Respondent's ID
2	4	1-7	Day of week
			1 – Monday, . . . 7 – Sunday
3	5-6	01-31	Day of month
4	7-8	01-12	January-December
5	9	6,7	Year
			Code last numeral only.
			1976
			1977
6,7,8	10,11,12		Source – Medium
			Three media may be coded. Code in same order as respondent, except where respondent spontaneously rank-orders media according to importance.
		0	Not mentioned
		1	Tribune (code this also when paper name is not mentioned)
		2	All other daily newspapers
		3	Weekly papers, including Evanston Review
		4	News magazine
		5	Book
		6	Television
		7	Radio
		8	Conversation
		9	Other

9,10,11

13-14,
15-16,
17-18

Source – Nature of offering

Code to correspond to "Source – Medium" category; for example, if first source mention is newspaper editorial, and newspaper is coded in column 10, editorial should be coded in columns 13-14.

1	News story
2	Editorial
3	Letter to editor
4	Columnist
5	Cartoon
6	Miscellaneous – ads
7	News magazine
11	TV news
12	TV special
13	TV talk show
14	TV family comedy
15	TV movie
16	TV – other
17	TV documentary/journalistic
18	TV political ad – candid
20	Radio talk show
21	Radio news
22	Radio drama
23	Radio political advertising of candidates
30	Conversation with friend
31	Conversation with family
32	Conversation with coworker
33	Conversation with others

221

Variable	Column	Code	Explanation
		34	Own thinking/experience
		40	Movies
		50	Books – fiction
		51	Books – nonfiction
		52	Academic books/journals
		60	Pamphlets, leaflets, newsletters
		70	Public meeting/convention/conference
12	21-22-23	1-999	Total Time
			List in minutes. Round seconds to full minutes upward. Beyond full minute, round upward and downward as indicated.
13	24-25-26	1-999	Story Time
			List in minutes
14	27-28	1-99	Time Delay
			List in hours, 1-94
		1 . . . 94	hours
		95	15 min. or less
		96	16-30 min.
		97	31-45 min.
		98	46-59 min.
		99	More than 94 hours
15	29		Attention Span
		1	Full
		2	Part
16	30		Recall
		1	Short
		2	Medium
		3	Long

Themes – Subject Categories (up to 3 may be coded)
Use codes in Appendix A, Variables 13-15.

17,18,19	31-32-33		
	34-35-36		
	37-38-39		
20	40	Novelty	
		1	New
		2	Old
		3	Old + new
21	41	Clarity	
		1	Clear
		2	Confused
		3	Clear and confused
22	42	Bias	
		1	None
		2	Some
		3	A lot
23,24,25	43-44,	Reasons for Interest	
	45-46,	Up to 3 reasons may be coded	
	47-48		
		01	General interest
		02	General entertainment
		03	Human interest
		04	Special interest
		05	General importance
		06	Personal importance
		07	Job-related importance
		08	Social life importance
		09	Circumstantial reasons

Variable	Column	Code	Explanation
		10	Appealing presentation
		11	Other
		12	Following previous story on same line
		13	Story unusual/shocking/very interesting
		14	Multiple exposure to same story
		15	Don't know
		16	Personally known/Evanston story, and so on
		17	Personally known similar situation
			Reactions to Story Substance
26,27,28	49-50, 51-52, 53-54		Up to 3 reactions may be coded
		01	Positive appraisal – likes what is going on. Considers it progress
		02	Negative appraisal – dislikes what is going on. Considers it detrimental
		03	Happiness reaction – story makes respondent or specified others feel good
		04	Unhappiness reaction – story makes respondent or specified others feel bad
		05	Indifference reaction – doesn't care what happens
		06	Fear/concern reaction – worried about this
		07	Relief/reassurance reaction – allays fears
		08	Surprise reaction
		09	No surprise – expected event – routine
		10	Restatement of facts of story
		11	Projections from story – what it implies for future and present. Includes mention of additional facts, speculations about causes
		12	Respondent's stand on the issue/person in question
		13	Questions concerning feasibility of story proposals
		14	Uncertainty– story unclear, insufficient information
		15	Interest of subject matter, high and low

16		Mixed reaction, positive and negative
17		Insignificant story; not worth bothering with
18		Significant (regardless of attitude toward issue)
19		Strange/weird
21		Other
22		Don't know
23		None

Reaction to Manner of Presentation
Up to 3 may be coded

29,30,31	55-56, 57-58, 59-60	01	Positive appraisal – likes how it is reported; glad it is reported
		02	Negative appraisal – dislikes how it is reported
		03	Annoyance
		04	Boredom
		05	Amusement – funny story
		06	Praise for particular columnist or TV or radio reporter
		07	Condemnation for particular columnist or TV or radio reporter
		08	References to story layout – page position, headline size, picture size, e.g.
		09	Comparison of various media
		10	Questions of accuracy
		11	Comments on sensationalism
		12	Too many ads/complaints about ads
		13	Positive appraisal of story subject (for example, on Today Show)
		14	Negative appraisal of story subject
		19	Other

Variable	Column	Code	Explanation
32,33,34	61-62, 63-64, 65-66		Spinoffs Up to 3 may be coded
		01	Relate story to past personal experience — "this reminds me of"
		02	Relate story to similar or relates stories or events in past (not necessarily personal experience)
		03	Relate story to future action by self
		04	Relate story to future action by others
		05	Speculation about how often similar things happen
35	71		Impact Level See Appendix A, Variable 16.
		1	Local
		2	State
		3	Regional
		4	National
		5	International
		6	Foreign
		7	All
36	72		Local Relevance to Chicago See Appendix A, Variable 17.
		0	No
		1	Yes

226

ANNOTATED BIBLIOGRAPHY

The literature search for this project has greatly benefited from access to the bibliographies compiled by the Center for Urban Affairs at Northwestern University for the Reactions to Crime project.

Abbott, Daniel, and James Calonico. "Black Man, White Woman — The Maintenance of a Myth: Rape and the Press in New Orleans." In *Crime and Delinquency*, edited by Marc Riedel and Terance Thornberry, pp. 141-53. New York: Praeger, 1974. Content analysis of rape portrayal in a New Orleans paper. The media data were compared with police rape statistics.

Antunes, George E., and Patricia A. Hurley. "The Representation of Criminal Events in Houston's Two Daily Newspapers." *Journalism Quarterly* 54 (1977): 756-60. Compares police and newspaper data.

Baker, Ralph, and Fred A. Meyer, Jr. *Evaluating Alternative Law-Enforcement Policies*. Lexington, Mass.: Heath, 1979.

_____, A. M. Corbett, and Dorothy Rudoni. "Citizen Evaluation of Police Services." American Political Science Association Paper, 1977.

Balkin, Steven. "Victimization Rates, Safety, and Fear of Crime." *Social Problems* 26 (1979): 343-58.

Baumer, Terry, and Fred DuBow. " 'Fear of Crime' in the Polls: What They Do and Do Not Tell Us." American Association for Public Opinion Research Paper, 1977.

Biderman, Albert D., Susan S. Oldham, Sally K. Ward, and Maureen A. Eby. *An Inventory of Surveys of the Public on Crime, Justice and Related Topics.* Washington, D.C.: U.S. Government Printing Office, 1972.

Block, M. K., and G. J. Long. "Subjective Probability of Victimization and Crime Levels: An Econometric Approach." *Criminology* 11 (1973): 87-93. An analysis of the relationship between crime levels and people's estimate of the likelihood of becoming crime victims.

Broach, Glen. "Dissonance Theory and Receptivity to Structural Perceptions of the Causes of Urban Crime." *Western Political Quarterly* 27 (1974): 491-99. The acceptability of the notion of structural causes of crime is examined.

Clark, David G., and William B. Blankenburg. "Trends in Violent Content in Selected Mass Media." In *Television and Social Behavior: Media Content and Control,* edited by George A. Comstock and Ali A. Rubinstein, vol. 1, pp. 188-243. Washington, D.C.: U.S. Department of Health, Education, and Welfare, 1972.

Cohen, Shari. "A Comparison of Crime Coverage in Detroit and Atlanta Newspapers." *Journalism Quarterly* 52 (1975): 726-30.

Cohen, Stanley. *Folk Devils and Moral Panics.* London: MacGibbon & Kee, 1972. Deals with role the media play in creating images of societal deviants.

_____, and Jock Young. *The Manufacture of News: Social Problems, Deviance and the Mass Media.* London: Constable, 1973. An excellent collection of essays analyzing mass media treatment of various types of social deviance.

227

Conklin, John E. *The Impact of Crime.* New York: Macmillan, 1975. Deals with direct as well as indirect effects of crime on society. The perceptions that individuals hold about crime and criminals are discussed, based in part on Boston survey data.

Culver, John H., and Kenton L. Knight. "Evaluating TV Impressions of Law-Enforcement Roles." In *Evaluating Alternative Law-Enforcement Policies,* edited by Ralph Baker and Fred A. Meyer, Jr., pp. 201-12. Lexington, Mass.: Heath, 1979.

Davis, James F. "Crime News in Colorado Newspapers." *American Journal of Sociology* 57 (1951): 325-30. Content analysis of crime reporting in four Colorado newspapers. Comparison with actual crime rates and with people's perceptions of crime.

Davis, John A. "Blacks, Crime and American Culture." In "Crime and Justice in America, 1776-1976." *Annals of the American Academy of Political and Social Science,* 1976, edited by Graeme R. Newman, vol. 423, pp. 89-98.

DiGennaro, Arthur F. "Crime Prevention — The Media and the Police." *Law and Order* 21 (1973): 50-53.

Dod, Suzie, Tony Platt, Herman Schwendinger, Greg Shank, and Paul Takagi. "Editorial: The Politics of Street Crime." *Crime and Social Justice* 5 (Spring-Summer 1976): 1-4.

Dominick, Joseph R. "Children's Viewing of Crime Shows and Attitudes on Law Enforcement." *Journalism Quarterly* 51 (1974): 5-12. Tests the relationship between children's attitudes about police and crime and their exposure to the mass media.

_____. "Crime and Law Enforcement in the Mass Media." In *Deviance and Mass Media,* edited by Charles Winick, pp. 105-27. Beverly Hills, Calif.: Sage, 1978. Brief review of the research literature for print and electronic media.

_____. "Crime and Law Enforcement on Prime Time Television." *Public Opinion Quarterly* 37 (1973): 241-50. Crime descriptions compared with crime statistics.

Doob, Anthony N., and Glenn E. MacDonald. "Television Viewing and Fear of Victimization: Is the Relationship Causal?" *Journal of Personality and Social Psychology* 37 (1979): 170-79.

Downs, Roger M., and David Stea. "Cognitive Maps and Spatial Behavior: Process and Products." In *Image and Environment,* edited by Roger M. Downs and David Stea, pp. 8-26. Chicago: Aldine, 1974. Explains how people form maps of their environment, including spatial information, evaluations, and the like.

Dulaney, William L. "Identification of Race in Newspaper Crime Stories." *Journalism Quarterly* 46 (1969): 603-5. Content analysis of story samples from 26 newspapers to determine patterns of suspect racial identification.

Erskine, Hazel. "The Polls: Causes of Crime." *Public Opinion Quarterly* 38 (1974): 288-98.

_____. "The Polls: Control of Crime and Violence." *Public Opinion Quarterly* 38 (1974): 490-502.

_____. "The Polls: Fear of Violence and Crime." *Public Opinion Quarterly* 38 (1974): 131-45.

———. "The Polls: Politics and Law and Order." *Public Opinion Quarterly* 38 (1974): 623-34.

Fischhoff, Baruch. "Attribution Theory and Judgment Under Uncertainty." In *New Directions in Attribution Research,* Volume 2, edited by John H. Harvey, W. J. Ickes, and R. F. Kidd, pp. 451-52. Hillsdale, N.J.: Erlbaum, 1976. A discussion of certain information processing theories.

Fishman, Mark. *Manufacturing the News.* Austin: University of Texas Press, 1980.

———. "Crime Waves as Ideology." Society for the Study of Social Problems Paper, 1977.

Friendly, Alfred, and Ronald Goldfarb. *Crime and Publicity: The Impact of News on the Administration of Justice.* New York: Vintage, 1968. The effects of news coverage on a suspect's right to fair trial are discussed. It is assumed that media coverage influences media audiences.

Furstenberg, Frank F., Jr. "Fear of Crime and Its Effects on Citizen Behavior." In *Crime and Justice: A Symposium,* edited by Albert Biderman, pp. 19-58. New York: Naiburg, 1972. Examines the various components of fear of crime and their behavioral consequences.

———. "Public Reaction to Crime in the Streets." *American Scholar* 40 (1971): 601-10.

Gans, Herbert J. *Deciding What's News: A Study of CBS Evening News, NBC Nightly News, Newsweek & Time.* New York: Pantheon, 1979.

Garofalo, James. *Local Victim Surveys: A Review of the Issues.* Law Enforcement Assistance Administration National Criminal Justice Information and Statistics Service. Washington, D.C.: U.S. Government Printing Office, 1977.

———. *Public Opinion About Crime: The Attitudes of Victims and Non-Victims in Selected Cities.* Law Enforcement Assistance Administration National Criminal Justice Information and Statistics Service. Washington, D.C.: U.S. Government Printing Office, 1977.

———. "Victimization and Fear of Crime in Major American Cities." American Association for Public Opinion Research Paper, 1977. Indicates that mass media information is the basis of public opinion.

Gerbner, George, and Larry Gross. "Living with Television: The Violence Profile." *Journal of Communication* 26 (1976): 173-201. A continuing annual study of violence profiles in television news and their effects on people's perceptions of the nature and extent of crime.

———. "The Scary World of TV's Heavy Viewer." *Psychology Today.* April 1976, pp. 41-45, 89. A popular version of the previously cited study.

———, Nancy Signorielli, Michael Morgan, and Marilyn Jackson-Beeck. "The Demonstration of Power: Violence Profile No. 10." *Journal of Communication* 29 (Summer 1979): 177-96.

Gordon, Margaret T., Project Director, Reactions to Crime Project, Center for Urban Affairs, Northwestern University. *Crime in the Newspapers and Fear in the Neighborhoods: Some Unintended Consequences.* Evanston, Ill.: Northwestern University, 1979.

Gould, Peter, and Rodney White. *Mental Maps.* New York: Penguin: 1974. Describes various studies of the formation and significance of mental maps.

Graber, Doris A. "Evaluating Crime-Fighting Policies: Media Images and Public Perspectives." In *Evaluating Alternative Law Enforcement Policies,* edited by Ralph Baker and Fred A. Meyer, Jr., pp. 179-99. Lexington, Mass.: Heath, 1979.

_____. "The Media and the Police." *Policy Studies Journal,* Vol. 7 Special Issue, 1978, "Symposium on Police and Law Enforcement Policy," pp. 493-500.

Greenberg, Bradley S. "Person-to-Person Communication in the Diffusion of News Events." *Journalism Quarterly* 41 (1964): 489-94. Telephone interviews shortly after news event to ascertain method of news transmission.

Harris, Frank. *Presentation of Crime in Newspapers: A Study in Methods in Newspaper Research.* Minneapolis: Sociological Press, 1932. Pioneering study of presentation of crime news in three Minneapolis newspapers in 1890, 1904-05, and 1921.

Haskins, Jack B. "The Effects of Violence in the Printed Media." In *Mass Media and Violence,* edited by David Lange, Robert Baker, and Sandra Ball, pp. 493-502. Washington, D.C.: U.S. Government Printing Office, 1969.

Henschel, Richard L., and Robert A. Silverman, eds. *Perception in Criminology.* New York: Columbia University Press, 1975.

Hindelang, Michael J. "Public Opinion Regarding Crime, Criminal Justice, and Related Topics." *Journal of Research in Crime and Delinquency* 11 (1974): 101-16. An analysis of public opinion poll data.

Howard, M. Katherine. "Police Reports and Victimization Survey Results: An Empirical Study." *Criminology* 12 (1975): 433-46. A comparison of images of crimes and criminals from police reports and from victimization studies in San Jose.

Hubbard, Jeffrey, Melvin DeFleur, and Lois DeFleur. "Mass Media Influences on Public Conceptions of Social Problems." *Social Problems* 23 (1975): 22-35. A comparison of perceptions of incidence of social problems between views of public, views of social agencies, and views of news media.

Humphries, Drew. "Newspapers and Crime Ideology: An Exploratory Study." Society for the Study of Social Problems Paper, 1977.

Jaehnig, Walter B., David Weaver, and Frederick Fico. "Reporting Crime and Fearing Crime in Three Communities." *Journal of Communication* 30 (Spring 1980).

Jones, Edward E., and George R. Goethals. "Order Effects in Impression Formation: Attribution Context and the Nature of the Entity." In *Attribution: Perceiving the Causes of Behavior,* edited by Edward E. Jones and George R. Goethals, pp. 27-46. Morristown, N.J.: General Learning Press, 1972. Deals with primacy and recency effects.

Jones, E. Terrence. "The Press as Metropolitan Monitor." *Public Opinion Quarterly* 40 (1976): 239-44. Content analysis of crime coverage of two St. Louis newspapers.

_____, and Edward Dreyer. "Environmental Influences of Electoral Attitudes and Behavior: The St. Louis Anti-Crime Referenda." Midwest Political Science Association Paper, 1971. Crime perceptions are compared to actual crime data.

Kanouse, David E., and L. Reid Hanson. "Negativity in Evaluations." In *Attribution: Perceiving the Causes of Behavior,* edited by Edward E. Jones and George R. Goethals, pp. 47-62. Morristown, N.J.: General Learning Press, 1972.

Karmen, Andrew. "How Much Heat? How Much Light? Coverage of New York City's Blackout and Looting in the Print Media." In *Deviance and Mass Media,* edited by Charles Winick, pp. 179-200. Beverly Hills, Calif.: Sage, 1978. Argues that the media ignore the social causes that produce looting.

Katz, Elihu, Jay G. Blumler, and Michael Gurevitch. "Utilization of Mass Communication by the Individual." In *The Uses of Mass Communications: Current Perspectives on Gratifications Research,* edited by Jay G. Blumler and Elihu Katz, pp. 19-32. Beverly Hills, Calif.: Sage, 1974. Brief review of uses and gratifications research.

Kelley, Clarence M. *Crime in the United States: Uniform Crime Reports 1976.* Washington, D.C.: Federal Bureau of Investigation, 1977.

Knopf, Terry Ann. "Media Myths on Violence." *New Society* 16 (1970): 856-59. Deals with violence and sensationalism in newspapers.

Lawton, M. Powell. *Psychological Aspects of Crime.* Philadelphia: Philadelphia Geriatric Center, 1974. Deals with reactions of elderly to crime.

Marzotto, Mary, Tony Platt, and Annika Snare. "A Reply to Turk." *Crime and Social Justice* 4 (Fall-Winter 1975): 43-45.

Meyer, Fred, Ralph Baker, Dorothy Rudoni, and A. M. Corbett. "Public Opinion on Police Services: Implications for Public Policy." Midwest Public Opinion Association Paper, 1977.

Meyer, John C., Jr. "Newspaper Reporting of Crime and Justice: Analysis of an Assumed Difference." *Journalism Quarterly* 52 (1975): 731-34.

Newman, Graeme R., ed. "Crime and Justice in America, 1776-1976." *Annals of the American Academy of Political and Social Science* 423 (1976). A symposium.

Ohlin, Lloyd E., and Henry S. Ruth, Jr., eds. "Combating Crime." *Annals of the American Academy of Political and Social Science* 374 (1967). A symposium.

Payne, David E. "Newspapers and Crime: What Happens During Strike Periods." *Journalism Quarterly* 57 (1974): 607-12. The effects of newspaper strike and normal periods.

————, and Kaye Price Payne. "Newspapers and Crime in Detroit." *Journalism Quarterly* 47 (1970): 233-38. Comparison of crime rates during newspaper strike and normal periods.

"Public Attitudes Toward Crime and Law Enforcement." *Task Force Report: Crime and Its Impact – An Assessment.* Washington, D.C.: U.S. Government Printing Office, 1967, pp. 35-95.

Quinney, Richard. *Critique of Legal Order: Crime Control in a Capitalist Society.* Boston: Little, Brown, 1974.

————. *The Social Reality of Crime.* Boston: Little, Brown, 1970.

Roshier, Bob. "The Selection of Crime News by the Press." In *The Manufacture of News,* edited by Stanley Cohen and Jock Young, pp. 28-39. Beverly Hills, Calif.: Sage, 1973.

Sasser, Emery L., and John T. Russell. "The Fallacy of News Judgment." *Journalism Quarterly* 49 (1972): 280-84. Discusses crime coverage in several newspapers.

Schudson, Michael. *Discovering the News: A Social History of American Newspapers.* New York: Basic Books, 1978.

Sears, David O., and Jonathan L. Freedman. "Selective Exposure to Information: A Critical Review." *Public Opinion Quarterly* 31 (1967): 194-213.

Sellin, Thorsten, and Marvin Wolfgang. *The Measure of Delinquency.* New York: Wiley, 1964. Contains scales for scoring the severity of crimes.

Sherizen, Sanford. "Social Creation of Crime News: All the News Fitted to Print." In *Deviance and Mass Media,* edited by Charles Winick, pp. 203-24. Beverly Hills, Calif.: Sage, 1978.

Skogan, Wesley G. "Citizen Satisfaction with Police Services." In *Evaluating Alternative Law-Enforcement Policies,* edited by Ralph Baker and Fred A. Meyer, Jr., pp. 29-42. Lexington, Mass.: Heath, 1979.

_____. "Measurement Problems in Official and Survey Crime Rates." *Journal of Criminal Justice* 3 (1975): 17-31.

_____. "Public Policy and the Fear of Crime in Large American Cities." In *Public Law and Public Policy,* edited by John A. Gardiner, pp. 1-17. New York: Praeger, 1977.

_____. "The Validity of Official Crime Statistics: An Empirical Investigation." *Social Science Quarterly* 55 (1974): 25-38.

Sparks, Richard F., Hazel G. Glenn, and David J. Dodd. *Surveying Victims: A Study of the Measurement of Criminal Victimization, Perceptions of Crime and Attitudes Toward Criminal Justice.* London: Wiley, 1977.

Springer, Larry. "Crime Perception and Response Behavior: Two Views of a Seattle Community." Ph.D. diss., Ann Arbor, Mich.: University Microfilms, 1974. Examines official and community crime perceptions.

Towers, Wayne M. "Reality, Pseudo-Reality, and Fantasy: The Reinforcement and Crystallization of Crime as an Issue, 1964-1973." Syracuse University Paper, 1976. Examines relations between official crime statistics, newspaper reporting, and public opinion polls on crime.

Tuchman, Gaye. *Making News: A Study in the Construction of Reality.* New York: Free Press, 1978.

_____. "Making News by Doing Work: Routinizing the Unexpected." *American Journal of Sociology* 79 (1973): 110-31. Discusses how news routines are developed by media personnel.

_____. "Objectivity as Strategic Ritual: An Examination of Newsmen's Notions of Objectivity." *American Journal of Sociology* 77 (1971): 660-79.

Turk, Austin. "The Mythology of Crime in America." *Criminology* 8 (1971): 397-411. Common misconceptions about crime are examined.

_____. "Prospects and Pitfalls for Radical Criminology." *Crime and Social Justice* 4 (Fall-Winter 1975): 41-45.

Tyler, Tom R. "Drawing Inferences from Experiences: The Effect of Crime Victimization Experiences Upon Crime-Related Attitudes and Behaviors." Ph.D. diss., University of California, Los Angeles, 1978.

U.S. Department of Justice. *Criminal Victimization in Eight American Cities: A Comparison of 1971/72 and 1974/75 Findings.* Washington, D.C.: Law Enforcement Assistance Administration, National Criminal Justice Information and Statistics Service, 1976.

——. *Public Opinion About Crime: The Attitudes of Victims and Nonvictims in Selected Cities.* Washington, D.C.: Law Enforcement Assistance Administration, 1977.

——. *Source Book of Criminal Justice Statistics, 1978.* Washington, D.C.: Law Enforcement Assistance Administration, 1979. See especially sec. 2, "Public Attitudes Toward Crime and Criminal Justice-Related Topics," pp. 285-359.

Van den Haag, Ernest. "No Excuse for Crime." In "Crime and Justice in America, 1776-1976." *Annals of the American Academy of Political and Social Science,* 1976, edited by Graeme R. Newman, vol. 423, pp. 133-41.

Zucker, Harold G. "The Variable Nature of News Media Influence." In *Communication Yearbook 2,* edited by Brent D. Ruben, pp. 225-40. New Brunswick, N.J.: Transaction Books, 1978.

INDEX

ABOUT THE AUTHOR

DORIS A. GRABER is professor of political science at the University of Illinois, Chicago Circle. She has combined a career of research and teaching with practical experience as a newspaper reporter and feature writer. Among her recent publications on the impact of the mass media on public attitudes and policies are *Verbal Behavior and Politics* (University of Illinois Press, 1976) and *Mass Media and American Politics* (Congressional Quarterly Press, 1980). She earned her B.A. and M.A. degrees in political science and economics at Washington University, St. Louis, and her Ph.D. degree in the field of public law and government at Columbia University, New York.